Wittgenstein *A Way of Seeing*

Wittgenstein *A Way of Seeing*

Judith Genova

Routledge / *New York & London*

Published in 1995 by
Routledge
29 West 35th Street
New York, NY 10001

Published in Great Britain in 1995 by
Routledge
11 New Fetter Lane
London EC4P 4EE

Library of Congress Cataloging-in-Publication Data

Genova, Judith.
    Wittgenstein : a way of seeing / Judith Genova.
        p.   cm.
    Includes bibliographical references and index.
    ISBN 0-415-91062-5 (cloth) — ISBN 0-415-91063-3 (pbk.)
    1. Wittgenstein, Ludwig, 1889-1951. I. Title.
B3376.W56G45 1995   96-8035
192—dc20   CIP

In memory of Jane Zukofsky 1939-1992
and Margaret Sala 1939-1993

Contents

Abbreviations

The following abbreviations refer to the major works of Wittgenstein and to editions of his lecture notes compiled by others.

BB
The Blue and Brown Books (Blackwell: Oxford, 1958)

CV
Culture and Value, ed. G. H. von Wright in collaboration with Heikki Nyman; trans. Peter Winch (Blackwell: Oxford, 1980)

LC
Lectures and Conversations on Aesthetics, Psychology and Religious Belief, ed. C. Barrett (Blackwell: Oxford, 1966)

LWI
Last Writings on the Philosophy of Psychology, vol. I, eds. G. H. von Wright and Heikki Nyman; trans. C. G. Luckhardt and Maximilian A. E. Aue (Blackwell: Oxford, 1982)

LWII
Last Writings of the Philosophy of Psychology, vol. 2, eds. G.H. von Wright and Heikki Nymann; trans. C.G. Luckhardt and Maximilian A.E. Aue (Blackwell: Oxford, 1992)

NB
Notebooks 1914-1916, eds. G. H. von Wright and G. E. M. Anscombe; trans. G. E. M. Anscombe (Blackwell: Oxford, 1961)

OC
On Certainty, eds. G. E. M. Anscombe and G. H. von Wright; trans. Denis Paul and G. E. M. Anscombe (Blackwell: Oxford, 1969)

PG

Philosophical Grammar, ed. Rush Rhees; trans. A. J. P. Kenny (Blackwell: Oxford, 1974)

PI

Philosophical Investigations, eds. G. E. M. Anscombe and R. Rhees; trans. G. E. M. Anscombe (Blackwell: Oxford, 1953)

PO

Philosophical Occasions 1912–1951, eds. James C. Klagge and Alfred Nordmann (Hackett Publishing: Indianapolis, 1993)

PR

Philosophical Remarks, ed. R. Rhees; trans. R. Hargreaves and R. White (Blackwell: Oxford, 1975)

RC

Remarks on Colour, ed. G. E. M. Anscombe; trans. L. L. McAlister and M. Schättle (Blackwell: Oxford, 1977)

RFGB

Remarks on Frazer's Golden Bough, ed. Rush Rhees; trans. A. C. Miles and R. Rhees (Brynmill: Retford, 1979)

RFM

Remarks on the Foundations of Mathematics, eds. G. H. von Wright, R. Rhees, G. E. M. Anscombe; trans. G. E. M. Anscombe, revised edition (Blackwell: Oxford, 1978)

RPP I

Remarks on the Philosophy of Psychology, vol. I, eds. G. E. M. Anscombe and G. H. von Wright; trans. G. E. M. Anscombe (Blackwell: Oxford, 1980)

RPP II

Remarks on the Philosophy of Psychology, vol. II, eds. G. H. von Wright and Heikki Nyman; trans. C.G. Luckhardt and M.A.E. Aue (Blackwell: Oxford, 1980)

TLP

Tractatus Logico-Philosophicus, trans. D. F. Pears and B. F. McGuinness (Routledge & Kegan Paul: London, 1961)

WLAA

Wittgenstein's Lectures: Cambridge, 1932–1935, ed. Alice Ambrose (Blackwell: Oxford, 1979)

WLDL

Wittgenstein's Lectures: Cambridge, 1930–1932, ed. Desmond Lee (Blackwell: Oxford, 1980)

WLFM

Wittgenstein's Lectures on the Foundations of Mathematics: Cambridge, 1939, ed. Cora Diamond (Harvester Press: Hassocks, 1976)

WLPP

Wittgenstein's Lectures on Philosophical Psychology, 1946–47, ed. P.T. Geach (University of Chicago Press: Chicago, 1988)

WVC

Ludwig Wittgenstein and The Vienna Circle, ed. Brian McGuinness; trans. Joachim Schulte and Brian McGuinness (Harper and Row Publishers: New York, 1979)

Z

Zettel, eds. G. E. M. Anscombe and G. H. von Wright; trans. G. E. M. Anscombe (Blackwell: Oxford, 1967)

Wittgenstein usually divided his writing into numbered "remarks," but not always. Citations of his work will sometimes follow the usual page-reference form, e.g. (*BB* pg. 11); but where only a number is given, the reference is to a remark rather than a page, e.g. (*PI* 46). Sometimes, the reference is to a part of the book as well as the remark, e.g. (*RC* III, 295). To indicate when I am not quoting the whole of a remark, I will use ellipses.

*[I believe it might interest a philosopher, one who can think **himself**,**
*to read my notes. For even if I have hit the mark only rarely, **he** would*
recognize what targets I had been ceaselessly aiming at.][1] *(OC pg. 50)*

Prominent among the targets at which Wittgenstein constantly aimed was
philosophy itself. With the eye of a practiced marksman, he hit his target
squarely, rather than rarely, challenging philosophy's emulation of science,
especially the latter's penchant for theory and its faith in progress. What has
philosophy to do, he asked, with either empirical data or mathematical certainty? Throughout his remarks, he denounced the peculiarities of philosophical expression and mocked the dynamics of its exchange. Often, he mar-
veled at philosophy's strange questions, e.g., "Are sense-data the material of
the world?" or "Can I know another's pain?" Simultaneously repelled and
attracted by philosophy, it became the bane of his existence:

> ...The real discovery is the one that makes me capable of stop-
> ping doing philosophy when I want to. The one that gives philoso-
> phy peace, so that it is no longer tormented by questions which
> bring *itself* in question. (*PI* 133)

and the brunt of his scorn and humor:

> I am sitting with a philosopher in the garden; **he** says again and
> again "I know that that's a tree", pointing to a tree that is near us.

---

* Like E.E. Cummings, Wittgenstein alters the physiognomy of his text to make a point. In
quoting Wittgenstein, I have tried to preserve the appearance of his text. Also, following his
practice, I have graphically marked his use of masculine pronouns to underscore the point
that not all native speakers or philosophers are men.

> Someone else arrives and hears this, and I tell **him**: "This **fellow** isn't insane. We are only doing philosophy." (*OC* 467)

While he eventually found a way of philosophizing that eased his anxiety, he never felt completely comfortable:

> You know I said I can stop doing philosophy when I like. That is a lie! I *can't*.[2]

Philosophy obsessed and tormented him.[3] From the beginning of his career until its end, he could not cease doing philosophy nor stop worrying about just what it was that he was doing.

His reservations were personal as well as intellectual. As the son of a highly successful Viennese businessman, philosophy seemed frivolous and impractical. His father pressured him to do something "important," like enter the family business.[4] While he rebelled, he also complied; if he were to practice philosophy, he would, like Marx, have to change the world:

> Yes, I have reached a real resting place. I know that my method is right. My father was a business man, and I am a business man: I want my philosophy to be business-like, to get something done, to get something settled.[5]

Philosophy would have to make some gains; problems would have to disappear to balance the ledger.

Like other revolutionary thinkers in the history of philosophy, Wittgenstein completely transforms the practice of philosophy, from reconceiving philosophy's goals to inventing new methods of inquiry and styles of discourse. His stylistic innovations are especially pertinent.[6] Style or how something is said determines for Wittgenstein what is said. The relationship is implicit in his practice and explicit in his ideas on the connection between form and content:

> Tell me *how* you are searching, and I will tell you *what* you are searching for. (*PR* III, 25)

> In philosophy it is not enough to learn in every case *what* is to be said about a subject, but also *how* one must speak about it. We are always having to begin by learning the method of tackling it. (*RC* III, 43)

> 'The question doesn't arise at all.' Its answer would characterize a

method. But, there is no sharp boundary between methodological propositions and propositions within a method. (*OC* 318)

Indeed, the "how" and the "what" are so closely tied for Wittgenstein that failure to grasp the former may lead to mistakes of comprehension in the latter. Similarly, understanding Wittgenstein depends on the right juxtaposition, the right presentation of a thought; the thing must be seen in the right light or else it will misfire, like Moore's attempts to defeat skepticism:

> When one hears Moore say "I *know* that that's a tree", one suddenly understands those who think that that has by no means been settled. The matter strikes one all at once as being unclear and blurred. It is as if Moore has put it in the wrong light.... (*OC* 481)

Wittgenstein fights hard to avoid Moore's mistake.[7] Style is his weapon for defeating theory and his trusted instrument for making thoughts perspicuous. Without his distinctive styles we would not recognize his voice, nor comprehend his purpose.

Unlike other targets, such as language or meaning, Wittgenstein never openly identifies philosophy as a primary subject of concern. Nowhere in the zillion remarks patiently recorded in his notebooks can one find an explicit declaration of his aims and intentions. Instead, cryptic and hostile sayings pepper the texts, such as "What is your aim in philosophy?—To shew the fly the way out of the fly-bottle" (*PI* 309) or "My aim is: to teach you to pass from a piece of disguised nonsense to something that is patent nonsense" (*PI* 464). Many factors conspire to create his attitude. In part, he is reluctant to propound and declare like a scientist or prophet. Instead, sarcasm seems a better teacher than sincerity for would-be lovers of wisdom. The results, however, are few clues and even fewer descriptions of his new way of doing philosophy.

In the early work, he speaks of his approach as a kind of Kantian "critique" delineating the boundaries of what can and cannot be said; in the later work, he refers to philosophy as a "therapy" aimed at disabusing people of their philosophical intentions. While these similes aid in grasping his new concept of philosophy, they are not quite accurate. When Wittgenstein borrows a concept from another thinker, he always crumples it a bit to tailor it to his own purposes (*CV* pg. 16). *Clarification* adds a new wrinkle to *critique*, making it less judgmental, and *performance* twists *therapy* into a more demonstrative activity. Philosophers become not poets, critics, or therapists for the later Wittgenstein, but performance artists whose only aim is to effect change.

Change in all its manifestations is Wittgenstein's life-long target. Enticing philosopher-flies to leave the neurotic comforts of ill-fitting ideas requires special handling in which even prodding insults have a place.

Despite the centrality of his concept of philosophy, it has received surprisingly little attention. K.T. Fann wrote a monograph years ago (1969), but except for a few chapters and articles here and there, nothing substantial was written until recently. Finally concentrating on Wittgenstein's dramatic transformation of philosophy's practices, Steven Hilmy's *The Later Wittgenstein: The Emergence of a Method* (1987) and James F. Peterman's *Philosophy as Therapy* (1992) began to give the topic the attention it deserves. Additionally, scholars like Cora Diamond and Ben Tilghman drew attention to the ethical character of Wittgenstein's work, arguing for a reappraisal of his philosophical goals.[8] These long-overdue attentions to a subject that transfixed Wittgenstein and changed the face of philosophical inquiry are most welcome.

Unfortunately, the labyrinthian character of Wittgenstein's thought makes it impossible to follow only one thread. Just as one cannot tease apart what he said from how he said it, one cannot isolate his concept of philosophy from the rest of his work. As with Parmenides' well-rounded truth, no matter where one starts in Wittgenstein's work, one eventually passes through all his moves. However, rather than be connected by logical implication, Wittgenstein's thoughts mirror each other and the whole: "one movement links thoughts with one another in a series, the other keeps aiming at the same spot" (*CV* pg. 7). Thus, one cannot speak only about his concept of philosophy; one must also address all the other targets of his work.

Wittgenstein's writing styles further complicate the problem of understanding him. The movable feast of quotes in the later work are as unwieldly as the immovable aphorisms of the earlier period. In both cases, the absence of a narrative argument structure with its soothing cadences of "and thus" make concluding anything about what Wittgenstein had to say risky business. One is always in danger of saying too much or too little. As with poetry, wrenching the thoughts from their embodiment invariably does them damage. One produces theory, the phenomenon Wittgenstein dreaded most, instead of change, the only thing that mattered to him.

Practically, these considerations cause many problems—the same problems Wittgenstein encountered—in trying to write or speak about his way of seeing. Not only must one tell the whole story to make sense of any particular part, but at every juncture one feels the need to tell it all over again:

> Each of the sentences I write is trying to say the whole thing, i.e. the
> same thing over and over again; it is as though they were all simply
> views of one object seen from different angles. (*CV* pg. 7)

Thus, repetitions and misstatements abound. While one tries to calm oneself with typical Wittgenstein asides such as "Don't let yourself get overwhelmed with questions; just take it easy" (*NB* 20.9.14), one soon becomes
pressed by, as Wittgenstein complained: "The crush of thoughts that do not
get out because they all try to push forward and are wedged in the door"
(*RFGB* pg. 3).[9] After suffering this squeeze for twenty years, I came to the
conclusion that there is no one, final presentation of his thought, but a variety of arrangements, some more perspicuous than others. In this effort, I
target his concept of philosophy and show how everything else falls into
place around it.

I am indebted to The Colorado College for grants over the years to
help in the preparation of this manuscript. Also, I thank the many friends
and relatives who patiently listened and waited for this text to be born—
especially my good friends and colleagues Jane Cauvel and Herving
Madruga, who also supplied editorial assistance, and my secretary, Rory
Maikoski, for her help with the back matter. I thank *Metaphilosophy* for
allowing me to use "Wittgenstein: A Way of Seeing" (24, No. 4, October
1993, 326–43). That material is an earlier version of the introduction to this
text. Lastly, I thank my lucky stars for my home in the peace and beauty of
the Garden of the Gods.

To ask, "What is your aim in philosophy?" and to reply, "To show the fly the way out of the fly-bottle" is...well, honor where it is due, I suppress what I was going to say; except perhaps this. There is something deeply exciting about philosophy, a fact not intelligible on such a negative account. It is not a matter of "clarifying thoughts" nor of "the correct use of language" nor of any other of these damned things. What is it? Philosophy is many things and there is no formula to cover them all. But if I were asked to express in one single word what is its most essential feature I would unhesitatingly say: vision.... What is characteristic of philosophy is the piercing of that dead crust of tradition and convention, the breaking of those fetters which bind us to inherited preconceptions, so as to attain a new and broader way of looking at things.... What is decisive is a new way of seeing and, what goes with it, the will to transform the whole intellectual scene. This is the real thing and everything else is subservient to it.[1]

What is so remarkable about this barely concealed attack on Wittgenstein is that it perversely identifies his later goal in philosophy, namely, to change a way of seeing, while denying that it was his goal. Of course, Wittgenstein would never have spoken so hyperbolically; nor would he have thought that "clarifying thoughts" or "the correct use of language" were damnable things. Yet, he would have agreed wholeheartedly with Waismann that the only thing that matters is a new way of seeing and the will to act on it:

> What do I mean when I say "the pupil's capacity to learn *may* come to an end here"? Do I say this from my own experience? Of course not. (Even if I have had such experience.) Then what am I doing with that proposition? Well, I should like you to say: "Yes, it's

true, you can imagine that too, that might happen too!"—But was I trying to draw someone's attention to the fact that **he** is capable of imagining that?—I wanted to put that picture before **him**, and **his** *acceptance* of the picture consists in **his** now being inclined to regard a given case differently: that is, to compare it with *this* rather than *that* set of pictures. I have changed **his** *way of looking at things*. (Indian mathematicians: "Look at this") (cf. *Z* 461). (*PI* 144)

Although minimally stated in this remark and positioned as a happy effect of his argument, rather than an intended goal, his desire to practice philosophy like Indian mathematicians is clear. He wants to make change possible:

A present-day teacher of philosophy doesn't select food for **his** pupil with the aim of flattering **his** taste, but with the aim of changing it. (*CV* pg. 17)

Indeed, even theoretical possibilities do not interest him; only change itself. If the new picture frees one from a fly-bottle, take it and run—no questions asked. Learning comes to an end when one cannot see the case differently, that is, when one becomes aspect-blind. Being aspect-blind makes one incapable of seeing shades of meaning and thus incapable of change (*PI* pg. 214). As linguistic animals, we have an infinite capacity for variation. The trick is to use it to escape fly-bottles.

Each remark in the *Investigations* repeats this scene of instruction. The direct address of the text invites readers to scrutinize a belief, to see it in this light instead of that, to vary the circumstances and stretch the imagination. His repeated demands to "suppose this" and "imagine that" urge us to stop reading and perform the experiment to see if it is effective. Wittgenstein hopes to change *our* beliefs, not those of some virtual or implied reader. Unlike Plato, for whom the proper philosophical stance was wonder, or Descartes, who made us doubt, or Heidegger, who shaped himself into a question-mark, Wittgenstein performs acts of supposition, feats of imagination. The goal of his arguments is to coax and prod us into recognizing that "it ain't necessarily so" and our acceptance that it "ain't" marks a turning-point in the way we see things. Once the new possibility is glimpsed, the hold of the previous way of seeing is broken, and we are free to explore familiar terrain in new ways. The style of the *Investigations* mirrors this goal and argument procedure precisely: the possible declamatory content of the remarks is sacrificed to the deed, to the illocutionary acts they perform. Never more than notes towards change, his remarks tell no stories, weave no morals; instead, they quietly invite us to see things differently.

To see his intentions in operation, consider the context of his satiric fly-bottle remark: it follows a passage which asks how philosophical problems get started in the first place:

> How does the philosophical problem about mental processes and states and about behaviorism arise?—The first step is the one that altogether escapes notice. We talk of processes and states and leave their nature undecided. Sometime perhaps we shall know more about them—we think. But that is just what commits us to a particular way of looking at the matter. For we have a definite concept of what it means to learn to know a process better. (The decisive movement in the conjuring trick has been made, and it was the very one that we thought quite innocent.) —And now the analogy which was to make us understand our thoughts falls to pieces. So we have to deny the yet uncomprehended process in the yet unexplored medium. And now it looks as if we had denied mental processes. And naturally we don't want to deny them. (*PI* 308)

Unaware that the question, in this case about mental processes, is already structured by a certain way of seeing, philosophers ensnare themselves. To ask whether the mental is a process or a state prior to determining whether either category is appropriate is to trap oneself in a fly-bottle. Since the question itself depends on a particular way of seeing, in this case a wrong way, it leads to further errors which multiply exponentially. Wittgenstein was not a behaviorist; he never wanted to deny mental processes. Given his antipathy to mental talk, however, he often sounds like one.[2] For Wittgenstein, all philosophical theories land us in similar pickles. Moore's defense of realism is another case in point. For Wittgenstein neither dogmatism nor skepticism, realism nor idealism, provide helpful ways of seeing. The solution is a new set of choices. As Richard Rorty has urged, one must change the subject.[3]

The context of remark 144 from the *Investigations*, quoted above, is equally instructive. The passage occurs at the beginning of Wittgenstein's discussion of the concepts of understanding and knowledge. Given its content, this placement suggests that getting someone to understand, especially when the mistake the pupil is making is systematic, involves a transformation of a way of seeing. In addition, this discussion begins just after a transition section, a transition from the end of what might be considered an introduction to the *Investigations* (133) to what can be thought of as the first chapter of that work, the discussion of knowledge and understanding (143).[4] The transition begins with the proposition that haunted the *Tractatus,* "This is how things are," (134) and continues with a discussion of propositions and pictures. As a path to the discussion of knowledge, this section is avowedly demonstrative. In fact, its main purpose is to demonstrate a method. Thus, he breaks into the flow of his thoughts on propositions and asks us to consider the effect of his argument:

> …What was the effect of my argument? It called our attention to (reminded us of) the fact that there are other processes, besides the one we originally thought of, which we should sometimes be prepared to call "applying the picture of the cube". So our belief that the picture forced a particular application upon us consisted in the fact that only the one case and no other occurred to us. "There is another solution as well" means: there is something else that I am also prepared to call a "solution"; to which I am prepared to apply such-and-such a picture, such-and-such an analogy, and so on.
>
> What is essential is to see that the same thing can come before our minds when we hear the word and the application still be different. Has it the *same* meaning both times? I think we shall say not. (*PI* 140)

This time the effect of his argument is to show that things can be otherwise than imagined. There are more possibilities to be considered. Once this dawns on the captive spirit, life goes on, either in new ways or with a renewed respect for the old. In either case, one's way of seeing has been transformed.

Almost the same remark is nested in a series of remarks in *Zettel* (*Z* 447–67) discussing the function and limitations of philosophy. At one point, he notes that direct argument against a position won't work, especially when one isn't arguing for any specific way of seeing, but only for the possibility of seeing things differently:

> On mathematics: "Your concept is wrong.—However, I cannot illumine the matter by fighting against your words, but only by trying to turn your attention away from certain expressions, illustrations, images, and *towards* the *employment* of the words." (*Z* 463)

By attending to the employment of words, he hopes one can overcome the entrenched pictures that hold us captive. Such attention produces a description of a language-game and the purpose of such a description is to either return us from the idling pictures of philosophy or change our practices when that is needed. Philosophy's goal is to encourage this change, whichever direction it takes.

Indeed, for Wittgenstein, philosophy has no other goal. Its theories can not be construed as scientific hypotheses about the nature of the world, nor as explanations about why things are the way they are.[5] Instead, they can only offer new ways of seeing, new songs:

> The "visual room" seemed like a discovery, but what its discoverer really found was a new way of speaking, a new comparison; it might even be called a new sensation. (*PI* 400)

> You have a new conception and interpret it as seeing a new object. You interpret a grammatical movement made by yourself as a quasi-physical phenomenon which you are observing. (Think for example of the question: "Are sense-data the material of which the universe is made?")

> But there is an objection to my saying that you have made a "grammatical" movement. What you have primarily discovered is a new way of looking at things. As if you had invented a new way of painting; or, again, a new metre, or a new kind of song.[6] (*PI* 401)

We mistake the visual room for the physical one and then foolishly think, like Bertrand Russell, that the world is made of sense-data. For Wittgenstein, the royal road to metaphysics is paved with similar mistakes:

> Philosophical investigations: conceptual investigations. The essential thing about metaphysics: it obliterates the distinction between factual and conceptual investigations. (*Z* 458)

If successful, new pictures make new scientific theories possible:

> ...One might also give the name "philosophy" to what is possible *before* all new discoveries and inventions. (*PI* 126)

Moore makes a similar mistake when he tries to prove realism by listing all the ordinary things he knows:

> "I know" is here a *logical* insight. Only realism can't be proved by means of it. (*OC* 59)

Even Wittgenstein mistook a way of seeing for a physical hypothesis when he claimed that language and the world shared a common logical form. By the time of the *Investigations*, however, he realized that this was philosophy's central mistake. From then on, he used philosophy solely to effect change. Thus, of his own work, he says:

> My "achievement" is very much like that of a mathematician who invents a calculus. (*CV* pg. 50)

He has invented a new way of speaking that makes new thoughts possible; however, he cannot anticipate what all those changes are.

His objection above to calling a new way of seeing a "grammatical movement" is important. It thwarts any attempt to see Wittgenstein as a mere voice of the status quo.[7] In Kuhn's language, a grammatical movement takes place within a paradigm; it advances the workings of "normal science".[8] The invention of a new way of seeing, on the other hand, is more like the discovery of a new grammar, a new form of life—"And to imagine a language means to imagine a form of life" (*PI* 19). In projecting how we might see things and in successfully applying the vision, we create change.

Wittgenstein in Wonderland

It came into my head today as I was thinking about my philosophical work and saying to myself: "I destroy, I destroy, I destroy—". (CV p. 21)

Waismann's attack is doubly curious coming as it does from one of Wittgenstein's life-long friends who, at one time, tried to play Plato to Wittgenstein's would-be Socrates.[9] One would have thought that he would have known better. Critique and clarification, while important in themselves, become tools for seeing in Wittgenstein's hands. What Waismann calls "vision" is the product of much spadework; one does not simply open one's eyes and see. Even in the *Tractatus*, clarification and critique served a larger purpose: "seeing the world aright" (*T* 6.54).[10] While the *Investigations* no longer promises such an ultimate way of seeing, it continues to use these techniques to transform our ways of seeing.

In all fairness to Waismann, Wittgenstein was not a very cooperative Socrates. Suspicious and afraid he would be misunderstood, as he had been in the *Tractatus,* he guarded his work fiercely, refusing to publish any of his later remarks. Once again, however, forces other than personality contributed to his reticence and reluctance. For example, his worries about how one actually affects change and whether, in fact, change itself is possible, conspire against his ever saying what he wanted to say directly. Also, his desire to avoid theory made it impossible for him to simply say, "see, it goes like this." Philosophical problems require a more subtle treatment. Both his early aphoristic style and his later prosaic one dramatically reflect his difficulties. In neither case can one directly read what he has to say. Rather, one must painstakingly piece remarks together in order to get the drift of his thought (*CV* pg. 78).

Despite the difficulties, however, I have never understood why so many, like Waismann, become so angry at Wittgenstein's pose as fly-chaser. Surely we have learned from Socrates' metamorphosis into a gad-fly, a sting-ray, and a midwife that things aren't always what they seem. In fact, except for the snub nose, there is a strong family resemblance between Wittgenstein and Socrates.[11] Both claim to offer no truths and propound no theories. They emphasize the activity of philosophy, the process of inquiry, and direct their critique at those truths held to be self-evident. For both, philosophy was an all consuming passion aimed at salvation. Socrates was so concerned that he not be mistaken for a sophist or rhetorician that he refused to write a word, while Wittgenstein twisted and contorted his prose so as to never be cofused with a scientist or a traditional philosopher. While he rarely mentions Socrates by name when he is berating philosophers for their failure to look at cases and utilize examples, he mentions this fact to Drury:

> It has puzzled me why Socrates is regarded as a great philosopher. Because when Socrates asks for the meaning of a word and people give him examples of how that word is used, he isn't satisfied but wants a unique definition. Now if someone shows me how a word is used and its different meanings, that is just the sort of answer I want. (cf. *PG* VI, 76)[12]

Despite some important differences, however, they shared a riddling, ironic style and managed to have dramatic effects on those with whom they came in contact. Perhaps the major difference between them is that where Socrates stresses our ignorance in favor of philosophical reconstruction, Wittgenstein champions our knowledge at the expense of philosophical theorizing. For Wittgenstein, knowledge is not the elusive carrot just beyond reach, but the daily product of our interactions with the world.

Socrates was, of course, ridiculed and eventually executed for his challenge to the pride of Athens. Who knows what would have happened to Wittgenstein had he been more outspoken. Indeed, I can hear the outrage now: "Why the gall of the man! Imagine, philosophers, named for their love of wisdom, and descended from the prophets and seers of yore, have nothing better to do than extract themselves from the fly-bottles of language." No doubt, the image conjures thoughts of wise homunculi running helter-skelter, caught in a web of nouns and verbs. "And to be told that all the theories amount to so much nonsense, that the complexities of a Plato or a Parmenides which inspired awe in all onlookers and hushed the noise of easy answers represent nothing more than misunderstandings caused by bumping one's head against the limits of language. What nerve!" Like Alice, and to the dismay of everyone concerned, Wittgenstein concludes his odyssey through the wonderland of philosophy with the impatient cry, "you're nothing but a pack of cards":

> Where does our investigation get its importance from, since it
> seems only to destroy everything interesting, that is, all that is great
> and important? (As it were all the buildings, leaving behind only
> bits of stone and rubble.) What we are destroying is nothing but
> houses of cards and we are clearing up the ground of language on
> which they stand. (*PI* 118)

While Waismann is right that one could not impart the excitement of philosophy or fathom its lofty niche in the history of Western Civilization from a literal reading of Wittgenstein's disparaging remarks, to become as angry as Waismann is to miss the satire of Wittgenstein's broadside at those who trade on being lovers of wisdom. His was a calculated insult intended to shake the intellectual complacency of that most blessed of species, human beings, especially the hubris of its reputedly most blessed members, i.e., most rational members, philosophers.[13] By challenging the long-standing myth that philosophers had privileged access to "all that was great and important" and that such access was necessary to solve philosophical problems, Wittgenstein hoped to secure a more humble role for philosophers, that of therapist, perhaps, or performer. Like Kant, who plays a seminal role in Wittgenstein's thinking, he begins by seeing philosophy as a form of critique—a critique, as he would say, of the pretensions that burden a philosopher's capacity to think (*OC* pg. 72). Critique, however, quickly transforms into clarification, providing a less intrusive role for philosophy, but one aimed clearly at change.

To see that irony was his intent, one must consider the analogy between captive flies and philosophers more carefully. Lured by the presence of some ideal form of sustenance, flies unwittingly trap themselves. Once caught, all their usual methods of dealing with the environment become ineffective; they have lost their way. Instead of seeking new methods to cope with their unusual circumstances, they stubbornly thrust themselves again and again against the glass, clinging to the illusion that freedom is only a matter of their persistence. Some make forays to the left or right of their battered position; others, the more stalwart of the species, manage to tour the whole bottle. In these cases, freedom is sometimes gained. The exit, it must be remembered, is always there in plain view:

> A **man** will be *imprisoned* in a room with a door that's unlocked and opens inwards; as long as it does not occur to **him** to *pull* rather than push it. (*CV* pg. 42)

One need only turn around—make an imaginative leap—to see the opening. For flies, however, this is impossible. Escape, when achieved, is always a matter of luck and determination. Their methods are instinctually rigid and their experiments random. Thus, most perish in what they thought would be the land of milk and honey.

In similar fashion, philosophers pursuing an ideal form of explanation entrap themselves. Viewing philosophy as either a form of ultraphysics or secular theology, they inadvertently bottle themselves in theories and systems which have lost all contact with reality: "A philosophical problem has the form: 'I don't know my way about'" (*PI* 123). Once lost, they become detached from the language-games of ordinary life. Wittgenstein likens it to a cinema where the lights are suddenly turned on (*Z* 233). Just as the images lose their solidity, words become mere shadows of their former meanings. With all the usual common sense ways of dealing with the world forgotten, the world becomes a strange and unsettling place:

> And here one must remember that all the phenomena that now strike us as so remarkable are the very familiar phenomena that don't surprise us in the least when they happen. They don't strike us as remarkable until we put them in a strange light by philosophizing. (*PG* IX, 120)

Accordingly, philosophers are easily misled by a one-sided diet of examples (*PI* 115), or pursue a misleading analogy (*PG* pg. 311), or become captive to a picture, (*PI* 115), or, most often, entangle themselves in their own rules (*PI* 125). In all cases, they do not realize that philosophical problems are unlike other kinds of problems. Since they behave more like problem children than well-behaved questions, they require special handling. While a question calls for an answer and a problem for a solution, a puzzle calls for a treatment or a new way of seeing:

> Why is philosophy so complicated? It ought, after all, to be *completely* simple. Philosophy unties the knots in our thinking, which we have tangled up in an absurd way; but to do that, it must make movements which are just as complicated as the knots. Although the *result* of philosophy is simple, its methods for arriving there cannot be so.
>
> The complexity of philosophy is not in its matter, but in our tangled understanding (cf *PR* X, III). (*PR* I, 2)

The main difference is that philosophical problems are of our own making, although not consciously. To resolve them, one must bring words back from their metaphysical use to their everyday employment (*PI* 116). Once one rearranges what one already knows, the problems disappear since they are a function of one's own blindness to what lies in plain sight.

Not realizing their predicament, however, philosophers behave like flies. Marshalling arguments on behalf of one reform or another, they batter their heads against the glass. Treating a philosophical puzzle as if it were an ordinary problem, they foolishly believe that logic or what the tradition has called "unaided reason" can help. For Wittgenstein, however, logic only facilitates life in the bottle, not escape from it. Without realizing it, we soon settle for the bottled world, transforming our ideals into idols to which we insist reality must correspond (*PI* 131). In this respect flies have the advantage: death for them in only a matter of hours, whereas for philosophers it may take centuries.

On the other hand, and this is Wittgenstein's main point, philosophers have the more important advantage: they are human. They can think! Not restricted to instinctual responses or logic's impoverished conception of thought, they can vary their methods and employ imagination to make the unpredictable leaps of thought requisite to escape a fly-bottle. Most succinctly, humans can see something *as* something else; we can transform our way of seeing—thus the importance of Wittgenstein's work on "seeing-as." Thought, for Wittgenstein, is not a simple validating machine, but a tool for discovery. Unlike flies, we can experimentally play with the situation and find the way out of the fly-bottle before reaching a point of exhaustion.

As Wittgenstein tells us, we too often forget our potential and behave like flies. Thus, the point of his satirical attack is to remind us of our unthinking and narrow ways. We trap ourselves in our own ideals and then reason ourselves into accepting fool's gold. We short-change thinking by treating it as a calculating machine and forget its capacity for new insight. Only by sharpening imagination—our ability to see something as something else—can we escape the fly-bottles of philosophy.

Contrary to Waismann and the many others who do not appreciate Wittgenstein's riddling style, his goal and the repeated message of his later works is to find a way of seeing that liberates philosophers, not pests, from the problems that tax their endurance. His task is not an easy one, as anyone who has tried to release a trapped animal knows. We cling to the familiar, especially when it has been two thousand years in the making. Yet change is possible. Indeed, for Wittgenstein, only philosophy, with its rethinking of what everyone already knows, can "break those fetters which bind us to inherited preconceptions, so as to attain a new and broader way of looking at things…." With all his worries about philosophy, peace comes to him when he realizes that philosophy's proper task is to describe a way of seeing, a *Weltbild*, as a corrective to wild theorizing and to change the picture when it is not the theorizing, but the practice, which is at fault.

The Politics of Change

*(The philosopher is not a citizen of any community of ideas. That is what makes **him** into a philosopher.) (Z 455)*

Often, Wittgenstein's remarks about philosophy are too harsh and minimizing to support such revolutionary aims. After all, he never says: "I want to change your way of seeing"; rather, he only non-committally puts another picture before us. In fact, he insists that philosophy can have no normative role:

Philosophy may in no way interfere the actual use of language; it can in the end only describe it.

For it cannot give it any foundation either.

It leaves everything as it is…. *(PI 124)*

> Philosophy simply puts everything before us, and neither explains nor deduces anything…. *(PI* 126)

How can one simultaneously create change and desist from interfering with the use of language? It appears an impossible task—like that of a traveler from the future who wants to help but dares not tamper with time and history, Wittgenstein is forced to pursue change from a distance. His reasons for this policy are many and intimately connected to the nature of philosophical problems.

The impersonal aspects of a book, for example, constrained his actions. Change, like doubt, requires a context. If the problem is not felt as a problem, then grounds for change are lacking. In fact, he could not possibly succeed unless the person being addressed already desired a change:

> A philosopher says "Look at things like this!" — but in the first place that doesn't ensure that people will look at things like that, and in the second place **his** admonition may come altogether too late; it's possible, moreover, that such an admonition can achieve nothing in any case and that the impetus for such a change in the way things are perceived has to originate somewhere else entirely. For instance it is by no means clear whether Bacon started anything moving, other than the surface of his reader's minds. Nothing seems to me less likely than that a scientist or mathematician who reads me should be seriously influenced in the way **he** works….I ought never to hope for more than an indirect influence. (*CV* pg. 61-62)

As Plato knew, when desire is lacking, philosophy is helpless. It cannot seek change generally, as a matter of policy, but only respond to individual needs. Even then, it can only act indirectly:

> I ought to be no more than a mirror, in which my reader can see **his** own thinking with all its deformities so that, helped in this way, **he** can put it right. (*CV* pg. 18)

The text can only serve as the occasion for one's own self-examination. While others might see their reflection in Wittgenstein's words, the texts are primarily directed at himself:

> Working in philosophy—like work in architecture in many respects—is really more a working on oneself. On one's own interpretation. On one's way of seeing things. (And what one expects of them.) (*CV* pg.16)

> A philosopher is a **man** who has to cure many intellectual diseases
> in **himself** before **he** can arrive at the notions of common sense.
> (*CV* pg. 44)

He could not set out to reform a culture, only himself—and hope that others
might profit from the knowledge.

Moreover, even in cases where he was persuaded that change was needed, he could only present possibilities, not untangle the puzzle for the other
person. He could not go further because he could not argue that the new way
is true while the old false. Wittgenstein cannot say "follow me" or "you ought
to change" because he knew better than to claim that truth is on his side:

> Supposing we met people who did not regard that as a telling
> reason. Now, how do we imagine this? Instead of the physicist, they
> consult an oracle. (And for that we consider them primitive.) Is
> it wrong for them to consult an oracle and be guided by it?—If we
> call this "wrong" aren't we using our language-game as a base from
> which to *combat* theirs? (*OC* 609)

> And are we right or wrong to combat it? Of course there are all
> sorts of slogans which will be used to support our proceedings.
> (*OC* 610)

There is no one final way of seeing, but a variety of ways whose only measure of success is relief from disquietude. If the change works, if it frees you
from the fly-bottle, that is sufficient. Even when one could point to some
truth, pointing to it alone would not suffice to change anyone:

> We must begin with the mistake and transform it into what is true.
> That is, we must uncover the source of the error; otherwise hear-
> ing what is true won't help us. It cannot penetrate when something is
> taking its place.
> To convince someone of what is true, it is not enough to state it;
> we must find the *road* from error to truth. (*RFGB* pg. 1)

If no other factor is taken into consideration, this one fact—that
Wittgenstein cannot appeal to truth or use logic to persuade—accounts for
his reluctance to openly say, "I want to change your way of seeing." There
are other factors as well.

The phenomenon of change itself perplexes him. Throughout the later
works he is bothered by the question, "What changes when a way of see-

ing is changed?" The conundrum originates from the definition of noticing an aspect:

> I contemplate a face, and then suddenly notice its likeness to
> another. I *see* that it has not changed; and yet I see it differently. I call
> this experience "noticing an aspect". (*PI* pg. 193)

Like the elusive aspects of the duck–rabbit picture, one is continually trying to grab hold of something which magically vanishes with the slightest
shift of vision:

> Now you try and say what is involved in seeing something *as* some-
> thing; it is not easy. These thoughts I am now working at are as hard
> as granite.[14]

Since the very definition of "noticing an aspect" maintains that we are seeing the *same* thing differently, one can understand Wittgenstein's pessimism
that philosophy leaves everything as it is. Reality itself does not change, only
our attitude towards it. The phenomena remain the same:

> But what is different: my impression? my point of view?—Can I
> say? I *describe* the alteration like a perception; quite as if the object
> had altered before my eyes.
> "Now I am seeing *this*", I might say (pointing to another picture,
> for example). This has the form of a report of a new perception.
> The expression of a change of aspect is the expression of a *new*
> perception and at the same time of the perception's being unchanged.
> I suddenly see the solution of a puzzle-picture. Before, there
> were branches there; now there is a human shape. My visual impres-
> sion has changed and now I recognize that it has not only shape and
> colour but also a quite particular 'organization'.—My visual impres-
> sion has changed;—what was it like before and what is it like now?—
> If I represent it by means of an exact copy—and isn't that a good
> representation of it?—no change is shewn. (*PI* pg. 195-96)

Indeed, in some sense, even the visual impression has not altered—an exact
copy of the initial impression would show no differences. Yet everything is
different! The puzzle is resolved and we act and see differently:

> For might not someone be able to describe an unfamiliar shape
> that appeared before **him** just as *accurately* as I, to whom it is familiar?
> And isn't that the answer?—Of course it will not generally be so. And
> **his** description will run quite differently. (I say, for example, "The

animal had long ears"—**he**: "There were two long appendages", and
then **he** draws them.) (*PI* pg. 197)

Again and again, Wittgenstein draws the conclusion that we think, see, and
act differently:

> If someone sees a smile and does not know it for a smile,
> does not understand it as such, does **he** see it differently from some-
> one who understands it?—**He** mimics it differently, for instance
> (cf. *PI* 74). (*PI* pg. 198)

Why then does he hesitate to credit the powers of a way of seeing?
In one sense, this section is completely typical; there is a distinction to be
made, even if it should not be made with the same emphasis as in the past.
The phenomena and our view of the phenomena should not be collapsed:

> The concept of a representation of what is seen, like that of a copy is
> very elastic, and so *together with it* is the concept of what is seen. The
> two are intimately connected. (Which is *not* to say that they are
> alike.) (*PI* pg. 198)

We must not forget that there are two uses of "see". On the other hand, if
we insist on this distinction in typical philosophical fashion, we are liable to
be led into a series of moronic questions like, where and when exactly is
the change occurring? Wittgenstein asks all these questions in part to
demonstrate the futility of treating philosophy like a science.
First, he tries to locate the possibility for change in the object itself:

> How would the following account do: "What I can see some-
> thing *as*, is what it can be a picture of."?
> What this means is: the aspects in a change of aspect are those
> ones which the figure might sometimes have *permanently* in a picture.
> (*PI* pg. 201)

Second, he tries our visual impression:

> "And is it really a different impression?"—In order to answer this
> I should like to ask myself whether there is really something different
> there in me. But how can I find out?—I describe what I am seeing
> differently. (*PI* pg. 202)

Finally, he also suggests that maybe cases of seeing-as are not really cases of
seeing, but of seeing plus interpreting or thinking:

> When I see the picture of a galloping horse—do I merely *know*

that this is the kind of movement meant? Is it superstition to think I *see* the horse galloping in the picture?—And does my visual impression gallop too? (*PI* pg. 202)

Eventually, he denies the last option and simply ignores the others. The discussion peters out without reaching any formal conclusion. There is no answer to the question, "exactly what changes when a way of seeing changes?" Like time and the aroma of coffee, change is not something that can be straight-forwardly measured. However, and this is the important lesson, just because we cannot locate the place of change we should not conclude that therefore change does not exist or that change is an illusion while reality is unchanging. Such conclusions are never convincing since they fly in the face of experience; in fact, they ultimately give philosophy a bad name. Their problem is that they misunderstand the nature of a philosophical investigation. Instead of denying our experience, the inability to locate the place of change should lead us to drop the object (the reference) out of consideration altogether.

Still, Wittgenstein's attitude towards philosophy is ambiguous. While I have shown that the claim "philosophy leaves everything as it is" should not be read as pessimistically as it has been, a lingering suspicion remains that Wittgenstein has not fully escaped this fly-bottle. And perhaps he hasn't; his lingering commitment to realism and his greater fear of relativism drove him to unwanted words.[15] Ultimately, idealism worried Wittgenstein more than realism. Without the distinction between "the phenomena themselves" and "our view of the phenomena," both relativism and idealism threaten to appear. True, he has solved this dilemma in other places, however, he refuses to appeal to it here. For example, he says:

> We have a colour system as we have a number system. Do the systems reside in *our* nature or in the nature of things? How are we to put it?—*Not* in the nature of numbers or colours. (*Z* 357)

> Then is there something arbitrary about this system? Yes and no. It is akin both to what is arbitrary and to what is non-arbitrary. (*Z* 358)

Wherever the systems reside (and Wittgenstein is not going to comment on where that may be), they are not arbitrary. Elsewhere, he is less reluctant to grant grammar or numbering and color systems their proper role:

> Essence is expressed by grammar. (*PI* 371)

Consider: "The only correlate in language to an intrinsic necessity is an arbitrary rule." It is the only thing which one can milk out of this intrinsic necessity into a proposition. (*PI* 372)

Grammar tells what kind of object anything is. (Theology as grammar.) (*PI* 373)

Perhaps, these remarks go too far since they can easily be misread for theoretical statements. Yet they make the point that the systems reside less in our nature or in the nature of the world than in the rule-governed structure of language. Whenever one gets into the position of asking, "But, doesn't something real correspond to our grammar?" or "Isn't there something behind the grammar to justify it?", Wittgenstein reminds us that even if there were if would be irrelevant. The social facts provide sufficient understanding of a way of seeing; one does not have to fall back upon a physical explanation:

But doesn't anything physical correspond to it? I do not deny that. (And suppose it were merely our habituation to *these* concepts, to these language-games? But I am not saying that it is so.) If we teach a human being such-and-such a technique by means of examples—that **he** then proceeds like *this* and not like *that* in a particular new case, or that in this case **he** gets stuck, and thus that this and not that is the 'natural' continuation for **him**: this of itself is an extremely important fact of nature. (*Z* 355)

Thus, he had an answer to his dilemma about the status of the "phenomena themselves": they are irrelevant. Why he did not avail himself of it when dealing with the problem of seeing-as and change, one can only speculate. Had he done so, however, I think he would have seen that philosophy leaves *nothing* the way it is.

Further complicating these substantial problems about the nature of change was his fear that we only exchange one *Weltanschauung* for another. The last thing Wittgenstein wanted was to simply exchange one world-view for another:

So I am trying to say something that sounds like pragmatism.
Here I am being thwarted by a kind of *Weltanschauung* (cf. *PI* 307–308 on Behaviorism). (*OC* 422)

Rather, he hoped to be able to avoid the temptations of any *one* picture and remain open to changing aspects, even as he he could not help being captured by the one he inhabited. Yet, as Cavell has noted, if Wittgenstein was successful, he had to have changed our way of seeing: "The answer to that question [*PI* 122] is, I take it, not No. Not perhaps, Yes, because it is not a *special*, or competing, way of looking at things. But not No; because its mark of success is that the world seem-be-different."[16] Thus, we too face his problem about change; things are both the same and different after Wittgenstein. While our way of seeing has been transformed, in some sense that Wittgenstein insisted we preserve, nothing has changed.

Lastly, Wittgenstein worried that philosophy's theoretical mode of discourse would have no effect on the way people lived. Like Marx, Wittgenstein believed that philosophy had to effect people's lives and not just talk about them:

> I am by means sure that I should prefer a continuation of my work by others to a change in the way people live which would make all these questions superfluous. (For this reason I could never found a school). [17] (*CV* pg. 61)

Frustrated that he could do nothing to directly effect change, Wittgenstein often gave in to pessimism and proclaimed that philosophy leaves everything as it is or that it teaches you how to move from disguised nonsense to patent nonsense (*PI* 464). Had he stuck to cases and solved his problem about the nature of change, I think he would have confidently concluded, as Gertrude Stein concluded, that nothing is the same after a change in our way of seeing:

> The only thing that is different from one time to another is what is seen and what is seen depends upon how everybody is doing everything. This makes the thing we are looking at very different and this makes what those describe it make of it, it makes a composition, it confuses, it shows, it is, it looks, it likes it as it is, and this makes what is seen as it is seen. Nothing changes from generation to generation except the thing seen and that makes a composition.[18]

As Ray Monk, Wittgenstien's biographer notes, philosophy leaves *nothing* the way it is.[19]

Given these considerations, it should be clear why Wittgenstein never bluntly says: "I want to change your way of seeing." Like Kierkegaard before him, he learned the arts of indirection. Philosophy could only be a catalyst for change. It could only interpose itself between the picture and the believer in such a way as to disrupt the felt necessary connection between the two and hope for the best. The strategy for accomplishing this was to demonstrate the relativity of ways of seeing. Anything that can be imagined can be otherwise; even the necessity of logical truths can be questioned once they are placed outside the system in which they have their life. What inhibits the skepticism which usually accompanies such relativism is the double recognition that while there is no final way the world is, forms of life constrain the world, giving temporary shape and articulation to its infinite potentiality. Thus, while all he can do is present possibilities, he is not merely pointing to the fact that we are capable of change; rather he seeks a change that issues in action, that transforms the lived world.

A Map of My Own

*I should not like my writing to spare other people the trouble of thinking. But, if possible, to stimulate someone to thoughts of **his** own. (PI pg. x)*

The following chapters explore the many facets of Wittgenstein's new way of seeing and doing philosophy. My procedure is to ask questions. I hope to ask every possible question about his concept of philosophy. The questions divide into three broad categories marked by the three main parts of the text: A Way of Seeing, Changing a Way of Seeing, Wittgenstein's Way of Seeing. Rather than begin with a question, however, I preface each section with a particularly apt or puzzling Wittgensteinian remark. Not coincidently, most of the ones I have chosen are by now well-known and familiar. The ensuing discussion in each section attempts to undo the disturbing character of the remark. I have found that untying knots in Witttgenstein's remarks unravels the knots in our thinking. The remarks themselves, as he well knew, are the vehicles of change:

> (The choice of our words is so important, because the point is to hit upon the physiognomy of the thing exactly, because only the exactly aimed thought can lead to the correct track. The car must be placed on the tracks precisely so, so that it can keep rolling correctly.) (*PO pg. 165*)

Consequently, I depend heavily on his exact words—although I rearrange them to produce a perspicuous map of his concept of philosophy.

Part I examines the concept of a way of seeing itself. It targets the two significant words in the expression "a way of seeing." Thus the first chapter concentrates on "way" and asks: What does Wittgenstein mean by *Die Übersehen* or a perspicuous representation? In the famous remark that prefaces chapter one (*PI* 122), Wittgenstein's declares that *Die Übersehen* describes how he sees things. What is distinctive about this way of seeing and how does it compare with his earlier way in the *Tractatus*, the view *sub specie aeternitatis?* Secondly and relatedly, how does a *"Weltbild,"* Wittgenstein's word for *way*, in the sense of content, differ from a *Weltanschauung?* Does it differ, thus confirming his desire to avoid theorizing? Lastly, how do both these concepts relate to the idea of *eine Lebensform* or form of life? What does the latter concept add, if anything, to that of a way of seeing?

Chapter two, then, focuses on the concept of "seeing" in the expression "a way of seeing" and asks why Wittgenstein almost always speaks of "ways of seeing" and not "ways of thinking." His choice of seeing over thinking and then, later in his career, of acting over seeing, is deliberate. The texts progress steadily from one to the other. Even if the remarks do not fully corroborate this observation, Wittgenstein spends enough time investigating the relations between our modes of learning, i.e., perceiving, conceiving, and doing, to warrant a detailed examination of them. What is seeing and how does it differ from thinking? When we see something as something else, are we mixing two different modes of learning or is seeing itself less dogmatic than it seems? How does acting affect seeing? All these questions are critical to Wittgenstein's resolution of the empiricism/rationalism debate and his development of a new way of seeing.

In Part II, chapters three and four trace Wittgenstein's conception of language and his struggles to develop a style of writing and speaking philosophy that successfully frees people from fly-bottles (the cave). Style embodies Wittgenstein's way of acting, and thus also his direct attempts to change our way of seeing or alert us to the need for change. Chapter three begins with Wittgenstein's early style in the *Tractatus* where he develops a rhetoric of logical *elucidations* to create clarity. Still heavily influenced by Kant and his sucessors in Germany/Austria, he is too invested in the business of constructing concepts to achieve full freedom from transcendental positions. Chapter four continues with the later work, exploring his new rhetoric of *reminders* and his conception of philosophy as performance. Playing the language-games of the *Investigations* retrains philosophers in the art of philosophy and provides new maps of the conceptual terrain.

Finally, chapters five and six of Part III attempt to answer a different set of questions: Why should we change? What is wrong with our old way of seeing, and how should we look at things? Convinced that Wittgenstein has changed our way of seeing and that philosophy has continuing effects on the way we live, I present what, for want of a better expression, I shall call "Wittgenstein's way of seeing." As noted earlier, I am as reluctant as Wittgenstein himself to speak of a distinctive way he saw things; yet, it is there. One can say, "Wittgentein disagrees with Descartes about this and rejects what Kant says about that." Besides, no study of his way of doing philosophy can be complete without some attempt at saying what changes he wrought. To accomplish this task in a brief and condensed way, I focus on his belief in the autonomy of language, logic, and world. Repeatedly, Wittgenstein insists that language, logic, and the world take care of themselves. I interpret these puzzling remarks as Wittgenstein's attempts to liberate meaning, truth, and sense, respectively, from their Kantian dependence on human consciousness. Essentially, then, the three sections of chapter five detail Wittgenstein's rejection of Kant's transcendental ego, his transcendental logic, and his metaphysical solution of transcendental idealism. The last chapter traces the effect of these autonomous systems on Wittgenstein's conception of knowledge. His thinking about knowledge defies many time-worn beliefs, e.g., that experience is necessary for knowing, or that knowledge is only possible when error is not, or even that knowing something needs authorization of some kind.

My goal is to allay all doubts, not only about the transforming power of philosophy, but about Wittgenstein's success in changing the way we see things. Afterall, nothing has been the same since him. Language, not reason, now distinguishes humans from the "brutes" and their more modern counterparts, the machines. In one form or another, language has affected every field of study. While Wittgenstein was not alone in creating the linguistic turn, he played a central role, especially in Anglo-American philosophy Under his leadership, philosophy has experienced the first major turning since Kant's Copernican Revolution over two hundred years ago. As he would say, he has created a new "'kink' in the 'development of human thought'" (*PO* pg. 113). By departing from Kant in a different way than does Hegel and all his progeny, Wittgenstein manages a different entry into the Postmodern world.

Part One *A Way of Seeing*

A main source of our failure to understand is that we do not command a
clear view [übersehen] *of the use of our words.—Our grammar is lacking in
this sort of perspicuity* [Übersichtlichkeit]. *A perspicuous representation produces just that understanding which consists of 'seeing connexions'. Hence the
importance of finding and inventing* intermediate cases.

The concept of a perspicuous representation [der übersichtlichen
Darstellung] *is of fundamental significance for us. It earmarks the form of
account* [Darstellungsform] *we give, the way we look at things* [die Art wie
wir die Dinge sehen]. *(Is this a* 'Weltanschauung'?) (PI *122*)

Wittgenstein calls his later way of seeing *die Übersichtliche Darstellung,* or, as
the expression is most often translated into English, a perspicuous representation.[1] Initially, he means *"way"* (die Art) in the sense of method or
style.[2] *Way,* like *form* (from *Darstellungsform)* in the *Tractatus,* does not so
much signify a *kind,* for Wittgenstein, as it does a *means* of representation. A
perspicuous representation does nothing more than survey, in engineering
fashion, a form of life. "Way" also signifies a kind. Its method frames a content; that is, presents a picture which differs from other pictures. And, as I
shall demonstrate in Part III, Wittgenstein's way of seeing is readily distin-
guishable from that of Modern Philosophy's, the period extending from
Descartes to Kant. Given his antipathy to past philosophy's psuedo-scientific aspirations, his worry about whether having a way of seeing is tantamount to having a *Weltanschauung* is not misplaced. As I indicated in my
introduction, he would have preferred not to be known for a distinctive or
competing way of seeing.

To distinguish his way of seeing clearly from that of a *Weltanschauung,*
Wittgenstein introduces the concept of a *Weltbild* in *On Certainty,* his last
writings. Das *Weltbild* is also a world-picture, but not one invented or
imposed by the inquirer. Rather, it is obtained by listening carefully to the
language of a form of life, simultaneously imagining other possibilities, in
order to discover what everyone already knows, albeit indistinctly. The goal
is to describe, or take the pulse of a form of life *(Lebensform),* not explain it
by drawing blood. In this sense, a *Weltbild* is a *Lebensform*; the two name the
same phenomenon from different perspectives: the epistemological and
ontological. The subtle differences between Wittgenstein's early talk of a
"form of account" in the *Tractatus* and his later choice of "way of seeing,"
for the *Investigations* further differentiate the two kinds of world-pictures.
Form, because it is usually tied to function, serves in an explanatory capac-

ity. One easily confuses it with the way things are. Way, on the other hand, is less exact and less exacting than form. It relies more on style than method and is thus ideal for describing a *Weltbild*. It only provides a channel or space to view a form of life, not a net for interpreting it. Way abandons form's static, structural take on the world for a dynamic, open-ended shot, which is interestingly more interventionist than theory.

The concept of seeing further elaborates Wittgenstein's conception of way as means; that is, it responds to the age-old question, How do we know? What equipment do we use to learn? The traditional tools have always been the senses and the mind. In turning to language, Wittgenstein discovers a new avenue for learning: the hand or its extension, the tongue. Learning requires a more interactive and immediate medium than either thinking or seeing provide. To accomodate this insight, Wittgenstein eventually names action as the closest activity of language. However, he first spends a good deal of time worrying about the relations between seeing and thinking.

Die Übersehen is fundamentally a way of looking, not thinking. Yet, such a polarization of thought and sight (or the senses more generally) betrays Wittgenstein's intentions in the later works. His goal in drawing our attention to the phenomenon of *seeing-as* is precisely to undermine Modern philosophy's strict separation of the senses and disrupt the empiricism/rationalism debate as well as mind/body dualism. *Seeing-as* weaves thinking and seeing together into an inextricable whole making it impossible to distinguish them. Additionally, it focuses attention on the actions of seeing and thinking rather than the states. I would call it "interpretative" seeing/thinking rather than "contemplative," except that Wittgenstein repeatedly denies the word "interpreting." Interpretation is too conscious, too deliberate to capture the unconscious actions of *seeing-as* for him. Yet, if we think of "interpretation" as an internal function of sight itself, the term would not be misleading. Commanding a clear view requires a close seeing that involves imaginative thinking. One has to be close and far simultaneously. In effect, neither objectivity, nor subjectivity solves philosophical problems; rather, activity alone dissolves them.

Chapter 1 Commanding a Clear View

...It disperses the fog to study the phenomena of language in primitive kinds of application in which one can command a clear view of the aim and functioning of the words.... (PI 5)

A good way to begin dispersing the fog obscuring Wittgenstein's use of a perspicuous representation is to compare it with his more primitive form of account in the *Tractatus,* the view, *sub specie aeternitatis.* (As Wittgenstein predicted, a better understanding of his later ideas can be achieved by comparing them with his earlier ones.) The main link between these two ways of seeing is the concept of a *Darstellungsform* or "form of representation." An *Übersehen,* whatever else it may be, is first and foremost a form of representation. While many important differences attend the change from *form* to *way,* a perspicuous representation remains a kind of "net" for describing reality. And for the *Tractatus,* everything depends on finding the right net. With the proper net, he claimed, one can describe the world completely.

His sensitivity to painting and music was the foundation for this idea; a visual or musical idea is so perfectly wedded to its embodiment (in the sense of a tautology) that one is not expressible without the other. If philosophy could find an equally suitable net, it too could achieve perfect expression. By *net,* Wittgenstein literally means the notation, or the actual *style* or way in which the method is inscribed. What Schubert wanted to say musically is perfectly expressed in the arrangement of notes provided by musical notation. Style for Wittgenstein embodies his method; it gives method physiognomic detail. A way of seeing is foremost a style of seeing, like a style of painting.

By "proper," Wittgenstein means a net that clarifies, rather than explains or theorizes. Clarity, Descartes as well as Wittgenstein claimed, is the single most important virtue for philosophical understanding:

> Typically it [scientific thinking] constructs. It is occupied with building an even more complicated structure. And even clarity is sought only as a means to this end. For me on the contrary clarity, perspicuity are valuable in themselves. (*CV* pg. 7)

A clear net not only frees one's psychologically from doubt and confusion, but objectively makes things perspicuous. Clarity's main virtue is that it reveals the connections between things and thus provides a view of the whole or the world-picture informing our form of life. A perspicuous representation is not interested in the details of any one particular piece of a puzzle; nor does it seek to penetrate phenomena to find their internal structure. Rather, it shows how things hang together. Wittgenstein's early search for a view of the whole provides the first clue to understanding his concept of a perspicuous representation.

Concomitantly, it reveals something about the nature of postmodern philosophy. The question that motivates Wittgenstein is not the greek one, "Of what is the universe made?" nor the medieval one, "Who is its maker?" nor its modern replacement, "How does the world work?" but the postmodern quandry, "Why does the world exist at all?"—the *that* of the world, its meaning. Like Heidegger, his contemporary, he was struck by the question, Why is there something rather than nothing?[3] Both thinkers, who otherwise seem poles apart, are fascinated with the brute fact of existence, the *that*, not the *how*. And they both agree that nothing in science addresses this question (*T* 6.52). Science reigns supreme in the domain of the *how*, but it is impotent in the world of the *that*. God is no scientist. Unlike Heidegger, however, Wittgenstein abandons any pretense of answering this question. The sense of the world lies outside it (*T* 6.41); no form of representation can comprehend it. The Parmenidian vision of Being (i.e., as one, whole, and everlasting) is a view for the Gods. The most Wittgenstein can do is show the impossibility of such quests, the limits of what can be said. His hope is that by seeing the world as a world, he might explain its meaning. From this perspective, the view *sub specie aeternitatis* precedes and contrasts nicely with Wittgenstein's later goal of an *Übersehen*.

From Eternity to Here

> *To view the world* sub specie aeterni *is to view it as a whole—a limited whole. Feeling the world as a limited whole—it is this that is mystical.* (T 6.45)

Near the end of the *Tractatus*, Wittgenstein wishes for a view of the world *sub specie aeterni,* a view, as he explains, from the timeless perspective of eternity (*T* 6.4311). Seeing the world aright: that is, after the scaffolding of Tractarian propositions are kicked away (*T* 6.54), is seeing it whole—in one glorious vision—instead of piecemeal or as an endless series of pieces. "Limited" reiterates the notion of the whole by emphasizing finiteness. We see the world as bounded and suspended in space.[4] We would then be in a position to see all the effects of every action as they ripple across the face of the globe: that is, the world waxing and waning as a whole (*T* 6. 43). He compares it to an artist's view:

> But it seems to me too that there is a way of capturing the world sub specie aeterni other than through the work of the artist. Thought has such a way—so I believe—it is as though it flies above the world and leaves it as it is—observing it from above, in flight. (*CV* pg. 5)

Read in conjunction with *T* 6.44, "It is not how things are in the world that is mystical, but that it exists," one deduces that the view of the whole reveals the *that* of the world (its sense) not the *how*. It is a view for the Gods or for those who see the world from afar.

Yet, the existence of the *Tractatus* suggests that such an experience, as he refers to it, a *feeling* of the world as a whole, may be possible if not seeable or thinkable.[5] Wittgenstein writes from such a feeling. In the early work, Wittgenstein, like Heidegger and *pace* Kant, renounces thinking to make room for feeling.[6] Yet one ought not say this too loudly. Unlike the thinkers of the late Nineteenth Century, who no doubt inspired his hope for feeling, Wittgenstein never claims theoretical status for feeling's capacity for knowledge. A feeling or presentment of the whole adds nothing to our knowledge of the world. Feelings must be felt in silence.

In the *Tractatus,* logic is the closest thing to Godliness. Since it is prior to the *how,* it creates a hidden access to the *that* (*T* 5.552). To experience the world as a whole, one must experience logic. Its precise, machine-drawn propositions lay bare the form of the world. Like x-rays, logical pictures penetrate the clutter of phenomena revealing the skeletal form beneath. With classic modernist sensibility, Wittgenstein believed that form underlay content, making it coherent. "How things stand" (*T* 4.5) was perspicuous by inspection of the logical connective tissue underlying content. Logic's cheat, however, is that it only provides a peek of the whole in miniature and from inside. Instead of leaving the world, and viewing it from afar, logic positions one inside the world swinging one's feet from a cosmic girder. Wittgenstein himself introduces the spatial metaphors of "inside/outside" and "close/far" to describe the view *sub specie aeternitatis*:

> The usual way of looking at things sees objects as it were from the midst of them, the view *sub specie aeternitatis* from outside.
>
> In such a way that they have the whole world as background.
>
> Is this it perhaps—in this view the object is seen *together with* space and time instead of *in* space and time?
>
> Each thing modifies the whole logical world, the whole of logical space, so to speak.
>
> (The thought forces itself upon one): The thing seen *sub specie aeternitatis* is the thing seen together with the whole of logical space.[7] (*NB* 7/10/16)

The object is beside space and time, not in it, like the illegitimate diagram of the visual field in the *Tractatus* (*T* 5.6331). In this view, the world is frozen, splayed flat in two dimensions, making the connections or states of affairs which an object can enter into clear. A version of seeing the whole is seeing the totality of connections for each object. Logic produces this picture—the full truth of how things stand—and provides the *Tractatus* with a language of reality. Yet, logic can only show the whole through the holes in its net. The inside view is intimate, but for Wittgenstein, it is still not as good as one from the outside.

Like Einstein who in one *gedanken* experiment imagined himself riding a light beam, Wittgenstein imagines himself sitting astride a girder of logic watching objects and events against the backdrop of the whole of space and time. Today's animated films easily produce such a spectacle. Each object affects the whole, but the change is orderly and static. At each moment, the world is different from the next, but change is accomplished by a progression of isolated still pictures. The objects cast no shadows, no unwanted pictures. Everything is still, movement is eliminated, even though change continues to happen. It is a peculiar picture, familiar voyerism from the history of philosophy, yet foreign to a post-*Investigations* generation where no such privileged views are possible. By the time of the *Investigations*, Wittgenstein had abandoned this religious picture and settled for a secular scene, an *Übersehen*. While the latter picture still desires a view of the whole, it has been drained of all mysticism.

The key difference in the later attempt to view the world as a whole is that Wittgenstein places himself amidst the concepts, on a level with them, instead of outside them or in some way underneath them. As Norman Malcolm noted, the drama between inner and outer plays an important role in Wittgenstein's thinking.[8] On one hand, one cannot get outside language, or distance oneself from a form of life. On the other, one cannot be content to simply be a citizen of any form of life (*Z* 455). To be committed to any community of ideas renders the philosopher aspect-blind and thus unable to see beyond the status quo. One must be free from any particular *Weltanschauung* or even *Weltbild* if one is going to see the numerous possibilities and changing aspects of a situation:

> I find it important in philosophizing to keep changing my posture,
> not to stand for too long on *one* leg, so as not to get stiff. (*CV* pg. 27)

Thus, at the same time as being on the inside, one must also seek the outside. The question is, How can one be both near and far, inside and outside, at the same time? (*See* pg. 70–75 for further discussion of this point.) The view from eternity was Wittgenstein's first strategy; a perspicuous representation is his second and more considered one.

In the *Investigations*, he relinquishes all exterior perspectives. Standing on a hill in the rolling landscape or on one of the labyrinthian streets of a city, he follows the thread of language wherever it leads, erecting signposts for innocent travelers (*CV* pg. 18). Mapping the linguistic domain, the way of seeing, must be done slowly. Human, native speaking cartographers, must walk among the concepts, handling and sorting them carefully. The image of a land of concepts, a parallel conceptual universe, illuminates Wittgenstein's project in the *Investigations* perfectly:

> I am trying to conduct you on tours in a certain country. I will
> try to show that the philosophical difficulties which arise in mathe-
> matics as elsewhere arise because we find ourselves in a strange town
> and do not know our way. So we must learn the topography by going
> from one place in the town to another, and from there to another, and
> so on. And one must do this so often that one knows one's way, either
> immediately or pretty soon after looking around a bit, wherever one
> may be set down (cf. *WLAA* pg. 43). (*WLFM* pg. 44)

One ambles from the concept of understanding to that of knowledge, pausing at reading on the way. No moonbeams carry one to a star to obtain an aerial view. Instead, the sense of the whole is achieved through an apprehension of the connections between concepts. Webs of connections suspend one just high enough to see forever. Finally in the later work, Wittgenstein fulfills his earlier insight that one cannot get outside of language (or the world). Wittgenstein knew this early on (*T* 5.61, *T* 5.6331). In fact, the limit to what can be said in the *Tractatus* is a direct function of the fact that one can not get outside of language; yet, he still longed for an external perspective and believed that logic could somehow provide it:

> Logic is kind of ultra-physics, the description of the 'logical structure of the world', which we perceive through a kind of ultra-experience (with the understanding, e.g.). (*RFM* I, 8)

The view *sub specie aeternitatis*, like so many other commandposts in the history of philosophy (e.g., God's omniscience, the disinterested spectator, the absolute spirit) promised objectivity, truth, and an escape from the subjectivity of fallible human perspectives. In good old cosmological fashion, the world breathes as a whole or not at all. A perspicuous representation, on the other hand, eliminates all superviews. Wittgenstein recognizes that even if there were such a thing as an all-seeing eye, it would not necessarily see all things at all times. The most perfect view is still an imperfect one. A perspicuous representation provides only a tentative map, not one for eternity. Things change, especially ways of seeing.

The wide disparity between the two views is captured in the very meaning of the word "*Übersehen*," the details of which are obscured by English translations. In German, *"die Übersehen"* implies a superficial view; things are spied quickly, roughly. One sees the whole, the connections between things, but the details are obscured. An *Übersehen* is not a careful, scientific scrutiny of the trees, but a glimpse of the forest. It seeks not what is hidden, but the blooming, buzzing confusion of the ordinary. While this may sound odd in light of Wittgenstein's admonitions against ignoring details and his demand that philosophy study things close up, a map of the whole is the only remedy for those who have lost their way:

> A philosophical problem has the form: "I don't know my way about". (*PI* 123)

Myopia is as much a cause of philosophical problems as long-sightedness. To escape a fly-bottle, one needs a map to get from point a to point b.

Further understanding of an *übersehen* comes from similes Wittgenstein uses to characterize his method. In the Introduction to the *Investigations,* Wittgenstein speaks of his remarks as "sketches," and of the whole of his book as a "sketch of the landscape":

> The philosophical remarks in this book are, as it were, a number of sketches of landscapes which were made in the course of these long and involved journeyings.
>
> The same or almost the same points were always being approached afresh from different directions, and new sketches made. Very many of these were badly drawn or uncharacteristic marked by all the defects of a weak draughtsman. And when they were rejected a number of tolerable ones were left, which now had to be arranged and some-times cut down, so that if you looked at them you could get a picture of the landscape. Thus this book is really only an album.
>
> (*PI* pg. ix)

The goal is a general picture showing how concepts hang together in the conceptual domain. Once again exactness, details, and painstaking analyses are sacrificed to the broad outline. In complete contrast to the precisely engineered pictures of the *Tractatus* where the limits of sense and nonsense were drawn to a millimeter, the sketches of the later works, the "remarks (*bemerkungen*)"—yet another word for a casual glance—could only give a tentative, rough, approximation of "how things stand":

> "What's ragged should be left ragged." (*CV* pg. 45)

Instead of a logical picture whose end points touched reality, a sweeping hand gesture, indicating a *this-here-now* would have to suffice. "Landscape" like "sketch" emphasizes seeing the whole at a glance, in one composite picture. Unlike the careful scrutiny of the logical gaze, an *Übersehen* implies a rough glance, one marked as much by its raggedness as its quickness.

Calling the book an "album" is also revealing. An "album" is a blank book; it offers a topos to collect things, e.g., family pictures, remarks. The *Investigations* is a collection of remarks or pictures on a variety of subjects. It is not a "book" in the ordinary sense, not a treatise, nor an essay. Yet, it is not a jumble or a heap; it is a whole, of sorts. Connections exist. There is an order, even if it is not always perspicuous. The album presents a record of a form of life. Wittgenstein strives not to impose an order through theory, but to discover the connections that already exist through observation, literally "re-marks." Wary not to make the metaphysical mistake of confusing conceptual investiagtions with physical ones, he is careful to place the connections in grammatical, not physical space *(Logische raum)*. Of course, as he himself laments, he is not completely successful. There are gaps and jumps; but the transitions are smooth enough for well-travelled readers to detect the lay of the land. "Sketch," "remark," "perspicuous representation," "album" reiterate in different ways the tenuous, open nature of Wittgenstein's style, his *way* of seeing.

Synchronic, although never explicitly used by Wittgenstein, offers yet another approach to the concept of a perspicuous representation:

> Disquiet in philosophy might be said to arise from looking at philosophy wrongly, seeing it wrong, namely as if it were divided into (infinite) longitudinal strips instead of into (finite) cross strips. This inversion in our conception produces the *greatest* difficulty. So we try as it were to grasp the unlimited strips and complain that it cannot be done piecemeal. To be sure it cannot, if by a piece one means an infinite longitudinal strip. But it may well be done, if one means a cross-strip.—But in that case we never get to the end of our work!— Of course, not, for it has no end.
>
> We want to replace wild conjectures and explanation by quiet weighing of linguistic facts. (*Z* 447)

A diachronic or historical inquiry tracing one concept both back to its roots and forwards towards its completion not only misconceives its goal in terms of causes and ends, but presumes that there is an end and a beginning. A synchronic picture, on the other hand, does not ask "why" either in terms of aetiology or teleology, but only describes the relations and interactions between concepts at one point in time. The synchronic picture describes how something works, but it can never justify itself as the right picture; it can never answer the question "why this picture and not another?" By "piece" he means a gestalt of the whole, rather than a fragment. Like a G curve in mathematics, each part gives a picture of the whole. One still has to piece things together—a piece is not a crystal ball—yet, by careful piecing, one can obtain a view of the whole. Whether dealing with infinite longitudinal strips or finite latitudinal ones, the task is endless. Philosophy has no end, just as it has no beginning.

The structural, synchronic nature of Wittgenstein's account is best seen in a series of remarks made on Frazer's *Golden Bough*:

> An historical explanation, an explanation as an hypothesis of the

development, is only *one* kind of summary of the data—of their synopsis. We can equally well see the data in their relations to one
another and make a summary of them in a general picture without
putting it in the form of an hypothesis regarding the temporal development....

"And all this points to some unknown law" is what we want to
say about the material Frazer has collected. I *can* set out this law in an
hypothesis of development, or again, in analogy with the schema of a
plant I *can* give it in the schema of a religious ceremony, but I can
also do it just by arranging the factual material so that we can easily
pass from one part to another and have a clear view of it—showing it
in a "perspicuous" [*übersichtlichen*] way.

For us the conception of a perspicuous presentation [a way of
setting out the whole field together by making easy the passage from
one part of it to another] is fundamental. It indicates the form in
which we write of things, the way in which we see things. (A kind of
"*Weltanschauung*" that seems to be typical of our time. Spengler)

This perspicuous presentation makes possible that understanding
which consists just in the fact that we "see the connections". Hence
the importance of finding *intermediate links*.

But in our case an hypothetical link is not meant to do anything
except draw attention to the similarity, the connection, between
the *facts*. As one might illustrate the internal relation of a circle to an
ellipse by gradually transforming an ellipse into a circle; *but not in
order to assert that a given ellipse in fact, historically, came from a circle*
(hypothesis of development) but only to sharpen our eye for a formal
connection.

But equally I might see the hypothesis of development as nothing but a way of expressing a formal connection. (*RFGB* pg. 8-9)

The remark about a perspicuous representation in the *Investigations* was
obviously lifted from this context. The cross-sectional view highlights connections, internal resemblances. One arranges facts to make these connections perspicuous. Because everything is visible, one is not tempted to offer
a theory connecting things as one is with the temporal dimension.[9]
Knowledge is not a matter of guessing meanings, offering explanations, or
other kinds of summaries that take law-like form, but of listening to and
observing the connections that obtain without interfering. A perspicuous
representation produces a synthesis, not an analysis. How we see things will

become evident with the right guidance; the framework for interpreting phenomena is already present in the phenomena. No external schemas or theories are needed.

The differences between the two approaches, offering a theory and describing a way of seeing, are many, but subtle. For example, Wittgenstein's philosophy is highly pragmatic, but he is not a pragmatist. He does not assume that he has discovered a framework that explains how the world is for all times. Rather, he is pragmatic to the extent that he believes that context and use are important for determining meaning. Wittgenstein's pragmatism is no more than heuristic, while Dewey's or Peirce's is a *Weltanschauung* and thus, for Wittgenstein, a potential prison. In fact, if one tries to identify Wittgenstein's philosophy about reality, no "ism" applies. For Wittgenstein, one arranges facts to display connections that exist independently of the mind of the knower. But, since the facts are the "cultural" ones of a way of seeing or form of life, the realism of discovery is tempered by a blurring of the subject/object distinction. One learns how to see things, not the way one ought to see them. The language-game, way of seeing, or form of life is not other than reality. They can not be separated. How we see things is not developed in a vacuum; it is related to the way things are, but not as its indubitable model.

Supporting Wittgenstein's belief in the worth of a synoptic or perspicuous view is a rejection of the mechanical world view where only external connections prevail; he favors an organic view, but one tempered by twentieth century structuralism. Things are related, only the dialectic between internal and external no longer provides a framework to understand those relations. They are not external in the sense that they are arbitrary; yet they are not internal in the sense that they are hidden and irreversible. "Then, what are they?" someone will surely ask. The proper answer is, "Who cares?" To want to say is to want to theorize. What Wittgenstein wants to do is *show* the fact of connectedness. The problem will disappear when one accepts these connections; then, one will no longer need to prove that they are connected.

Proof is still another concept Wittgenstein uses to speak about a perspicuous representation. What makes a proof a proof for Wittgenstein is that it shows the derivation (the connection) of one line from another. In Kantian terms, a proof constructs a concept:

> Proof, one might say, does not merely shew *that* it is like this, but: *how* it is like this. It shews *how* 13+14 yield 27.

"A proof must be capable of being taken in [*übersehbar*]"
means: we must be prepared to use it as our guide-line in judging.

When I say "a proof is a picture"—it can be thought of as a cinematographic picture.

We construct the proof once for all.

A proof must of course have the character of a model.

The proof (the pattern of the proof) shews us the result of a procedure (the construction); and we are convinced that a procedure regulated in *this* way always leads to this configuration.

(The proof exhibits a fact of synthesis to us.) (*RFM* II, 22)

Again distinguishing between the *that* and the *how*, Wittgenstein this time focuses on the how. The how may not be mystical, but neither is it obvious. A renewed respect for the how of things fills the *Investigations*. Using the language of the *Tractatus,* the proof provides "a model," and at the time of the composition of this remark, a guarantee of how something is. In contrast to Frazer, the structural character of a proof describes more convincingly than an historical explanation. The latter kind of explanation while developmental and therefore connective is always causal and temporal and irrelevant to the philosophical issue. Frazer approached the task of understanding how people saw things from the wrong point of attack. He hoped to say something about *why* people saw things the way they did. For Wittgenstein this is impossible. All one can do is show how they saw things. Thus, discovering the missing links between the apes and ourselves would not prove the truth of evolutionary theory, but only confirm the hypothesis of evolution as we have constructed it. A proof is the most formal version of a perspicuous representation. Less sketchy than a collection of remarks, it still only shows how to get from one point to another and not that the last step is inevitably true. Ironically, Wittgenstein takes one of the most exalted concepts of traditional philosophy, proof, and gives it one of the most ordinary interpretations. To prove something is to show how it is related to something else. A proof is a record of a connection, nothing more.

Comparing Wittgenstein's two attempts at a view of the whole, one can say that *die Übersichtliche Darstellung* is a secular version of the view *sub specie aeternitatis*. It remains a commandpost of sorts, but one subject to all the limitations of an aerial view. While it remains an extension of the human eye, it is a natural extension, and not some supernatural all-seeing eye. It solves problems by helping one to find one's way about. With it, one can see the *Weltbild*, the world picture that informs a form of life as Wittgenstein does most concertedly in *On Certainty*. One cannot justify or explain the way we see things, since one can only see the map, not the territory. (For Wittgenstein, this famous saying can be misleading. He would say, it is best not to think there is something we cannot do, some territory or noumena which resists our mapping; rather think of the territory as an alternative series of pictures which could materialize if our proofs were different.) Hopefully, one can see enough to correct the idling theories of philosophers and help to point people in the right direction.

Making Problems Disappear

It is not our aim to refine or complete the system of rules for the use of our words in unheard-of ways.

For the clarity that we aiming at is indeed complete *clarity. But this simply means that the philosophical problems should* completely *disappear....* (PI 133)

An *Übersehen* promises to *dissolve* philosophical problems.[10] Dissolution is a special kind of destruction. Like images fading on a screen, problems lose their contours and intensities when illuminated by the right light. They fade, leaving only the faintest ghosts. "Dissolve" however, has deeper resonances. Like the chemical sense, where "to clarify" means to purify, the treatment envisioned by perspicuous representation rids language of its pictorial impurities. The philosopher–alchemist distills words, refines them into pure actions. From a religious perspective, a perspicuous representation offers absolution from philosophical temptation. Yet only certain kinds of problems respond to such treatment.

Repeatedly, Wittgenstein argues that philosophical problems, unlike scientific ones, are not "real" problems, but puzzles caused by misunderstanding the grammar of language:

....Let us consider a particular philosophical problem, such as "how is it possible to measure a period of time, since the past and the future aren't present and the present is only a point?" The characteristic feature of this is that a confusion is expressed in the form of a question that doesn't acknowledge the confusion, and that what *releases* the questioner from **his** problem is a particular alteration of **his** method of expression. (*PG* X, 141)

The riddling quality of the question derives from the picture of time as something stretching behind and ahead of us. (Interestingly, the picture is created by words. Later, in Chapter 5, I shall say more about the relation between words and pictures.) The fact that a riddle presents itself shows that something is wrong with the picture of time as a road stretching to infinity. If it were appropriate, no riddle would exist and time could be measured as imagined. Philosophical problems are deep precisely because they are rooted in our conceptual universe. To realize the inappropriateness of the picture, however, is to dissolve the problem. That is the moment of truth:

> Here we come up against a remarkable and characteristic phenomenon in philosophical investigation: the difficulty—I might say—is not that of finding the solution but rather that of recognizing as the solution something that looks as if it were only a preliminary to it. "We have already said everything. —Not anything that follows from this, no, *this* itself is the solution!"
>
> This is connected, I believe, with our wrongly expecting an explanation, whereas the solution of the difficulty is a description, if we give it the right place in our considerations. If we dwell upon it, and do not try to get beyond it.
>
> The difficulty here is: to stop. (*Z* 314)

New expressions bring new pictures. Hopefully, the new picture will not lead to new puzzles.

Wittgenstein's problems in the *Tractatus* with "naming" is an instructive example:

> "A *name* signifies only what is an *element* of reality. What cannot be destroyed; what remains the same in all changes." But what is that?—Why, it swam before our minds as we said the sentence! This was the very expression of a quite particular image: of a particular picture which we want to use. For certainly experience does not shew us these elements. (*PI* 59)

With the hindsight of the *Investigations*, he mocks his tendency in the *Tractatus* to be captivated by this Platonic picture of naming and glad that he never, like Russell, makes the mistake of arguing that "this" is the only truly proper name. Russell is a paradigm example of a philosopher being led into a *reductio absurdum* by the pictures of language. Indeed, if one considers some of the strange problems and theories occupying the philosophers of Cambridge and Oxford in the first half of this century,

Wittgenstein's depreciating view of philosophical problems is not so surprising, e.g., Can I know whether someone else is in pain or has a mind?; Are sense-data the ultimate constituents of reality? I pick some of those mentioned by Wittgenstein in the course of his remarks since these were obviously his examples of philosophers gone amuck:

> "I can only *believe* that someone else is in pain, but I *know* it if I am." —Yes, one can make the decision to say "I believe **he** is in pain" instead of "**He** is in pain." But that is all.—What looks like an explanation here, or like a statement about a mental process, is in truth an exchange of one expression for another which, while we are doing philosophy, seems the more appropriate one.
>
> Just try—in a real case—to doubt someone else's fear or pain. (*PI* 303)

Confronted with philosophical problems such as these one cannot help but smile at Wittgenstein's treatment and urge him to dissolve more problems. Mesmerized by the pictures created by language, philosophers lose sight of reality and ask questions and produce answers that would never occur under ordinary circumstances. Cut off from the rest of the world, philosophers deny what everyone else admits and affirm what strikes others as odd. No wonder Wittgenstein views philosophy as a kind of madness!

His main strategy for achieving perspicuous representation is a rearrangement of the data:

> It was true to say that our considerations could not be scientific ones. It was not of any possible interest to us to find out empirically 'that, contrary to our preconceived ideas, it is possible to think such-and-such'—whatever that may mean. (The conception of thought as a gaseous medium.) And we may not advance any kind of theory. There must not be anything hypothetical in our considerations. We must do away with all *explanation*, and description alone must take its place. And this description gets its light, that is to say its purpose, from the philosophical problems. These are, of course, not empirical problems; they are solved, rather by looking into the workings of our language, and that in such a way as to make us recognize those workings; *in despite of* [sic] an urge to misunderstand them. The problems are solved, not by giving new information, but by arranging what we have always known. Philosophy is a battle against the bewitchment of our intelligence by means of language (cf. *PI* 119, *PI* 123). (*PI* 109)

Nothing empirical, nor hypothetical is needed to solve philosophical puzzles. Rather, because of their origin in linguistic confusion, they respond to re-mapping or rearranging of what one already knows. Wittgenstein practices what he preaches; he is constantly rearranging his remarks, copying them from one notebook to another in an effort to make them perspicuous. While it sounds effortless, almost magical, the job is not easy. Our continual need to misunderstand, to capitulate to temptation, complicates the task. As he reminds us often, the problems are deep, even if they are ephemeral (*PI* 111).

Most often, he exhorts us to examine things closely. Again and again, as he attacks Socratic tendencies in philosophy, he urges us to draw near and study things close to:

> ...In order to see more clearly, here as in countless similar cases, we must focus on the details of what goes on; must look at them *from close to.* (*PI* 51)

Yet, an *Übersehen* counsels against getting too close. It misses details and requires the distant perspective of a non-citizen. But, how does one assume a perspective that overlooks much and also respects Wittgenstein's injunction to study details and examine cases? In fact, if philosophical problems are a result of taking language on holiday i.e., of distancing oneself from the everyday, how can a perspicuous representation achieve the clarity that dissolves philosophical problems?[11]

One strategy Wittgenstein uses is to maintain a double perspective, alternating back and forth between a view of the whole, and a view of the part. His remarks shamelessly flaunt the law of excluded middle: "'But this isn't *seeing!*'—'But this is seeing!'—It must be possible to give both remarks a conceptual justification" (*PI* pg. 203). To some his method is indecisive; to others, it is a good way to circumscribe the area of contention. Exactness and preciseness are not necessary for the clarity Wittgenstein seeks. Inexactness cannot be a reproach because the details of one tree or the character of one bush are unimportant when one is sketching the landscape or mapping the world as a whole. Besides, there is no one standard of exactness, but a variety of conventions which gain their rigor from the goal. Concepts like "game," "language," and even "exact" have no fixed boundaries, but depend on the context:

> If I tell someone "Stand roughly here"—may not this explanation work perfectly? And cannot every other one fail to?...(cf. 65–89). (*PI* 88)

Thus, for Wittgenstein's purposes, the rough sketches, which trace the family resemblances between concepts, are entirely sufficient:

> The pedigree of psychological concepts: I strive *not* after
> *exactness*, but after a synoptic view (*sondern Übersichtlichkeit*). (*Z* 464)

While the borders between concepts might be vague, the general picture is in focus and provides a working diagram with which to proceed.

Another possible strategy that preserves one's distance yet brings words back from their metaphysical to their everyday use is to send for them; that is, have someone else do the thinking. Yet, for Wittgenstein, only a personal journey ensures the word's safe return. As he often remarks, no one can think for anyone else (*PI* pg. x). Each one of us must make the journey and, no doubt, repeatedly, once one is bitten by the philosophical bug. Wittgenstein knew that, as humans, all of us would one day or another be bitten. Cure requires a slow, painful process:

> In philosophizing, we may not *termina*te a disease of thought. It
> must run its natural course, and *slow* cure is all important. (That is
> why mathematicians are such bad philosophers.) (*Z* 382)

Philosophers must travel to distant suppositional lands and walk the perimeters of a problem, despite the danger of being cut-off from a language-game:

> "It is only by thinking even more crazily than philosophers do that
> you can solve their problems." (*CV* pg. 75)

Indeed, the danger is not in the going, but in the failing to return. Holidays are not criminal; in fact, they are necessary for doing things in a new way and even for appreciating the old ways.[12] All too often, however, we overstay our vacation and exchange the real, everyday world for the glamorous temptations of theoretical make-believe—ergo "I cannot know another's pain." Importantly, the reason for returning to the case is not just one's civic responsibilities to others, as Plato suggested, but one's own health and sanity. One returns transformed and armed with a way of seeing that dissolves philosophical problems and makes room for new ones to form.

One point worth reiterating is that distancing does not secure objectivity, truth, or any other of the promised jewels of rational exploration. It only allows for possibilities that cast the familiar in a new light. In the double perspective, the suppositional move reminds us that we only think we know, while the move back to a specific form of life confirms that we do know it. It brings us home. Wittgenstein calls the process of coming home a move from disguised nonsense to patent nonsense (*PI* 464):

> To the *philosophical* question: "Is the visual image of this tree compos-
> ite, and what are its component parts?" the correct answer is: "That
> depends on what you understand by 'composite'." (And that is of
> course not an answer but a rejection of the question.) (*PI* 47)

The common sense answer, the one that wisely says, it depends on conditions, on your definition, etc., rejects the desire for absolutes. There is no
answer; in a certain sense, trees are neither composite nor simple. But neither are they fundamentally anything else; that is, we have no better grid of
concepts to fully explain trees. We have chosen to speak of them in this way;
if it helps, use it. If we feel that our knowledge of trees is expanded by speaking of them in this way, we may continue. However, things can go wrong.
Someone with a philosophical bent can come along and push our picture to
its limits revealing either the absurdity of our belief or the mayhem of the
particular inquiring mind. The common sense answer, "it depends," eliminates both the problem and the philosophical answers previously offered.
The solution involves giving examples and not some essence of the examples. To want more, to want to either ground the case, to explain why things
are the way they are, or to state a rule that will function as law is the temptation of philosophy, not its task. Thus the commonsense reply thwarts philosophy because it shows that explanation has no place:

> A rule stands there like a sign-post.—Does the sign-post leave no
> doubt open about the way I have to go? Does it shew which direc-
> tion I am to take when I have passed it; whether along the road or
> the footpath or cross-country? But where is it said which way I am
> to follow it; whether in the direction of its finger or (e.g.) in the
> opposite one?—And if there were, not a single sign-post, but a chain
> of adjacent ones or of chalk marks on the ground—is there only *one*
> way of interpreting them?—So I can say, the sign-post does after all
> leave no room for doubt. Or rather: it sometimes leaves room for
> doubt and sometimes not. And now this is no longer a philosophical
> proposition, but an empirical one. (*PI* 85)

It replaces astonishment with acceptance or acknowledgement. Wittgenstein
calls it therapy because we have been skinned of our illusions. Our desire to

find "logical musts" is a disease of thought inherited from past conceptions of the world and philosophy. The cure is a new conception of philosophy. Returned to the patent nonsense of commonsense, all one can do is articulate the norms of the way of seeing or point to the differences between cases. When we have reached the norms, Wittgenstein says we have reached rock-bottom; that is, "this is how we do it":

> …But if it is *a priori,* that means that it is a form of account which is very convincing to us. (*PI* 158)

In other cases, problems disappear because of the recognition that there is no certain convention to which one can appeal; either one can say "it depends" or an empirical question lurks behind the philosophical one.

Once one sees the variety of cases and the family resemblances between them, the attempt to establish an *a priori* generalization is thwarted. There is no one answer, but a variety of answers depending on a variety of factors. The moral is: Look to the circumstances! "Patent nonsense" adds nothing to our knowledge, but it does bring peace. Wittgenstein would have liked to hear what unappreciative viewers of a Picasso announce readily: "Anybody could have done that." We expected so much and got so little. Common-sense thwarts further philosophical speculation. Philosophy is put to rest—for the moment.

Wittgenstein's praise of common sense, however, is not a simple acceptance of empiricism:

> The limits of empiricism are not assumptions unguaranteed, or intuitively known to be correct: they are ways in which we make comparisons and in which we act. (*RFM* V, 18)

In looking, we come up against conventions, not facts of nature. Eventually, explanations come to an end. The way of seeing cannot be justified; it has no ultimate explanation. Even the laws of nature are just descriptions, but ones we treat as standards. As Moore said with respect to the predicate "good," one can always ask, "but why?" There is no end to the potential string of "whys." Philosophy can only find some peace when it is prepared to stop and accept something as an explanation. Of course, one can always ask, "But, why should we accept something as an explanation?" And the answer is, for true philosophical problems, ones that torment their bearer, it is not a question of should or should not, but of relieving the disquietude that plagues one. If one is like Wittgenstein, problems drive one mad, the resolution of disquietude is paramount.

One can also dissolve philosophical problems by moving from patent nonsense to disguised nonsense (*PI* 524):

> But now it is also correct to use, "I know" in the contexts which Moore mentioned, at least *in particular circumstances.* (Indeed, I do not know what "I know that I am a human being" means; but even that might be given a sense.)
>
> For each one of these sentences I can imagine circumstances that turn it into a move in one of our language-games, and by that it loses everything that is philosophically astonishing. (*OC* 622)

By using imagination to invent cases, even the most outrageous propositions can be given a sense. No *a priori* boundary separates sense from nonsense. While these imaginings may not necessarily have an application in our form of life, the possibility of creating a context eliminates the original strangeness of the proposition and thus quiets the need to say something general. Whether one is moving from disguised to patent nonsense or the other way round, the strategy is to make the strange ordinary or the ordinary strange. Problems disappear and philosophy stops, at least for the moment. It rests because it accomplishes something. One need no longer bring philosophy itself into question; it has a purpose.

Wittgenstein is not eliminating philosophy, nor is he exempting himself from the group of philosophers who are tempted by language. On the contrary, he calls these quandaries "deep disquietudes" (*PI* 111) and recognizes that no strategy will ever completely eliminate them. The disease cannot be helped. Philosophers are just ordinary people, who by asking certain questions and expecting certain answers, are led into a kind of insanity. As long as language tempts us, there will be philosophical problems. The task, then, is to eliminate philosophy of a certain kind: the kind practiced by previous philosophers, especially those surrounding Wittgenstein in England and Vienna. The goal is to eliminate the conception of philosophy as an exact, scientific form of inquiry giving general, *a priori* answers like: "'This' is the only proper name."

Of Shifting Riverbeds and Moving Waters

The propositions presenting what Moore 'knows' are all of such a kind that it is difficult to imagine why anyone should believe the contrary. e.g. the proposition that Moore has spent his whole life in close proximity to the earth. Once more I can speak of myself here instead of speaking of Moore. What could induce me to believe the opposite? Either a memory, or having been told. Everything that I have seen or heard gives me the conviction that no **man** *has ever been far from the earth. Nothing in my picture of the world (Weltbild) speaks in favour of the opposite. (OC 93)*

But I did not get my picture of the world by satisfying myself of its correctness; nor do I have it because I am satisfied of its correctness. No: it is the inherited background against which I distinguish between true and false. (OC 94)

The propositions describing this world-picture might be part of a kind of mythology. And their role is like that of rules of a game; and the game can be learned purely practically, without learning any explicit rules. (OC 95)

It might be imagined that some propositions, of the form of empirical propositions, were hardened and functioned as channels for such empirical propositions as were not hardened but fluid; and that this relation altered in time, in that fluid propositions hardened, and hard ones became fluid. (OC 96)

The mythology may change back into a state of flux, the river-bed of thoughts may shift. But I distinguish between the movement of the waters on the river-bed and the shift of the bed itself; though there is not a sharp division of the one from the other. (OC 97)

These remarks from *On Certainty* introducing Wittgenstein's alternative concept of world-picture, *Das Weltbild,* are among the most vivid and moving of Wittgenstein's writings. Everthing can change; nothing is final. Knowledge, like nature, is subject to erosion and the winds of change. His comparison of certain knowledge with mythology evokes ancient memories of philosophy's first quarrel. Philosophy prided itself on surpassing myth; logos provided a method for distinguising between true and false beliefs and for grounding knowledge on a firmer footing than authority and tradition. Yet, rather than shun myth, Wittgenstein incorporates it into his talk. Myth is not opposed to logic, but an ally in the knowing-game. It has a role in reasoning. Acceptance of the rules of the games precedes all inquiry. But the status of these rules is more mythological than logical. The anti-foundational metaphor of shifting riverbeds further underscores the geological time-frame that Wittgenstein intends by the concept of a world-picture. What we know with certainty, we have known for a very long time and will continue to believe until there is a major shift in our thinking. Thoughts form a riverbed which allows one to step into the same river twice, even though Heraclitus is still right: because the bed itself may shift, all remains in flux. The way of seeing of a form of life is as hard as rock which is to say as soft as rubble from a geological perspective. Furthermore, no rigid line distinguishes between the hardened propositions and the more fluid ones. Movement back and forth guarantees the relativity of perception and the possibility for change.

Among the first "theses" established by these remarks is that the beliefs that comprise a *Weltbild* are all incorrigible; they are neither true nor false, but rules or norms that channel thinking in certain directions. The beliefs are ordinary, everyday thoughts that no one (except philosophers) would think of questioning. They are a varied lot, including such stalwarts as "12x12=124," "this is my hand," "Cows don't stand on their heads and laugh." Inclusion in a world-picture turns not on the kind of proposition, but on its position in a system of beliefs. Empirical propositions serve as norms of description. The beliefs that stand fast for us, that is, what we take as certain, comprise the riverbed of our thoughts, our form of life.[13] They are neither true nor false.

Another important feature of these propositions is that they have not been explicitly learned, nor is belief in them a matter of their truth-status:

> In general I take as true what is found in text-books, of geography for example. Why? I say: All these facts have been confirmed a hundred times over. But how do I know that? What is my evidence for it? I have a world-picture. Is it true or false? Above all it is the substratum of all my enquiring and asserting. The propositions describing it are not all equally subject to testing. (*OC* 162)

We learned them when we learned a form of life, during a time when correct did not matter. Yet, our commitment to the world-picture is not irrational, not a matter of blind faith. Squeezed between the choice of myth or reason (logic), philosophers have made it impossible to obtain an adequate understanding of the status of these beliefs. We are neither completely irrational nor rational in accepting such beliefs; rather they impress themselves on us in the course of interacting with the world. While they seem completely natural, inevitable, we must remember that that is an illusion of a form of life. The riverbed can always shift, making new beliefs plausible. Both skepticism and dogmatism are undermined by the riverbed metaphor; the river runs under or through them.

The beliefs of a *Weltbild* function normatively not descriptively; they tell us how the world ought to look to "normal" observers, not how it does look to the omniscient eye. For the most part, we are unaware of the subtle directions provided by our way of seeing and mistake them for descriptions of the world. The results of such confusions are, of course, metaphysics. Recognizing their normative status is the first step to seeing the world aright:

> We know that the earth is round. We have definitively ascer-
> tained that is round.
>
> We shall stick to this opinion, unless our whole way of seeing nature changes. "How do you know that?" I believe it. (*OC* 291)

> Further experiments cannot *give the lie* to our earlier ones, at most they may change our whole way of looking at things.
> (*OC* 292)

Bed-rock is reached when we refuse to acknowledge a challenge to our form of life.

Another word Wittgenstein uses for world-picture is "*Bezugssystem*" or frame of reference:

> The *truth* of certain empirical propositions belongs to our frame of reference [Bezugssystem]. (*OC* 83)

In other terms, propositions that comprise a frame of reference describe the logic or grammar of our way of seeing, what we treat as *a priori*:

> …It is a logical proposition; for it does describe the conceptual (lin-
> guistic) situation. (*OC* 51)
> …And everything descriptive of a language-game is part of logic.
> (*OC* 56)
> When we say "Certain propositions must be excluded from doubt," it sounds as if I ought to put these propositions—for exam-
> ple, that I am called L.W.—into a logic book. For if it belongs to the description of a language-game, it belongs to logic…(*OC* 628)

To be part of logic, grammar, or the frame of reference means to be descriptive of the way of seeing itself, e.g., the labeling system for color names

(*PI* 50), and not of the scene seen. These propositions become rules for see-ing. They make sense of the world by giving a frame to our questions and assertions. However, they do this not by corresponding with the facts, not by being necessarily true, but by being believed:

> Here we see that the idea of 'agreement with reality' does not have any clear application. (*OC* 215)

In fact, these propositions are among the least grounded of all:

> At the foundation of well-founded belief lies belief that is not founded. (*OC* 253)
> The difficulty is to realize the groundlessness of our believing. (*OC* 166)

In a marvelous image, Wittgenstein overturns the usual picture of foundations:

> I have arrived at the rock bottom of my convictions.
> And one might almost say that these foundation-walls are carried by the whole house. (*OC* 248)

Like the molten core that now constitutes our picture of the earth's interi-or, rather than the fixed rock of earlier pictures, the top holds the bottom in place. Thus, when one describes the logic of a world-picture one is not explaining anything, nor justifying practices, but only describing the beliefs that stand fast. Of course, one can use the description as an explanation; that is, one can decide to treat the description normatively. It must be noted however, that this remains a decision.

In all these ways and more, the world-picture named by the German word "*Weltbild*" differs radically from that named by "*Weltanschauung.*" A *Weltbild* does not consist of hypotheses; it is not a theory. One does not invent it, but acquires it as if by osmosis. The propositions of a *Weltbild,* like all those Moore worries about, can neither be confirmed nor falsified. They are outside the knowledge game:

> It is clear that our empirical propositions do not all have the same status, since one can lay down such a proposition and turn it from an empirical proposition into a norm of description.
> Think of chemical investigations. Lavoisier makes experiments with substances in his laboratory and now he concludes that this and that takes place when there is burning. He does not say that it might happen otherwise another time. He has got hold of a definite world-picture—not of course one that he invented; he learned it as a

child. I say world picture [Weltbild] and not hypothesis, because it is the matter-of-course foundation for his research and as such also goes unmentioned. (*OC* 167)

A *Weltanschauung,* on the other hand, is a special or competing way of seeing things. Its propositions are offered in the spirit of hypotheses and theories. It proposes new knowledge and thinks of itself in competition with science. It mistakes a conceptual investigation for a physical one and concludes by saying things like, "Sense-data are the material of the universe," or "The world and language share a common logical form." Both behaviorism and pragmatism are examples of *Weltanschauungen,* from which Wittgenstein struggles to disassociate himself. While he agrees with a number of the ideas professed by these views, he does not hold these views in the same way. A *Weltanschauung* forgets its status as *a* way of seeing and parades itself as *the* way of seeing. It takes itself too seriously, as the ultimate explanation and foundation of our convictions. In contrast, the concept of a *Weltbild* completely avoids the knowledge game.

The extent to which Wittgenstein wished to avoid the knowledge-game can best be seen in his efforts to avoid such concepts as "hypothesis," "assumption," "presupposition," "inference," etc., as well as "truth," "argument," and "reason." The whole vocabulary of knowledge is out of place when discussing the certainty provided by a *Weltbild:*

> No one ever taught me that my hands don't disappear when I am not paying attention to them. Nor can I be said to presuppose the truth of this proposition in my assertions, etc., (as if they rested on it) while it only gets sense from the rest of our procedure of asserting. (*OC* 153)

> That is to say, the *questions* that we raise and our *doubts* depend on the fact that some propositions are exempt from doubt, are as it were like hinges on which those turn. (*OC* 341)

> But it isn't that the situation is like this: We just *can't* investigate everything, and for that reason we are forced to rest content with assumption. If I want the door to turn, the hinges must stay put. (*OC* 343)

> My *life* consists in my being content to accept many things (cf. OC 411). (*OC* 344)

Assumptions and presuppositions belong to the game of reason and knowledge. They are formal propositions adopted at will to advance a position. The beliefs of a *Weltbild,* on the other hand, are not learned in a context in which a question makes sense, nor can they be exchanged or adopted at will. Thus, Wittgenstein prefers the similes of "hinges," "bedrock," and "pivots" to describe their status. No one would think of a "hinge" as an assumption. These similes are taken from the physical world to emphasize the fact that while our beliefs form a system, it is not a knowledge system, but an ungrounded way of acting. Both Hume and Moore mistake the status of this system when they try to use it as an example of certain knowledge. As Wittgenstein would say, it is not quite right to say "we presuppose" these beliefs; we just accept them, or rather, trust them:

> I really want to say that a language-game is only possible if one trusts something (I did not say "can trust something"). (*OC* 509)

These ideas become even clearer when we consider what Wittgenstein has to say about the manner in which we acquire a world-picture.

In two remarks already quoted, Wittgenstein indicates that we acquire a world-picture as a child through informal and tacit processes. We never learn it explicitly, but inherit it from a culture. To highlight this difference, Wittgenstein attempts to draw a distinction between "learning" and "acquiring":

> I do not explicitly learn the propositions that stand fast for me. I can *discover* them subsequently like the axis around which a body rotates. This axis is not fixed in the sense that anything holds it fast, but the movement around it determines its immobility. (*OC* 152)

> …This system is something a human being acquires by means of observation and instruction. I intentionally do not say "learns."(*OC* 279)

Learning is something we do when we explicitly set out to acquire knowledge. Acquiring begins at the onset of life and is gained by doing and observation. As in the learning of a native language, one acquires the practice first and learns the rules later. Since we normally do not make such a hard distinction between "acquiring" and "learning," Wittgenstein goes so far as to compare "acquiring" with an instinctual process to help distinguish it from "learning":

> The squirrel does not infer by induction that it is going to need stores next winter as well. And no more do we need a law of induction to justify our action or our predictions. (*OC* 287)

But that means I want to conceive it as something that lies beyond being justified or unjustified; as it were, as something animal. (*OC* 359)

I want to regard **man** here as an animal; as a primitive being to which one grants instinct but not ratiocination. As a creature in a primitive state. Any logic good enough for a primitive means of communication needs no apology from us. Language did not emerge from a kind of ratiocination. (*OC* 475)

Just as animals are programmed to store food for subsequent winters, humans are programmed into a world-picture. They acquire certain beliefs from their interactions with nature and their culture. These beliefs stand outside the process of inquiry, testing and justification, not because they are true, but because of the way they are learned. However, it is important to remember that in drawing this distinction, Wittgenstein is not offering an hypothesis on human nature; rather, in trying to get us to see the difference between the beliefs of a *Weltbild* and those of the latest scientific theory, for example, he is comparing it, drawing an analogy to instinctual response and animal behavior. The analogies ought not to be taken in the spirit of assertion, but rather as an attempt to get us to see things in one light rather than another.

His discussion raises another important question, "How does this acquiring take place?" As Plato would say, "Who are the teachers? " Wittgenstein's answer to this question further illustrates the distinctive character of the beliefs of the *Weltbild* and also his own difficulties with an analogy between acquiring and instinctive response. The answer is, of course, that we learn them from culture and from experience. To say that we learned them from experience creates a number of problems. For example, Wittgenstein asks, How does mute experience teach? Moreover, since experience seems to be a world of demonstrative facts, how does it teach us while all the time showing that things can be otherwise than we experience them. The matter is a delicate and difficult one since Wittgenstein both wants to challenge the illusion that experience teaches us anything while all the time defending experience as a teacher. Need I add that this is a classic example of Wittgenstein's philosophical need to both assert and deny the same proposition?

Consider the following passages challenging experience's authority:

But isn't it experience that teaches us to judge like *this*, that is to say, that it is correct to judge like this? But how does experience *teach* us, then? *We* may derive it from experience, but experience does not direct us to derive anything from experience. It is the *ground* of our judging like this, and not just the cause, still we do not have a ground for seeing this in turn as a ground. (*OC* 130)

> One wants to say "All my experiences shew that it is so." But how do they do that? For that proposition to which they point itself belongs to a particular interpretation of them.
>
> "That I regard this proposition as certainly true also characterizes my interpretation of experience." (*OC* 145)

Experience is not sacrosanct; there is always an interpretation of experience. Since experience produces the illusion of hard fact or rather, we allow experience this place, it is crucial to remember that when we say experience teaches, we ought to be saying an interpretation of experience teaches. Accordingly, we say,"one acquires the world-picture entirely from the culture which has interpreted experience for us." On the other hand, it is absurd to say that experience requires an interpretation or a "mastery of a technique." Just as with the concept of "seeing-as", there are two concepts of experience: one where it makes sense to talk about interpretation, and one where this is out of place. As with that other concept, the line distinguishing them is marginal. In our daily interactions with the world, we simply experience things and do not first frame our experiences, e.g., the famous example of a child learning that fire burns. Thus, Wittgenstein agrees that experience teaches, only not isolated propositions:

> One such [empirical propositions that count as certain for us] is that if someone's arm is cut off it will not grow again. Another, if someone's head is cut off, **he** is dead and will never live again.
>
> Experience can be said to teach us these propositions. However, it does not teach us them in isolation; rather, it teaches us a host of interdependent propositions. If they were isolated I might perhaps doubt them, for I have no experience relating to them. (*OC* 274)

Inherent in the notion of experience is the idea of multiple instances, repeatable occurrences and interconnected beliefs; that is, we experience a way of seeing and thus cannot use experience to justify that way of seeing. We learn the correct judgements themselves and not rules for judging:

> Can one learn this knowledge? Yes; some can. Not, however, by taking a course in it, but through "*experience*". Can someone else be

a **man's** teacher in this? Certainly. From time to time **he** gives **him** the right *tip*. This is what 'learning' and 'teaching' are like here. (*PI* pg. 227)

What one acquires here is not a technique; one learns correct judgements. There are also rules, but they do not form a system, and only experienced people can apply them right. Thus, there is nothing wrong with saying we learn from experience as long as we realize that a) what was learned could have be otherwise and b) experience would not teach without a context. Indeed, experience is a teacher in spite of itself because this is the way we treat it. If instruction and experience conflict, we will choose in favor of experience. It is always innocent until proven guilty. Even though we can not use experience as the ground for what we believe as an empiricist might want to, it nevertheless is the ground: that is how we treat it. The trick is to remember that it is matter of our treating it in such a way, rather than it being in such a way.

The world-picture like a form of life is not equivalent to any specific content; it is a variable, grammatical notion meant to point to a shifting, unstable set of beliefs. "Set of beliefs" is already too rigid. The *übersehen* or method of seeing in the later works discovers these beliefs, the content of our current world-picture. Pointing to these beliefs is useful to correct idling philosophical theories, but they can never represent the truth, the "this is how things stand." This is what we believe, this is the form of our life. One can say no more. But if one says it right, philosophy will find peace. Questions will dissipate; colors will reappear as the world regains its rough ground and its many dimensions. Life will be livable again.

Chapter 2 Don't Think, Look!

Consider for example the proceedings that we call "games". I mean board-games, card-games, ball-games, Olympic games, and so on. What is common to them all?—Don't say "There must be something common, or they would not be called 'games'"—but look and see whether there is anything common to all.— For if you look at them you will not see something that is common to all, but similarities, relationships, and a whole series of them at that. To repeat: Don't think, but look!... (PI 66)

The word "see" in the expression "a way of seeing" is not fortuitous. Wittgenstein explicitly means to speak of "a way of seeing" and not "a way of thinking." Not only does he rarely use "thinking,"[1] but he repeatedly thematizes the differences between it and seeing:

> One cannot guess how a word functions. One has to *look at* its use and learn from that.
>
> But the difficulty is to remove the prejudice which stands in the way of doing this. It is not a *stupid* prejudice. (*PI 340*)

Surprisingly, for a philosopher, he insists that looking, not thinking, remedies philosophical ignorance. One would have thought that seeing only reproduces the status quo; not so for Wittgenstein. Sounding like Bacon chastising his mathematically-minded contemporaries, Wittgenstein cautions that adequate deductions only follow from the meticulous examination of data. Don't guess, he admonishes; be there, look, observe.[1]

Getting philosophers to look, however, has difficulties of its own. As Wittgenstein remarks, philosophers resist looking and once more, they do so with good reason. Looking has its drawbacks too, most notably, the myopia that cannot see the forest for the trees. Pointless empiricism is as directionless as rational confabulation. He notes a similar ambivalence surrounding the examination of details:

> If I am inclined to suppose that a mouse has come into being by spontaneous generation out of grey rags and dust, I shall do well to examine those rags very closely to see how a mouse may have hidden in them, how it may have gotten there and so on. But if I am convinced that a mouse cannot come into being from these things, then this investigation will perhaps be superfluous.

> But first we must learn to understand what it is that opposes such an examination of details in philosophy. (*PI* 52)

For the most part, philosophers have treated details as minutiae. Instead of such a knee-jerk reaction against the fine print, Wittgenstein wants us to become sensitive to the possible solutions that looking and details provide.

Wittgenstein's own practice reflects philosophy's long-standing ambivalence about seeing versus thinking, details versus wholes, and examples versus exceptions. At every opportunity, he calls upon thinking to picture alternatives either real or imagined to what is seen. Indeed, practically every other remark in the later work asks us "to think (*denken*) this" or "imagine (*vorstellen*) that," or just "suppose (*annehmen*)." The *Investigations* is unimaginable without these memorable *gedenken* experiments. Yet, he also just as regularly mocks his and philosophy's penchant for supposition:

> Could one imagine a stone's having consciousness? And if anyone can do so—why should that not merely prove that such image-mongery is of no interest to us? (*PI* 390)

> …Where (outside philosophy) do we use the words "I can imagine **his** being in pain" or "I imagine that…" or "Imagine that…"?… (*PI* 393)

Imagings and supposings have their place, but they have their faults too.

His dilemma is, of course, not new. One immediately recognizes in his contortions philosophy's age-old battle between rationalism and empiricism first initiated by Socrates and the Sophists and replicated endlessly ever after. Determined to exit this fly-bottle, Wittgenstein tries a variety of solutions. As I shall argue, he finally abandons them both and even their dialectic for "acting":

> Giving grounds, however, justifying the evidence, comes to an

end;—but the end is not certain propositions' striking us immediately *as* true, i.e. it is not a kind of *seeing* on our part; it is our *acting*, which lies at the bottom of the language-game (cf. *OC* 110, 232, 395, 411, 414.) (*OC* 204)

"A way of acting," not seeing, finally identifies the critical factor in a form of life. The progression from the *Tractatus* to *On Certainty* is marked by a steady advance from thinking through seeing to acting. In the end, for Wittgenstein, as well as in the beginning, is the deed:

> …und schreib getrost
> "Im Anfang war die Tat." (*OC* 402)

"I'll Teach You Differences"[2]

> *You think that after all you must be weaving a piece of cloth: because you are sitting at a loom—even if it is empty—and going through the motions of weaving. (PI 414)*

According to the hints provided by the already quoted remarks, the main difference between thinking and seeing is that thinking, like language, glosses over differences. Aloof in its conceptual tower, thinking treats everything as variations of the same:

> Seeing life as a weave, this pattern (pretense, say) is not always complete and is varied in a multiplicity of ways. But we, in our conceptual world, keep on seeing the same, recurring with variations. That is how our concepts take it. For concepts are not for use on a *single* occasion (cf. *Z* 568). (*RPP* II, 672)

Concepts are meant to generalize, to bulk experience. Percepts, on the other hand, are meant to particularize. In fact, by crossing wires, *thinking* tends to *see* identities and essences, where *seeing*, in contrast, *thinks* differences. (The ultimate goal is to find a skill tuned to family resemblances.) While we ordinarily picture thinking as more liberating than seeing, Wittgenstein reminds us that thinking can be as conservative as other modalities. Instead of liberating one from provincialism, thinking can imprison one in ritualized beliefs.

His own use of thinking in the *Tractatus* is, for Wittgenstein, an instructive case in point. Again and again in the *Investigations*' sustained critique of

Tractarian thinking (*PI* 89–133), Wittgenstein draws attention to thinking's potential for error and illusion:

> Thought is surrounded by a halo.—Its essence, logic, presents an order, in fact the a priori order of the world: that is, the order of *possibilities*, which must be common to both world and thought. But this order, it seems, must be *utterly simple*. It is *prior* to all experience, must run through all experience; no empirical cloudiness or uncertainty can be allowed to affect it—It must rather be of the purest crystal. But this crystal does not appear as an abstraction; but as something concrete, indeed, as the most concrete, as it were the *hardest* thing there is (*Tractatus Logico-Philosophicus* 5.5563).... (*PI* 97)

Radiating order, thought can find no foothold in reality; it can only remake it. Deprived of the friction provided by the rough ground, thinking loses itself. What is worse, it deceives itself into thinking that it *sees* what it thinks:

> We want to say that there can't be any vagueness in logic. The idea now absorbs us, that the ideal '*must*' be found in reality. Meanwhile we do not as yet see *how* it occurs there, nor do we understand the nature of the "must". We think it must be in reality; for we think we already see it there (cf. *PI* 95, 103, 104, 114). (*PI* 101)

Bound as it is to logic, it idealizes reality according to the patterns suggested by logic's network of symbols. We easily get trapped in logic's sublimed order and lose sight of the disorder of things. Wittgenstein's cry, "Back to the rough ground" (*PI* 107), is comparable to Husserl's battle-cry, "Back to the things themselves," only Wittgenstein would not have distinguished between the things themselves and how they are seen. No such ontological split guided his way. Rather, he only means for us to avoid illusion and delusion.

Seeing, on the other hand, shows the family resemblances between concepts (*PI* 67), the connections that criss-cross the conceptual domain. It resists faulty generalizations and theoretical musts, discovering differences, not essences. Above all, seeing refuses what is hidden and supposedly more fundamental. It demands that we consider what is open to view. Moreover, seeing is grounded in the shared world. It connects us to each other as well as to the world. By not losing sight of its applications, seeing resists the temptation to get lost in theoretical possibilities. From thinking's distant, theoretical standpoint, everything seems methodologically possible, even if thoroughly unworkable. Where the *Tractatus* insisted and depended upon keeping logic and its application apart (*T* 5.557), the *Investigations* proceeds by doing just the opposite: it demands that logic and its application overlap:

> The sense of a sentence—one would like to say—may, of course, leave this or that open, but the sentence must nevertheless have *a* definite sense. An indefinite sense—that would really not be a sense *at all*.—This is like: An indefinite boundary is not really a boundary at all. Here one thinks perhaps: If I say "I have locked the **man** up fast in the room—there is only one door left open"—then I simply haven't locked **him** in at all; **his** being locked in is a sham. One would be inclined to say here: "You haven't done anything at all" An enclosure with a hole in it is as good as *none*.—But is that true? (*PI* 99)

Wittgenstein's frustrating and philosophically deflating answer is, "maybe!" He argues that it depends on the physical conditions of the person and the door and also how we use "locked." Since logic cannot determine these things *a priori,* the answer awaits an application of the rules in particular circumstances.

The problem with thinking is that it gives rise to grand schemes, marvelous, perfectly symmetrical visions of, for example, the boundaries of a concept; however, since the application is never considered, thinking begins to idle. Following the tempting call of language, philosophers lose themselves in the fun and games of speculation and forget the needs of the everyday:

> "But this supposition surely makes good sense!"—Yes; in ordinary circumstances these words and this picture have an application with which we are familiar.—But if we suppose a case in which this application falls away we become as it were conscious for the first time of the nakedness of the words and the picture. (*PI* 349)

Words become naked without the dress of their circumstances. This telling reversal, since words are usually thought of as the dress of facts, reveals the vulnerability of words. Philosophers injudiciously seize them, becoming image-mongers, peddling consistent systems regardless of their applicability in the lived world. Unlike mathematicians and logicians who may play with their symbols generating trains of formal truths, philosophers, for Wittgenstein must look from the very beginning to the application, i.e., towards an interpretation in the domain of the everyday. Otherwise, the task of devising an interpretation at a latter date becomes either arbitrary and mysterious, or one is tempted to think as the *Tractatus* did that the application is guaranteed beforehand by the ontological structure of reality.

Clinically speaking, thinking's neurosis is that it lacks boundaries; in its limitless domain, everything is possible (*PI* 218). Our imaginative abilities can make sense of even the wildest assertion; that is, we can imagine a context for every thought. Thus, the skeptic obtains a foothold because if everything is thinkable, then nothing is knowable:

> "But how can a rule shew me what I have to do at *this* point? Whatever I do is, on some interpretation, in accord with the rule."—That is not what we ought to say, but rather: any interpretation still hangs in the air along with what it interprets, and cannot give it any support. Interpretations by themselves do not determine meaning…(*PI* 198)

However, thinkability or imaginability is not necessarily the criterion for reality. As Wittgenstein so often says, just because something is thinkable or imaginable does not mean that it is actually possible under the circumstances:

> Philosophers who think that one can as it were use thought to make an extension of experience, should think about the fact that one can transmit talk, but not measles, by telephone.
>
> Nor can I experience time as limited, when I want to, or my visual field as homogeneous etc. (*Z* 256)

Similarly, just because the skeptic can imagine a doubt or another interpretation does not mean that we do not know what we thought we knew:

> I said that the application of a word is not everywhere bounded by rules. But what does a game look like that is everywhere bounded by rules? whose rules never let a doubt creep in, but stop up all the cracks where it might?—Can't we imagine a rule determining the application of a rule, and a doubt which *it* removes—and so on?
>
> But that is not to say that we are in doubt because it is possible for us to *imagine* [denken] a doubt. I can easily imagine someone always doubting before **he** opened **his** front door whether an abyss did not yawn behind it, and making sure about it before **he** went through the door (and **he** might on some occasion prove to be right)—but that does not make me doubt in the same case. (*PI* 84)

Thinking something does not make it so and to think so is to engage in a particularly bad form of argument which encourages us to believe that thinking can accomplish more than action and practice allow (*PI* 345).

In contrast, seeing keeps in touch with its application. It proceeds by example and description, forsaking theory and explanation. Examples are not an indirect means in default of a better one (*PI* 71). On the contrary, they provide form of life training and offer objects of comparison (*PI* 130) to help eliminate theoretical possibilities. Sight provides the antidote to theory and spares us the false moves of previous philosophy:

> Isn't what I am saying: any empirical proposition can be transformed into a postulate—and then becomes a norm of description. But I am suspicious even of this. The sentence is too general. One almost wants to say "any empirical proposition can, theoretically, be transformed...", but what does "theoretically" mean here? It sounds all too reminiscent of the *Tractatus*. (*OC* 321)

This remark helps measure the depth of Wittgenstein's distrust of thought's theorizing. Even when it looked like he had some general proposition to utter, he feared its over-general consequences. No doubt, his earlier unqualified and rationalist faith in unaided reason, which led him to believe that language by itself mirrors the structure of reality, made him especially wary. He had never *looked* at thinking then. He had not begun with an *investigation* into the concept of thinking. In contrast, teaching schoolchildren and observing how they actually learn language reminded him that it takes human agents to apply the calculus and make language meaningful.[3]

With his turn to seeing, then, Wittgenstein not only abandons the picture theory of meaning, his search for essences and foundations, but also his faith in logic's ability to describe the world. He abandons a methodology and a long time prejudice of philosophers against looking, giving examples, examining details, and remaining within the domain of the everyday. While sight encounters many obstacles on its journey, they are—with effort—manageable and make progress, when there is any, real instead of illusionary. Unlike Prospero, philosophers cannot don the cape of thought and wave some magic equations to get reality straight; they must descend to Caliban's mud and look and see:

> A picture is conjured up which seems to fix the sense *unambiguously*. The actual use, compared with that suggested by the picture, seems like something muddied. Here again we get the same thing as

in set theory: the form of expression we use seems to have been designed for a god, who knows what we cannot know; **he** sees the whole of each of those infinite series and **he** sees into human consciousness. For us, of course, these forms of expression are like pontificals which we may put on, but cannot do much with, since we lack the effective power that would give these vestments meaning and purpose.

In the actual use of expressions we make detours, we go by sideroads. We see the straight highway before us, but of course we cannot use it, because it is permanently closed. (*PI* 426)

Overwhelmingly, the concept of seeing dominates the rhetoric and methodology of the *Investigations* and culminates in the specific way of seeing recommended in that work, *die Übersehen* (*PI* 122). Yet, in turning to seeing, Wittgenstein is not recommending any simpleminded empiricism. In fact, he is critical of strict empiricist methods and never tires of poking fun at the naiveté of empiricists:

Don't always think that you read off what you say from the facts; that you portray these in words according to rules. For even so you would have to apply the rule in the particular case without guidance. (*PI* 292)

His reservations are evident in his constant questioning about how it is that we learn from experience, or how it is that experience teaches us such-and-such. Neither seeing nor experience is sacrosanct; they both easily wallow aimlessly in a mass of information without a guiding interpretation. As he commented, the philosopher's prejudice against looking is not a *stupid* one.

But, what is it that philosophers have a right to fear about looking? Well—provincialism, loss of vision, disjointed facts, error, and a large part of their human potential. Thinking accomplishes much that sight can never attain. Thinking shows the range of possibilities; it allows an exploration of the terrain in advance of sight. Without it, we would surely be, as I suggested in my introduction, like flies in the fly-bottle banging stupidly against the glass. There would be no inventions, nor discoveries, without thought's sighting possibilities. Nor, I might add, would there be the book, *The Philosophical Investigations,* which depends as much on thinking's picturing possibilities as it does on seeing's concrete cases. The point is that, on their own, both the techniques of looking and thinking are limited, especially as they are polarized by the conflicting claims of empiricists and rationalists. Since there is no third possibility, e.g., feeling or intuition, which surpasses these options, one must reconfigure these ways of knowing so as to make them usable.

To draw from Wittgenstein's practice, his main strategy is to interweave them, alternating back and forth between "seeing connections" and "inventing intermediate cases" (*PI* 122). The continuation of the opening remark of this chapter illustrates this point nicely:

> …Look [*Shau*] for example at board-games, with their multifarious relationships. Now pass to card-games; here you find many correspondences with the first group, but many common features drop out, and others appear. When we pass next to ball-games, much that is common is retained, but much is lost.—Are they all 'amusing'? Compare chess with noughts and crosses. Or is there always winning and losing, or competition between players? Think [*Denk*] of patience…. (*PI* 66)

Thinking's inventions investigate the problem to find the right point of attack. An *investigation* is a formal concept for Wittgenstein and marks his approach to problems:

> …We need to realize that what presents itself to us as the first expression of a difficulty, or of its solution, may as yet not be correctly expressed at all. Just as one who has a just censure of a picture to make will often at first offer the censure where it does not belong, an *investigation* is need in order to find the right point of attack for the critic. (*OC* 37)

> Concepts lead us to make investigations; are the expression of our interest, and direct our interest. (*PI* 570)

Once the range of possibilities is at hand, seeing returns us to the rough ground. It grades the suppositions and cancels those which fail to have an application. While the suppositions allow skepticism a moment's hold, sight's cavalry charges in at the last minute to reaffirm our trust that only some applications make sense, i.e., belong to our form of life. The style of the *Investigations* employs this strategy. To say anything philosophical, one must make at least two moves. The first move supposes, to open the possibilities, while the second looks to cases and closes the range. Nothing can be said in one all encompassing theoretical or aphoristic statement. Differences must be recognized, especially the difference between what thinking discovers may be the case and what sight reminds us is the case *according to a specific form of life.* However, to comfortably move between seeing and thinking, further transformations had to be made. They had to be brought closer together. Picture mediates their differences. As Wittgenstein comes to realize, thinking need not be the "gaseous medium" of the *Tractatus* and seeing need not be the wide-eyed innocence of classical empiricism.

Thinking as Picturing

We want to say: "When we mean something, it's like going up to someone, it's not having a dead picture (of any kind)." We go up to the thing we mean.
(PI 455)

Immediately after concluding his discussion of the logic of facts in the *Tractatus* (1s and 2.0s), Wittgenstein asserts that, "We picture facts to ourselves" (*T* 2.1). Following the critical discussion of the logic of depiction (*T* 2.1s and 2.2s), he then immediately turns to thinking:

A logical picture of facts is a thought. (*T* 3)

'A state of affairs is thinkable': what this means is that we can picture it to ourselves. (*T* 3.001)

The totality of true thoughts is a picture of the world. (*T* 3.01)

While nothing is said directly, the sequence of concepts makes the point that thinking is a picturing. From the beginning of his career to its end, Wittgenstein never abandons the view that thinking is a form of picturing. One readily finds it in the middle works:

…But in my view, if it [the child] thinks, then it forms for itself pictures and in a certain sense these are arbitrary, that is to say, in so far as other pictures could have played the same role…. (*PR* 1, 5)

Thinking is quite comparable to the drawing of pictures.
(*PG* pg. 163)

And, it is ever present in the later ones:

Here it happens that our thinking plays us a queer trick. We want, that is, to quote the law of excluded middle and to say: "Either such an image [*Bild*] is in his mind, or it is not: there is no third possibility!" …. We use a picture; the picture of a visible series which one per-

son sees the whole of and another not. The law of excluded middle
says here: It must either look like this, or like that. So it really—and
this is a truism—says nothing at all, but gives us a picture.... (*PI* 352)

What changes from the early works to the later is the concept of picture,
not the association of thinking with picturing. In the later works,
Wittgenstein stresses the dynamic activity of calculating with pictures,
i.e. using them according to rules, rather than the static fact of having a picture. The *activity* of thinking rather than the *having* of thoughts takes center
stage in the later works.

Wittgenstein's beginning is noteworthy. He never asks, "why" we make
pictures of facts; rather, he begins his thoughts with the fact that we do. The
reason is that such a question would be tantamount to asking, Why we
think? and for Wittgenstein, that question could only lead to metaphysics. He makes this point dramatically when he tells his readers to avoid
the question, "why?":

> It often happens that we only become aware of the important
> *facts*, if we suppress the question "why?"; and then in the course of
> our investigations these facts lead us to an answer. (*PI* 471)

The same point is reiterated more amusingly elsewhere:

> People who are constantly asking 'why' are like tourists who stand in
> front of a building reading Baedeker and are so busy reading the his-
> tory of its construction, etc., that they are prevented from *seeing* the
> building. (*CV* pg. 40)

Asking philosophers not to ask "why" is as impossible as asking them not
to think. Nevertheless, for Wittgenstein, the question must be avoided
because it leads to a discussion of causes and origins and away from a
description of thinking's activities. In the *Investigations,* Wittgenstein thematizes this beginning; he speaks of accepting certain things as part of our natural history:

> What we are supplying are really remarks on the natural history
> of human beings; we are not contributing curiosities however, but
> observations which no one has doubted, but which have escaped
> remark only because they are always before our eyes. (*PI* 415)

We simply are the kind of beings who think, picture facts. There is no further qualification, no way of pushing back to an earlier beginning. Nothing
would show *why* we think (*PI* 468), or rather, while a variety of answers are

appropriate, no single response or finite conjunction of responses is satisfying. The question, no matter what curiosity dictates, is not answerable. However, this is so not because our minds are inadequate, but because the answer, such as it is, is already known, but not formulable. It is something we know, but cannot succinctly say.

While we might be convinced to accept this beginning without further protest, we need not be as accomodating about Wittgenstein's identification of thinking with picturing. Here too, Wittgenstein simply asserts that thinking is a picturing. Russell questions him about this in a letter early on. Wittgenstein's impatient response reflects both the depth of his assumptions and an interesting reluctance to wholeheartedly embrace his assimilation of thinking to picturing:

> (2) "...But a Gedanke is a Tatsache: What are its constituents and components, and what is their relation to those of the pictured Tatsache?" I don't know *what* the constituents of a thought are but I know *that* it must have such constituents which correspond to the words of language. Again the kind of constituents of thought and of the pictured fact is irrelevant. It would be a matter of psychology to find out. (4) Does a Gedanke consist of words? No! But of psychical constituents that have the same sort of relation to reality as words. What those constituents are I don't know. (*NB* pg. 129)

A similar kind of denial is found in other remarks:

> Suddenly I smile and say "...". When I smiled the thought had occurred to me.
>
> Of what did it consist? It consisted of nothing at all; for the picture or word, etc., which may perhaps have appeared was not the thought. (*RPP* II, 34)

The Preface to the *Tractatus* also maintains that thought itself cannot be talked about, only the expression of thoughts. Thus, it is not the case that to talk about the latter is automatically to talk about the former. Thinking is still not picturing. Picturing provides a good *simile* for understanding thinking, but is not identical with it. Besides, Wittgenstein would argue, "I am not really interested in the constituents of things, but in their logic, in the way the constituents are related. Structure is all."

Interestingly, Wittgenstein deduces the pictorial quality of thought from thought's relation to language. He reasoned since language is a pictorial medium, then so is thought:

Now it is becoming clear why I thought that thinking and lan‑
guage were the same. For thinking is a kind of language. For a
thought too is, of course, a logical picture of the proposition, and
therefore it just is a kind of proposition. (*NB* 12.9.16.)

While this passage is in the past tense, nothing in the *Tractatus* implies a
change of heart:

In a proposition a thought finds an expression that can be per‑
ceived by the senses. (*T* 3.1)

In a proposition a thought can be expressed in such a way that
elements of the propositional sign correspond to the objects of the
thought. (*T* 3.2)

Thought speaks through language; language makes it vocal and percepti‑
ble. As thought's dummy, language imprints on thought its pictorial quali‑
ties. Translation from one to the other is guaranteed by the logic of depic‑
tion (*T* 4.015) which is what makes any picture into a picture in the first
place. Just as language mediates the differences between thinking and pic‑
turing, picture mediates the possible differences between thought and lan‑
guage. Rather than anchor the argument in one sure premise, Wittgenstein
relies on the mutual entailment of a related group of propositions: Language
is a picturing, thinking is a language, and thinking is a picturing.

The last premise in the argument is that speaking and writing are kinds
of picturing. Language is a pictorial medium (*T* 4.0s) and if thinking takes
place in language, thinking pictures as well. To argue language's pictorial
character, he asks us to acknowledge its origins in hieroglyphics:

In order to understand the essential nature of a proposition, we
should consider hieroglyphic script, which depicts the facts that it
describes.

And alphabetic script developed out of it without losing what
was essential to depiction. (*T* 4.016)

Yet, he recognized that language's pictorial quality might not be obvious,
especially since one usually considers pictures the opposite of discursive
words:

At first sight a proposition—one set out on the printed page, for
example—does not seem to be a picture of the reality with which it
is concerned. But no more does musical notation at first sight seem

to be a picture of music, nor our phonetic notation (the alphabet) to
be a picture of our speech.

And yet these sign-languages prove to be pictures, even in the
ordinary sense, of what they represent. (*T* 4.011)

Obviously everything turned on the nature of picturing whose analysis was
of course the centerpiece of the *Tractatus.*[4]

Following Heinrich Hertz, the Nineteenth century physicist,
Wittgenstein first identified picturing with modeling:

"A picture is a model of reality." (*T* 2.12)

A model portrays the structural organization of a state of affairs. As a model,
a picture offers a diagram or blueprint of the internal workings of a fact.
Models are graphic, spatial, and highly visual. Sense depends on structure,
semantics on syntax. Pictorial form connected the model to that which it
modeled. It was as if our very ability to picture facts, i.e., to think them, guaranteed their sense. All this changes, however, in the later work where having
a picture, even if it is a model, is no longer sufficient for making sense.

Instead of the structure of a state of affairs or a picture, Wittgenstein turns
to a picture's interactions with its context. The role the picture serves within
its larger environment is what enables pictures to make sense. To distinguish
this later view from the earlier one, I shall use the concept of *scene*. *Scene*
replaces *model* as the best simile for *picture*. As pictures, propositions paint a
scene or tell a story. They narrate visually to connect. In this schema, time and
action are just as important as space and relation. Scene incorporates the live
action as well as the physical space of the state of affairs. A picture becomes
meaningful as it is incorporated into the intentional situation. "Bring me a
slab" becomes a substitute for the action, only by its birth in the scene. A
scene is a visualization of a language-game. Pictures can not be detached from
the context which gives them life. Concomitantly, using pictures, calculating
with them, becomes Wittgenstein's main simile for thinking.

The simile of calculating was present in the earlier work (*T* 6.2331);
however, at that time Wittgenstein did not see its potential. In the later
works, calculating becomes the activity that manipulates pictures and also
serves as the simile which disassociates thinking from imagining:

It is as a calculus that thinking has an interest for us; not as an
activity of the human imagination.

It is the *calculus* of thought that connects with extra-mental reality.
(*PG* pg. 160)

"But mustn't I know what it would be like if I were in pain?"—
We fail to get away from the idea that using a sentence involves
imagining something for every word.

We do not realize that we *calculate*, operate, with words, and in
the course of time translate them sometimes into one picture, sometimes into another.—It is as if one were to believe that a written
order for a cow which someone is to hand over to me always had to
be accompanied by an image of a cow, if the order was not to lose its
meaning. (*PI* 449)

In contrast to the *Tractatus*, the picture on its own no longer reaches out to
reality; rather, language users are needed to apply the picture and decide
whether it is appropriate:

Every sign *by itself* seems dead. *What* gives it life?—In use it is
alive. Is life breathed into it there? or is the *use* its life? (*PI* 432)

"Everything is already there in...." How does it come about that
this arrow ➜ *points*? Doesn't it seem to carry in it something besides
itself?—"No, not the dead line on paper; only the psychical thing, the
meaning, can do that."—That is both true and false. The arrow points
only in the application that a living being makes of it.

This pointing is *not* a hocus-pocus which can be performed only
by the soul. (*PI* 454)

Calculating or using signs according to rules which are sensitive to a context and environment produces meaning.

In fact, language's capacity for producing pictures is uncontrol-
lable. Willy-nilly, language gives rise to pictures. Since the range of these
pictures is much wider than any particular form of life, there is no guarantee that the picture will make sense. When pictures clash with their application, we are prevented from seeing things as they are:

A *picture* held us captive. And we could not get outside it, for it
lay in our language and language seemed to repeat it to us inexorably.
(*PI* 115)

Only by operating or calculating with pictures and experimenting with
their applications can one make contact with the world. Merely having a
picture or being capable of imagining one is not enough:

There is lack of clarity about the role of *imaginability [Vorstellbarkeit]* in our investigation. Namely, about the extent to which it ensures that a proposition makes sense. (*PI* 395)

It is no more essential to the understanding of a proposition that one should imagine anything in connection with it, than one should make a sketch from it. (*PI* 396)

Instead of "imaginability" one can also say here: representability by a particular method of representation. And such a representation *may* indeed safely point a way to further use of a sentence. On the other hand a picture may obtrude itself upon us and be of no use at all. (*PI* 397)

Besides making the point that for symbolic animals like ourselves, one need not translate sentences into pictures in order to understand them, these passages highlight the differences and similarities between Wittgenstein's earlier view of "methods of representation" and his later approach.

In order to think anything, one still needs a method or form of representation; a method is a necessary condition for thinking; a method may become insufficient, however, when the pictures produced by it are inappropriate. The only way to test the picture is to apply it, i.e., vary its components, invent related cases, draw its consequences. This is the real burden of thinking, not just producing a picture. Thinking is activity, movement. The key is to recognize the difference between the determination of a sense and its employment:

What I always do seems to be—to emphasize a distinction between a determination of a sense and the employment of a sense. (*RFM* pg. 80)

For the later Wittgenstein, the two are not always synonymous.

A similar point can be made about "calculating." When Wittgenstein uses the word "calculate," he depends upon a formal notion of the word. In mathematics, to speak of a calculus is to speak about a method of calculating. One does not just calculate; one calculates according to rules, which give the grammar of operating with the symbols. A calculus is, then, a language-game which is not just a method of representation, but a method plus rules for its application. *Language-game* replaces *method of representation* in the later work. It stresses not only the situation, but the practical consequence that one must practice thinking. One learns to think through practice.

Thinking is a ramified concept, which, like language or game, has no essence. To learn about it, one must observe how the word is used in a variety of contexts (*PI* 316, 328):

> "How can one learn the truth by thinking? As one learns to see a face better if one draws it." (*Z* 255)

By drawing the face, we become better acquainted with its details and over-all shape. Most likely we will have to make a number of renditions as we realize that our first efforts didn't see the face at all, or rather subsumed the particular face under some general schemata for faces, which we didn't even know we had until it stood in the way. Only by getting down and working with the actual face can we get to know not only how to express that particular face but faces in general. Similarly, thinking must be practiced. We must exercise it on some particular problem, trying to sharpen language (thinking's tool) so as to fit a particular case more comfortably. As with drawing, this kind of calculating teaches about the general as well as the particular. In more familiar Wittgenstein words, thinking is grounded in its applications. Above all, one must resist the temptation to introspect, i.e., to picture thinking as something which goes on exclusively in the head and thus can only be studied privately:

> One of the most dangerous ideas for a philosopher is, oddly enough, that we think with our heads or in our heads. (*Z* 605)

> The idea of thinking as a process in the head, in a completely enclosed space, gives **him** something occult. (*Z* 606)

Once grabbed by this picture, thought's grasp of reality is miraculous and mysterious. All of a sudden the question, how does thought manage to describe reality?, is attractive. The temptation is so great that Wittgenstein urges us not to picture thinking as a mental activity at all. Instead, he reminds us how thinking interlocks with our activities and cannot be separated from them:

> Of course we cannot separate **his** 'thinking' from his activity. For the thinking is not an accompaniment of the work, any more than of thoughtful speech. (*Z* 101)

Thinking does not run along side language breathing life into it:

> Thinking is not an incorporeal process which lends life and sense to speaking, and which it would be possible to detach from

speaking, rather as the Devil took the shadow of Schlemiehl from the ground… (cf. *PI* 329). (*PI* 339)

Rather thinking takes place in and with language as it does in so many of our other activities. In part, Wittgenstein's reintroduction of language users has raised these problems, which the magical realism of the *Tractatus* had circumvented. Subjectivity and the temptation to see thinking as a private mental process is to be fought anew.

One strategy that Wittgenstein uses to facilitate our understanding that thinking is not a mental process is to distinguish between thinking and imagining:

> The boundary line that is drawn here between 'thinking' and 'not thinking' would run between two conditions which are not distinguished by anything in the least resembling a play of images. (For the play of images [*Das Spiel der Vorstellungen*] is admittedly the model according to which one would like to think of thinking.) (*Z* 94)

Thinking cannot be thought of as a play of images. True, Wittgenstein often uses the words "*denken*" and "*vorstellen*" interchangeably as in the remarks just quoted about the limits of imaginability (*PI* 395–97); however, this does not happen as often as the English translations make it seem:

> Look at a stone and imagine [*denk*] it having sensation. One says to oneself: How could one so much as get the idea of ascribing a sensation to a thing?… (*PI* 284)

Nevertheless, it does happen and for a good reason; thinking is more closely related to imagining than either is to seeing. Consider the slight change which takes place between the same statement made in the *Notebooks* and in the *Tractatus*:

> 'A situation is thinkable' ('imaginable') means: we can make ourselves a picture of it. (*NB* 1.11.14)

> 'A state of affairs is thinkable [*denkbar*]': What this means is that we can picture it to ourselves. (*T* 3.001)

The move from "imagine" to "think" is small, but important. Obviously, Wittgenstein is moving away from Schopenhauer's sense of representation and back to Kant's as he continues to work through the latter's problems about representation. Yet, the difference between the two verbs is not that great. As in the *Tractatus* and following Kant, *das Bild* or picture has more to do with form and shape and with forming and shaping than it does with images and imagining. A picture is not an image and has a different set of implications:

> ... The image of pain is not a picture and *this* image is not replaceable in the language-game by anything that we call a picture.—The image of pain [*Die Vorstellung des Schmerzes*] certainly enters into the language-game in a sense; only not as a picture [*als Bild*] (cf. *Z* 636). (*PI* 300)

> An image is not a picture, but a picture can correspond to it. (*PI* 301)

> "Yes, but the image itself, like the visual impression, is surely the inner picture, and *you* are talking only of differences in the production, the coming to be, and in the treatment of the picture." The image is not a picture, nor is the visual impression one. Neither 'image', nor 'impression' is the concept of picture, although in both cases there is a tie-up with a picture, and a different one in either case. (*Z* 638)

The difference is that the image is truly a mental picture:

> The mental picture [*Vorstellungsbild*] is the picture which is described when someone describes what he images. (*PI* 367)

As such, the image is a private affair like a private language and thus cannot be evaluated for correctness, nor be communicated. So there is nothing public about images and thus they cannot connect with the external world; they might even be composed in an idiosyncratic method of representation:

> Auditory images, visual images—how are they distinguished from sensations? Not by "vivacity".
> Images tell us nothing, either right or wrong, about the external world. (Images are not hallucinations, not yet fancies).
> While I am looking at an object I cannot imagine it.
> Difference between the language-games: "Look at this figure!" and: "Imagine this figure!"
> Images are subject to the will.
> Images are not pictures. I do not tell what object I am imagining by the resemblance between it and the image.

> Asked "What image have you?" one can answer with a picture. (*Z* 621)

Thus, the force of the distinction is to dissuade us from the picture of thought as a private and unique phenomenon, which takes place in the head with the inner eye. Rather, we are to picture thinking as a play of schemata arising from the public realm of language. These pictures are not incorrigible but allow room for error. Yet, despite the distinction, Wittgenstein still does not want to leave us with the picture of an image as a superlikeness of the fact:

> "The image must be more like its object than any picture. For, however like I make the picture to what it is supposed to represent, it can always be the picture of something else as well. But it is essential to the image that it is the image of *this* and of nothing else." Thus one might come to regard the image as a super-likeness. (*PI* 389)

Images, like pictures, still retain a distance from phenomena. They exist within a method of representation and thus are as constructed as any picture. The important point is that they have no privileged position with respect to our thinking and, in fact, are poorer sources of a way of seeing than the pictures embedded in ordinary language.

"Picture" must be interpreted loosely in the later works, i.e., as closer to scene, than to image, visual picture, or anything that is strictly visual and spatial. Thinking's picturing must be understood, primarily, as an activity, like walking. It is a natural part of human action, not a report on action. To stress these connections, Wittgenstein more often than not speaks of thinking as a kind of seeing and seeing as a kind of acting.

Seeing as Acting

We find certain things about seeing puzzling, because we do not find the whole business of seeing puzzling enough (cf. RPP II, 372). (PI pg. 212)

Wittgenstein discusses the interconnections between seeing and thinking most concertedly in Part II, Section XI of the *Investigations*. The section is unusual, although paradigmatic, in the context of both the *Investigations* and Wittgenstein's later work as a whole. It is unusual because the discussion of seeing-as is longer and more systematic than his treatment of any other topic in the text, and it is also clearly demarcated from the rest of the remarks. Indeed, it feels more like a normal chapter in a book. Even his treatment of the topic is more traditional; he tests hypotheses and explores theoretical avenues one would have thought closed to him in the later work. Yet, it is paradigmatic because, in the end, his more familiar style and voice achieve mastery. No conclusions are reached, no temptations breached. Yet our questions about seeing and thinking have passed. Thinking and seeing cannot be demarcated and explained in scientific fashion. Seeing involves thinking and vice-versa. Philosophy cannot will them apart. Science can, but the conclusions reached will not speak to the philosophical questions raised. He ends by recognizing that "What has to be accepted, the given, is—so one could say—*forms of life*" (*PI* pg. 226). The end is especially poignant in light of the valiant effort Wittgenstein mounts to not end this way.

The section begins by confidently distinguishing between two uses of "see:" the first, a simple, direct seeing; the other less direct, the seeing of a resemblance or something like happiness. Wittgenstein calls the latter, "seeing an aspect" or seeing one thing in terms of another:

> I contemplate a face, and then suddenly notice its likeness to another. I *see* that it has not changed; and yet I see it differently. I call this experience "noticing an aspect". (*PI* pg. 193)

Critical to this experience is the recognition that while one is seeing something different when one notices an aspect, the perception itself is unchanged:

> The expression of a change of aspect is the expression of a *new* perception and at the same time of the perception's being unchanged. (*PI* pg. 196)

While the section ostensibly devotes itself to understanding this fascinating phenomenon, it is just as much about what I shall call, for convenience sake, "plain seeing." In fact, seeing an aspect is primarily a tool for getting us to rethink the concept of seeing more generally:

> The concept of 'seeing' makes a tangled impression. Well, it is tangled.—I look at the landscape, my gaze ranges over it, I see all sorts of distinct and indistinct movement; *this* impresses itself sharply on me, *that* is quite hazy. After all, how completely ragged what we see can appear! And now look at all that can be meant by "description of

what is seen."—But this just is what is called description of what is seen. There is not *one genuine* proper case of such description—the rest being just vague, something which awaits clarification, or which must be swept aside as rubbish (cf. *PI* 291, 292). (*PI* pg. 200)

Seeing is not the simple camera-like activity we ordinarily take it to be; that is, as we look at the world, our seeing is not simply informed by facts, but organized by contexts and patterns, prior personal histories, anticipatory beliefs, and even *ad hoc* imaginary flights. By focusing on seeing-as, he hopes to undermine any faith in naive realism, while all the time keeping in touch with the rough ground that seeing provides. Seeing-as shows us the multiplicity involved in seeing.

Wittgenstein himself suggests that he has ulterior motives in analyzing seeing-as; he says that it will illuminate a component of meaning, namely, experiencing the meaning of a word:

> The importance of this concept lies in the connection between the concepts of 'seeing an aspect' and 'experiencing the meaning of a word.' For we want to ask "What would you be missing if you did not *experience* the meaning of a word?" (*PI* pg. 214)

What is it to experience the meaning of a word and what in the world is the connection between noticing an aspect and experiencing the meaning of a word? By reminding us that meanings are also experienced, perhaps Wittgenstein is trying to tell us that meaning, like seeing, requires more than first meets the eye. In particular, it is not just an intellectual activity but a visceral one, just as seeing is not just visceral, but cognitive. Use creates customs which are imbibed in the learning process. We live and act these meanings. Meanings reach into the very fabric of our form of life. Talking lions would be incomprehensible precisely because of the connection between meaning and experience: "If a lion could talk, we could not understand **him**" (*PI* pg. 223). Lion talk would not translate into human talk because the forms of life do not overlap. Within a form of life, however, communication still falters because of the infinite possibilities for seeing an aspect or experiencing the meaning of a word.

Wittgenstein first offers the most obvious explanation for our ability to see something as something, namely, that the experience is half visual, half thought:

> But since it is the description of a perception, it can also be called the expression of thought.—If you are looking at the object,

you need not think of it; but if you are having the visual experience expressed by the exclamation, you are also *thinking* of what you see.

> Hence the flashing of an aspect on us seems half visual experience, half thought. (*PI* pg. 197)

However, he quickly rejects this hypothesis:

> Is being stuck looking plus thinking? No. Many of our concepts *cross* here. (*PI* pg. 211)

> Do I really see something different each time, or do I only interpret what I see in a different way? I am inclined to say the former. But why? To interpret is to think, to do something; seeing is a state. (*PI* pg. 212)

While the reasoning is suspect (i.e., thinking is a doing, seeing a state), Wittgenstein is clear that seeing-as is not a special case of seeing where thinking has been added. The problem is twofold. On one hand, seeing a smiling face, for example, requires no interpretation; we just see it as we would a face. Interpreting is far more conscious an activity and always involves offering hypotheses (*PI* 201). True, sometimes aspect seeing requires interpretation; as he says, it requires imagination to see the triangle as a figure that has fallen over (*PI* pg. 207); however, our daily lives are filled with cases which we would not ordinarily classify as requiring interpretation. On the other hand, seeing may be as interpretative as seeing-as:

> But how is it possible to *see* an object according to an *interpretation*?—The question represents it as a queer fact; as if something were being forced into a form it did not really fit. But no squeezing, no forcing took place here. (*PI* pg. 200)

Seeing is not an activity which takes place merely with the eyes:

> ...For isn't it a misleading metaphor to say: "My eyes give me the information that there is a chair over there"? (*PI* 356)

Thoughts of all sorts course through our seeing and help give it shape. Information can only occur in a context that has rules and a point. One cannot see bare facts (*PI* 292). In the more unusual cases, we recognize the thoughts and their possible interpretations; we feel their presence and are tempted to think that we are dealing with something that cannot be called seeing. To think this is to ignore all the codes and contexts which make seeing itself possible. No forcing takes place in arguing for the possibility of seeing an object according to an interpretation. While normal cases of seeing do not raise the feeling of interpretation, it may have been there in certain circumstances:

> One doesn't '*take*' what one knows as the cutlery at a meal *for* cutlery; any more than one ordinarily tries to move one's mouth as one eats, or aims at moving it. (*PI* pg. 195)

When no interpretation takes place, we are in the midst of a "fossilized" way of seeing. *Theoretically*, then, the only thing that separates seeing from seeing-as is the practice, the form of life, or, as Wittgenstein might say, the difference between normal and abnormal cases.

Yet one must be careful; the appeal to theory can quickly lead to metaphysics, and eventually leads to reading Wittgenstein as if he were a neo-Kantian. The way to avoid this is to remember that we daily distinguish between the experiences of seeing something and then suddenly seeing it in a new way. We *don't*, even though we theoretically *can*, take cutlery for cutlery. Indeed, in some sense, *we can't,* although *others might.* We don't paint like the Egyptians, and it is even fair to say that given our form of life, we can't (*PI* pg. 230). These differences are critical and blurred by the move to theory. The importance of noting the differences is to ensure that we do not tempt the skeptic to argue; "ah, since we are always interpreting, nothing is real, sure, or permanent." For Wittgenstein, on the other hand, within the context of a *Weltbild,* much is taken as knowledge. While seeing is obviously affected by a whole variety of things and is only possible on condition that we can see things otherwise than as they are in the normal course of events, we simply describe what we see and forget about philosophical considerations.

Before collapsing one use into the other, the only honest recourse is to maintain steadfastly two uses of "see," while knowing that there are no necessary or sufficient conditions for maintaining two. The principle of the identity of indiscernibles would have us collapse them, but that would miss fine nuances:

> I see that an animal in a picture is transfixed by an arrow. It has struck it in the throat and sticks out at the back of the neck. Let the picture be a silhouette.—Do you *see* the arrow—or do you merely *know* that these two bits are supposed to represent part of an arrow?
> (Compare Kohler's figure of the interpenetrating hexagons.)

"But this isn't *seeing*!"—"But this is seeing!"—It must be possible to give both remarks a conceptual justification.

But this is seeing! *In what sense* is it seeing? (*PI* pg. 203)

To give both remarks a conceptual justification is to remember the times when we are reluctant to call a case of seeing-as a case of seeing. There's a difference even though the two concepts are related.

Yet, this section, as I indicated earlier, is full of false starts. Often Wittgenstein seems content with a dichotomizing approach. For example, in one critical remark he suggests that we are born seeing, but not born seeing-as:

"Now **he's** seeing it like *this*", "now like that" would only be said of someone *capable* of making certain applications of the figure quite freely.

The substratum of this experience is the mastery of a technique.

But how queer for this to be the logical condition of someone's having such-and-such *experience*! After all, you don't say that one only 'has toothache' if one is capable of doing such-and-such.—From this it follows that we cannot be dealing with the same concept of experience here. It is a different though related concept.

It is only if someone *can do*, has learnt, is master of such-and-such, that it makes sense to say **he** has had *this* experience.

And if this sounds crazy, you need to reflect that the *concept* of seeing is modified here. (A similar consideration is often necessary to get rid of a feeling of dizziness in mathematics.)

We talk, we utter words, and only *later* get a picture of their life. (*PI* pg. 208)

The suggestion that to play the seeing-as game requires an ability to do something, whereas the seeing game requires no preparation, is a red herring and contrary to what he argued earlier both in the text and in this section. Earlier, Wittgenstein argued forcefully against the possibility of a private language; you learned the concept pain (*PI* 384), or what it is to have a toothache, when you learned a language. If pain requires mastery, then so does seeing. True, we use "see" or "experience" as primitive activities, but to think they actually are is a mistake. While Wittgenstein understands this perfectly, he often sounds as if he doesn't in Part II, Section XI. He skates so closely to the edge in this section to dramatize the temptations of philosophical analysis and perhaps convince us once and for all that philosophy is not a science.

His discussion about the differences between imagining and seeing helps to further the distance of seeing from thinking:

> I might also have said earlier: The *tie-up* between imagining and seeing is close; but there is no *similarity.*
>
> The language-games implying these concepts are radically different—but hang together. (*Z* 625)

> What is imaged is not in the same *space* as what is seen. Seeing is connected with looking. (*Z* 628)

> "Seeing and imaging are different phenomena".—The words "seeing" and "imaging" have different meanings. Their meanings relate to a host of important kinds of human behavior, to phenomena of human life. (*Z* 629)

If instead of "imagining" we read "thinking" in these passages, Wittgenstein's choice of the expression, "ways of seeing" rather than "ways of thinking" becomes perspicuous. Seeing, unlike thinking, cannot as easily take a holiday from a form of life. Neither experience, nor seeing are as flexible as imagination and thought. And it is precisely this lack of flexibility that makes seeing an attractive concept for exploring a form of life.

Another way to articulate the distinction between seeing and thinking is to borrow Wittgenstein's distinction between satisfied and unsatisfied concepts. Thinking, unlike seeing, is a satisfied concept. In the *Investigations,* Wittgenstein uses this distinction to differentiate between the concepts of thinking and those of believing, hoping, expecting, intending, and understanding:

> "A plan as such is something unsatisfied." (Like a wish, and expectation, a suspicion, and so on.
>
> By this I mean: expectation is unsatisfied, because it is the expectation of something; belief, opinion, is unsatisfied, because it is the opinion that something is the case, something real, something outside the process of believing. (*PI* 438)

He draws the distinction between these phenomena and thinking as follows:

> A proposition, and hence in another sense a thought can be the 'expression' of belief, hope, expectation, etc. But believing is not thinking. (A grammatical remark.) The concepts of believing, expecting, hoping are less distantly related to one another than they are to the concept of thinking. (*PI* 574)

Thinking, unlike these other concepts, does not need the context of the situation to complete itself. It can go merrily on its way without paying homage to the reality principle. Thus, while it would not be completely appropriate to call thinking a mental activity, it is less of a mistake than calling meaning a mental activity:

> "When I teach someone the formation of the series....I surely mean **him** to write....at the hundredth place." Quite right; you mean it. And evidently without necessarily thinking of it. This shews you how different the grammar of the verb "to mean" is from that of "to think." And nothing is more wrong-headed than calling meaning a mental activity! Unless, that is, one is setting out to produce confusion. (It would also be possible to speak of an activity of butter when it rises in price, and if no problems are produced by this it is harmless.) (*PI* 693)

This is also the point of his jibe at Plato's account of thinking in the Theatetus:

> Socrates to Theatetus: "And if someone thinks mustn't **he** think *something?*"—Th. "Yes, **he** must."—Soc.: "And if **he** thinks something, mustn't it be something real?"—Th.: "Apparently."
> And mustn't someone who is painting be painting something— and someone who is painting something be painting something real!—Well, tell me what the object of a painting is: the picture of a **man** (e.g.), or the **man** that the picture portrays? (*PI* 518)

The intentionality of thought does not require that one think something real, or rather, what is real is so varied and indeterminable that the qualification "real" adds nothing to one's point. In the *Zettel* version of this remark, the point is clearer. It begins in the same way, but instead of speaking about painting it speaks of the difference in grammar between, for example, the word "kill" and that of "think":

> ...If we put the word "kill" in place of "have an idea of" in this argument, then there is a rule for the use of this word: it makes no sense to say "I am killing something that does not exist". I can imagine [*Vorstellen*] a stag that is not there, in this meadow, but not kill one that is not there... (*Z* 693)

Only a thinking that reaches out to its application, which calculates its plausibility, thinks something real. Seeing, like an intention, is embedded in a situation and only completed by its surroundings. Once freed from the naiveté of empiricism, seeing, especially with its possibilities for seeing-as, can accomplish all that thought needs. Thus, in worrying about the "as" structure of sight, Wittgenstein shows us a seeing that thinks. A thoughtless sight would be as meaningless as a thoughtless language. When he says, "think such-and-such" or "imagine such-and-such," he is asking us to see something in another way, to see it *as*. By varying the original perception, one can see both its elasticity and its hardness.

The message for philosophers is that philosophical sight, like that of artistic sight, must be informed both by the practices of the world and the ever-present array of new possibilities. The philosopher can never fully join a way of seeing or the opportunities for changing aspects disappear. Always tetter-tottering between two ways of seeing, philosophers can point to the way we see things if that is necessary to solve a philosophical problem or point to a new way of seeing if that is what is required. This strategy helps to curb thought's infinite domain. Sometimes, the experiment results in a new way of seeing, other times, the variations are discarded to retain the original perception. Whether one changes or not depends upon how the new perception hooks up with other thoughts and to what extent it has been allowed to overturn our whole way of seeing. Seeing, even in its wildest hallucinatory flights, is capable of staying in touch with the rough ground. The injunction to look, not think, then, does not condemn philosophy to a pure empiricism, but only provides a correction to an unadulterated rationalism.

Ultimately, the true test of what we see or think is the way we act:

> How could human behavior be described? Surely only by sketching the actions of a variety of humans, as they are all mixed up together. What determines our judgement, our concepts and reactions, is not what *one* **man** is doing *now*, an individual action, but the whole hurly-burly of human actions, the background against which we see any action. (*Z* 567)

Concepts are too general for his purposes, just as perceptions are too particular. Only actions provide pictures, which, while particular and concrete, can nevertheless be sometimes used in general ways, i.e., to describe the *Weltbild* of a particular form of life. "Actions speak louder than words," for Wittgenstein. In the end, "a way of acting" is the true test of what we see. Acting finesses the quarrels between seeing and thinking and is the strategy that frees us from endless disputes in the fly-bottle. Changing a way of acting is Wittgenstein's final goal. To do this, however, he had to change the way philosophers acted, specifically, he had to change the way they wrote and spoke philosophy. Perhaps the best way to discuss Wittgenstein's ideas about "a way of acting" is to examine his own behavior, i.e., his styles of philosophizing.

Part Two *Changing a Way of Seeing*

My difficulty is only an—enormous—difficulty of expression. (NB 8.3.15)

At this point I am trying to express something that cannot be expressed. (NB 22.11.14)

What is most difficult here is to put this indefiniteness, correctly and unfalsified, into words. (PI pg. 227)

Naturally, my aim must be to say what statements one would like to make here, but cannot make significantly. (OC 76)

It is so difficult to find the beginning. *Or, better: it is difficult to begin at the* beginning. *And not try to go further back. (OC 471)*

Here I am inclined to fight windmills, because I cannot yet say the things I really want to say. (OC 400)

All his life, Wittgenstein had difficulty saying what he wanted to say. Try as he may, he could never quite say what he believed philosophy needed to say. Remarks like those above punctuate his writings, testifying to the persistence of the problem. He voices the same frustrations and apologies in the Prefaces to both his major works:

> Here I am conscious of having fallen a long way short of what is possible. Simply because my powers are too slight for the accomplishment of the task.—May others come and do it better. (*T* pg. 5)

> I should have liked to produce a good book. This has not come about, but the time is past in which I could improve it. (*PI* pg. x)

The practice of philosophy: the everyday business of producing philosophical thoughts in either written or oral form tormented him.

Typically, he blamed himself, pointing sometimes to vanity and other times to ineptitude:

> Broad was quite right when he says of the *Tractatus* that it was highly syncopated. Every sentence in the *Tractatus* should be seen as the heading of a chapter, needing further exposition. My present style is quite different; I am trying to avoid that error.
>
> I thought when I gave up my professorship that I had at last got

rid of my vanity. Now I find I am vain about the style in which I am able to write.[1]

Undoubtedly, personal factors played a part in his struggles with language; however, they do not tell the whole story.[2] As Wittgenstein remarked with respect to another issue: "There is something universal here; not just something personal" (*OC* 440). More than other factors, his attitude towards language along with his conception of what philosophy needed to say in order to be significant and worthwhile caused his difficulties.

In the early work, when he shared his predecessors grandiose visions for philosophy, language was the main culprit:

> The proposition that only the present experience has reality appears to contain the last consequence of solipsism. And in a sense that is so; only what it is able to say amounts to just as little as can be said by solipsism. For what belongs to the essence of the world simply *cannot* be said. And philosophy, if it were to say anything, would have to describe the essence of the world. (*PR* V 54)

Language only talks about how things are, not what they are, nor why they are the way they are, nor why they could not be otherwise than the way they are, and it was these latter subjects that Wittgenstein believed were the truly important things for philosophy to study. Those who ignored the limits of language by uttering theories like "realism" or "idealism" spoke nonsense (*PR* V 55). In the later work, on the other hand, when his ideas about what philosophy needs to say change, his view of the limits of language became less consequential. In fact, one might say that now philosophy failed language, rather than the other way round. Instead of being thwarted by the impossible, the hidden, recondite truths that cannot be said, Wittgenstein found himself plagued by the obvious, the ordinary, everyday platitudes that everyone fails to notice. As he acidly remarks, philosophy's task is to teach us to pass from disguised nonsense to patent nonsense (*PI* 464).

Occasionally, Wittgenstein acknowledged these more substantive roots of his discursive difficulties: "my thoughts were soon crippled if I tried to force them on in any single direction against their inclination.—*And this was, of course, connected with the very nature of the investigation*" (*PI* pg. ix, emphasis mine). He realized, that is, when self-doubt did not cloud his judgment, that his troubles were a function of the unhappy interaction of two variables: language and philosophy. Unlike the Greeks who considered language philosophy's greatest friend, indeed, the gift that first made philosophy possible, Wittgenstein had reservations about language's potential to declare philosophy's intentions. He was not at all sure about whether any system of signs could or should bear its messages. Torn between his expectations for philosophy and his reservations about language, Wittgenstein often felt speechless. In one biting remark, he literally describes himself as stuttering:

> I never more than half succeed in expressing what I want to express. Actually not as much as that, but by no more than a tenth. That is still worth something. Often my writing is nothing but "stuttering." (*CV* pg. 18)

Although harsh, his analogy is not entirely farfetched. Like the stammering order he quips about in the *Investigations* (*PI* 433), his remarks literally falter as they desperately struggle to say what he wants to say. As evidence, witness the way he supplements his words with wild rhetorical and punctuational signs—dashes, quotation marks, exclamation points, diagrams, font variations, demonstrative pronouns (invariably *italicized*), sentence spacings, temporal and spatial indexes, etc.—in his effort to make the signs speak. The dashes holding one sentence to another are especially revealing in their graphic attempt to comfort the stutterer. Nor are the syncopations or omissions of the early work immediately redressed by the excesses of the later ones. While he knew that his problem was general, namely, that nothing could help a misfiring sign, he nevertheless tried everything possible, short of telepathy, to make his meaning perspicuous. Clearly, he hoped that style, the *how* something is said, might push beyond the stutter, carrying what could not be said with it.[3]

Generally speaking, style is a constant but denied aspect of philosophical writing. Since Socrates, philosophers have been loath to associate with rhetoric or any form of discourse which uses a device-like style to persuade. Aware of language's power to deceive and coerce, Plato joined Socrates in his campaign against the poets. Truth, even at the expense of consensus, was the prize. And Wittgenstein, despite his obsession with style, is as worried about it as the others:

> If I am thinking about a topic just for myself and not with a view to writing a book, I jump about all round it; that is the only way of thinking that comes naturally to me. Forcing my thoughts into

an ordered sequence is a torment for me. Is it even worth attempting now?

I *squander* an unspeakable amount of effort making an arrangement of my thoughts which may have no value at all. (*CV* pg. 28)

Yet, given his beliefs about the nature of philosophy, he could not resist its temptations nor the opportunities it provided. For example, if discovery in philosophy depends not on new facts, but on a rearrangement of what one already knows, then style might be just the tool to negotiate the conflicting demands of language's limits and philosophy's intentions. Furthermore, Wittgenstein's exploration of the foundations of mathematics convinced him that proof was nothing more than a style of explanation:

When the truth of one proposition follows from the truth of others, we can see this from the structure of the propositions. (*T* 5.13)

If the truth of one proposition follows from the truth of others, this finds expression in relations in which the forms of the propositions stand to one another: nor is it necessary for us to set up these relations between them, by combining them with one another in a single proposition; on the contrary, the relations are internal, and their existence is an immediate result of the existence of the propositions. (*T* 5.131)

Logic was itself a rhetorical form. It did not discover truth, but only displayed it. Perhaps when used judiciously, style would not embarrass a philosopher, especially when persuasion, not truth, was precisely what the doctor ordered; that is, when one is stuck in a fly-bottle, or trapped in a way of seeing that logic seems only to mire further, or when one meets with another form of life where definitions are not shared, the only thing to do is use language's wits to change a way of seeing. Indeed, what else but style can suffice when one's goal is ultimately not to say anything, but to do something. Wittgenstein wanted words to act, not describe, nor explain. His point was to change the way we see things. He wanted us to see the world aright; to show us, if not "how things stand," then "how we see things." Only in light of this goal could philosophy suffer its fate of saying the obvious, what everyone always already knows.

While the two styles he develops during his life-time differ dramatically, both testify to his life-long search for a viable form of philosophical discourse, one that would allow him to speak easily and unhaltingly. In neither period can he be said to have written a textbook or a familiar kind of philosophical treatise. Rather, his "books" are like self-help manuals for doing philosophy. "Watch me," they urge; "Do as I do." We learn by apprenticing ourselves to his style or the actual behaviour of his works. Turning resolutely from Socrates and the heritage he bequeathed to philosophy, Wittgenstein renounces the age-old and vicious dichotomy between logic and rhetoric in his struggle to say what needs to be said.[4]

Chapter 3 *Saying the Impossible*

Man possesses the ability to construct languages capable of expressing every sense, without having any idea how each word has meaning or what its meaning is—just as people speak without knowing how the individual sounds are produced.

Everyday language is a part of the human organism and is no less complicated than it.

It is not humanly possible to gather immediately from it what the logic of language is.

Language disguises thought. So much so, that from the outward form of the clothing it is impossible to infer the form of the thought beneath it, because the outward form of the clothing is not designed to reveal the form of the body, but for entirely different purposes.

The tacit conventions on which the understanding of everyday language depends are enormously complicated. (T 4.002)

Entering the world of the *Tractatus* is like entering the C.I.A.: everything is said in code and all is suspect, especially language. Language, philosophy's indispensible mask, disguises thought, cloaking, like Descartes's doubt, the forms beneath it. Wittgenstein says little to explain his distrust. In fact, he appears to have inherited a ready-made skepticism about language from his Viennese friends and teachers: Schopenhauer, Mauthner, and Karl Kraus.[5] In his position as editor of *Die Fackel*, Kraus, for example, abused his adversaries for their misuse of so much as a comma. Language was the very index of civilization for him; if it was compromised, so was the moral fabric of a culture. Sharing these sentiments, Wittgenstein railed at language's penchant for obfuscation and generalization, as well as its clumsy, whimsical nature. "Temptress, bewitcher, devil's aide," he shouts; "instead of revealing thought, you conceal it". Notoriously, he blames language for all of philosophy's woes and proclaims that all philosophical problems are the results of bumping heads against the limits of language (*PI* 119) or that: "...Philosophy is a battle against the bewitchment of our intelligence by means of language" (*PI* 109).

Sometimes Wittgenstein sounds like an eighteenth-century moralist cautioning against the excesses of the linguistic imagination instead of a twentieth-century realist unafraid of language's charms. Despite his zealous attack, most of the time he recognizes that language's failure is due to a functional disparity between it and thought. The problem is mechanical, not mystical. His analogy between clothes and the body, and language and thought, shows how. Just as clothes are made for an endless variety of different reasons, warmth, protection, embellishment, concealment, seduction, etc., language exists for an equally plentiful set of purposes. No one ever promised that language would or should live in one-to-one correspondence with thought. While this makes it difficult to read the logic of facts or thoughts directly from propositions, it can eventually be accomplished with the special tools of logical analysis. All one has to do is explain the logic of all depiction. With this, the nature of all being will be revealed:

> My *whole* task consists in explaining the nature of the proposition.
>
> That is to say, in giving the nature of all facts, whose picture the proposition *is*.
>
> In giving the nature of all being (cf. *T* 5.4711). (*NB* 22.1.15)

He is convinced that language's secrets can be divulged with an exposé of its representational devices.

Thus, Wittgenstein's attitude toward language is ambivalent from the beginning. On the one hand, he is suspicious of it for apparently no reason. On the other, as the central remark from the *Tractatus* and others indicate, Wittgenstein is certain that language can express every sense and that its shortcomings can be overcome:

> What is the ground of our—certainly well-founded—confidence that we shall be able to express any sense we like in our two-dimensional script? (*NB* 26.9.14)

Despite all the "peculiar crotchets and contrivances" (*T* 5.511) of logic, and language more generally, both manage to represent, to be meaningful. The question is, how does language do it, how is representation possible? Like Kant before him, Wittgenstein begins his philosophical career puzzled by language's representing ability; how is it possible for mathematics or language to describe the world:

> The 'experience' that we need in order to understand logic is not that something or other is the state of things, but that something *is:* that, however, is *not* an experience.
>
> Logic is *prior* to every experience—that something *is so.*
>
> It is prior to the question 'How?', not prior to the question 'What?' (*T* 5.552)

> And if this were not so, how could we apply logic? We might put it in this way: if there would be a logic even if there were no world, how then could there be a logic given that there is a world? (*T* 5.5521)

Is it just a coincidence that the ever so human sign systems established by human thought and imagination relate to the world? While both Kant and Wittgenstein consider this an unlikely possibility, they are hard pressed to understand how language does it. How do the squiggles of a mathematical system predict reality? Of one thing Wittgenstein is sure: without understanding how one thing represents another, there can be no talk of truth and knowledge. Meaning precedes truth and makes it possible:

> …But in order to be able to say that a point is black or white, I must first know when a point is called black, and when white: in order to be able to say, '"*p*" is true (or false)', I must have determined in what circumstances I call '*p*' true, and in so doing I determine the sense of the proposition…(*T* 4.063)

If science and philosophy are to continue, they have to show how representation is possible—ergo the linguistic turn.

Russell and Frege (and Brower) paved the way for this turning by introducing Wittgenstein to symbolic logic and the tools of analysis. Their advances in understanding the logical structure of language inspired his project. Representation was possible, even reliable, with the proper understanding of language's logical scaffolding. However, Heinrich Hertz's development of a theory of mathematical modeling was even more influential and also more directly inspired by Kant. Extending Kant's constructional method for mathematical knowledge to physical concepts, Hertz believed that it was possible to show how physics describes the world. Following in Hertz's footsteps, and armed with the logical weapons developed by his friends and teachers, Wittgenstein developed the picture theory of meaning, which uses ordinary language as a construction of thought in the same manner as Kant used the figures of geometry and the numbers and letters of algebra to construct mathematical concepts. In an elegant *tour de force*, Wittgenstein showed how "The possibility of all imagery, of all our pictorial modes of expression, is contained in the logic of depiction" (*T* 4.015).[6] Most importantly for the reigning psychologism of the day, he showed how language does this without human help. As he repeated throughout his works and in a variety of different ways, language takes care of itself: "We must recognize *how* language takes care of itself" (*NB* 26.4.15) Language expresses what needs to be said without our doing anything. Philosophy need not worry about language; it has a voice of its own.

Constructing Concepts

Philosophical *knowledge is the* knowledge gained by reason from concepts; *mathematical knowledge is the knowledge gained by reason from the* construction *of concepts. To* construct *a concept means to exhibit* a priori *the intuition which corresponds to the concept* (A 713, B 741).[1]

Elaborating on the differences between mathematical and philosophical knowledge in the final section of *The Critique of Pure Reason*, the "Transcendental Doctrine of Method," Kant argues that in order for synthetic *a priori* propositions to be possible, that is, for thought to relate to the world in a pure, *a priori* fashion, a non-empirical intuition is needed:

> For the construction of a concept we therefore need a *non-empirical* intuition. The latter must, as intuition, be a *single* object, and yet nonetheless, as the construction of a concept (a universal representation), it must in its representation express universal validity for all possible intuitions which fall under the same concept. Thus, *I construct a triangle by representing the object which corresponds to this concept either by imagination alone, in pure intuition, or in accordance therewith also on paper, in empirical intuition—in both cases completely a priori, without having borrowed the pattern from any experience. The single figure which we draw is*

empirical, and yet it serves to express the concept, without impairing its uni-versality (A 713, B 741, emphasis mine).[7]

While Kant does not bring in schemata at this point in his exposition, it nevertheless is the faculty of imagination that mediates the disparities between concepts and objects by providing the non-empirical intuition:

> The *image* is a product of the empirical faculty of reproductive imagi-nation; the schema of sensible concepts, such as of figures in space, is a product and as it were, a monogram, of pure *a priori* imagination, through which, and in accordance with which, images themselves first become possible (*A* 142, *B* 181).

The figure of a triangle used to illustrate the properties of the concept tri-angle do not consign those properties to the realm of sense since the figure is a schema, not an image. The same holds for the language used to discuss algebra. Instead of *schemata*, Wittgenstein speaks of *pictures*. Pictures are Wittgenstein's version of non-empirical intuitions.

Theoretically, as Kant notes, only mathematical concepts can be so constructed because only the concept of quantity allows a construction by *a priori* schemata:

> for it is the concept of quantities only that allows of being construct-ed, that is exhibited *a priori* in intuition; whereas qualities cannot be presented in any intuition that is not empirical (*A* 715, *B* 743).

Thus, the plane figures of geometry represent what Kant calls "an ostensive construction," and the numbers of algebra a "symbolic construction" (*A* 717, *B* 745). They provide, as Wittgenstein later says, a picture or physiog-nomy of the concepts. Because the pictures being used are not drawn from experience, *a priori* or certain knowledge is possible:

> There cannot be a hierarchy of the forms of elementary proposi-tions. We can foresee only what we ourselves construct. (*T* 5.556)

Hintikka interestingly traces Kant's method to Euclid. He notes that: "Euclid never does anything on the basis of the enunciation (πρσταγιγ) alone. In every proposition, he first applies the content of the enunciation to a particular figure which he assumes to be drawn....This part of a Euclidean proposition was called the *setting-out or ecthesis* (εκθεσιγ, in Latin, *expositio*). It is perhaps no accident that Kant used the German equivalent for setting-out (*darstellen*) in explaining his notion of construction, and that he used the term exposition for a process analogous to that of mathematical construction."[8] Neither Kant nor Wittgenstein wanted these pictures or constructions to be taken as mental images; they were not simply subjective products, but artifacts of language itself—part of the symbolic process.

The implications of the possibility of constructing concepts is revolutionary for philosophy. No longer need knowledge based on "images" or other sensible aids necessarily be relegated to secondary status, as Plato maintained, since some representations did not carry a bodily or empirical taint.[9] Instead of Descartes' "unaided reason," reason could accept aids, thus making possible an understanding of how certain knowledge is possible without a foundation either in God or subjectivity. Given the pure character of the construction, Kant, and both Hertz and Wittgenstein after him, argue that:

> whatever follows from the universal conditions of the construction
> must be universally valid of the object of the concept thus constructed
> (*A* 716, *B* 744).

The Rationalists dream of *a priori*, apodictic knowledge of the world was possible because representational systems carry the possibility of truth and falsity. Once again, this was possible because imagination mediated through non-empirical schemata the relation between concepts and objects, thought and the world.

For Kant, the drawback is that philosophy, because it uses concepts other than quantity, could not avail itself of the constructional method. Yet he nevertheless makes limited use of the method to develop his transcendental metaphysics. Because "it is schemata, not images of objects, which underlie our pure sensible concepts" (*A* 141, *B* 181) and because "schemata are thus nothing but *a priori* determinations of time [a quantity] in accordance with rules" (*A* 145, *B* 185), certain philosophical constructions can be obtained. Specifically, Kant constructs first the forms of sensibility and then the twelve categories of the understanding which allow for knowledge of the conditions of experience. Other concepts, like God, Freedom, and Immortality, can only be thought and not known since they cannot be constructed; there is a limit to knowledge, if not to thought.

Adapting this method for a justification of science, Hertz formulates a similar principle of construction:

> We form for ourselves images or symbols of external objects and the
> form which we give them is such that the necessary consequents of
> the images in thought are always the images of the necessary *conse-*
> *quents in the nature of the things pictured. In order that this requirement may*

be satisfied, there must be a certain conformity between nature and thought.
(emphasis mine).[10]

Unfortunately, Hertz's adaptation completely misses the point of Kant's Copernican Turn. Instead of schemata mediating the relation between thought and the world, Hertz returns to a pre-critical belief in a conformity between the two. Kant's whole point is to avoid just this move because there is no privileged access to nature and thus no way of knowing whether there was a correspondence. Nature is opaque; to be known it has to be constructed; that is the point of his transcendental turn.

Excited by the modeling aspects of Hertz's theory, Wittgenstein elaborates his picture theory of meaning, which shows how propositions, or any other concatenation of signs, picture reality. To picture something is to use a notational system to construct a situation: "In a proposition a situation is, as it were, constructed by way of experiment." (*T* 4.031) The cautionary, "as it were," reminds us that the signs do not actually build the spatial–temporal fact; only a different spatial–temporal facsimile and the experimental nature of the effort allows for truth by making falsity possible. "Like a *tableau vivant*," the construction presents a state of affairs in logical space (*T* 4.0311). Since all forms of representation depend on the logic of depiction, the results are quite general (*T* 4.015).

Wittgenstein's picture theory is made possible by two insights; the first makes representation possible; the second limits its scope. Both thoughts are expressed in one critical comment:

> The possibility of propositions is based on the principle that objects have signs as their representatives.
>
> My fundamental idea is that the 'logical constants' are not representatives; that there can be no representatives of the *logic* of facts. (*T* 4.0312)

The first half of the remark announces the only necessary condition needed to make modeling possible. Names (signs), by going proxy for objects, allow propositions (pictures) to reproduce the structural relationships of the facts they represent. The existence of names makes everything else possible (just like the existence of objects). If the mathematical multiplicity is preserved, representation makes knowledge possible (*T* 4.04). By taking propositions as models, or to put the point another way, by restricting pictures to models, Wittgenstein makes representation completely independent of language-users. The picture by itself attaches to reality:

> *That* is how a picture is attached to reality; it reaches right out to
> it. (*T* 2.1511)

It is laid against reality like a measure. (*T* 2. 1512)

Language, not "man" or God, is the measure of all things. It literally speaks
for itself since, like some naturally evolving system, it is one with the structure of things.

However, as the second part of *T* 4.0312 indicates, there is a price to
pay for making language as independent as the rocks, namely, it becomes
as dumb as them regarding its own existence. In particular, no picture can
depict its pictorial form, that which makes it a picture in the first place (*T*
2.171). The method of representation or pictorial form used to construct
the picture can depict or say anything; except it can not talk about itself:

> A picture represents its subject from a position outside it. (Its
> standpoint is its representational form.) That is why a picture repre-
> sents its subject correctly and incorrectly. (*T* 2.173)

> A picture cannot, however, place itself outside its representational
> form. (*T* 2.174)

Language has no self-referential capacity; no meta-language can elude the
properties of the original language. Thus, one can never say, for example,
what logical form is:

> Propositions can represent the whole of reality, but they cannot
> represent what they must have in common with reality in order to be
> able to represent it—logical form.
>   In order to be able to represent logical form, we should have to
> be able to station ourselves with propositions somewhere outside
> logic, that is to say outside the world. (*T* 4.12)

> Propositions cannot represent logical form: it is mirrored in them.
> What finds its reflection in language, language cannot represent.
> What expresses *itself* in language, *we* cannot express by means of
> language.
>   Propositions *show* the logical form of reality.
>   They display it. (*T* 4.121)

Logic is in our eyes, so to speak, and we can never see the eye together with
what it sees (*T* 5.6331). As the ultimate form of representation, logic is prior
to all experiences and all experiences are already in logical form. We expe-

rience that something *is so*, the how of things, the facts, but never the *what*, the fact that something is, the substance of the world (*T* 5.55).

The factor mitigating this limitation is that what language cannot say, it shows in its very deployment. One can be confident about the human capacity for expression because pictures express by showing more than they say. Thus Wittgenstein is able to redraw the boundaries of thought through language. In his view, while a wedge can no longer be driven between what can be thought (the realm of faith) as opposed to known, one can be erected between what can be said as opposed to shown. Opting for a more consistent view, if not more complete, Wittgenstein asserts that while language expresses every sense, it cannot always do this by speaking or saying. Instead, some truths show themselves in the very deployment of language. Knowledge is limited, only by our ability to articulate what is known.

The solution was elegant. Kant's subjectivism was eliminated since the subject or transcendental ego had become unnecessary to the modeling of the world. Instead, the picture reached right out to reality, laying against it like a measure. Language users were incidental to the process of representing. Language and logic were autonomous and could take care of themselves. The gap between knowledge and thought closed. The seventeenth-century rationalist belief that the real and the rational are one was confirmed. Language and thought followed the logic of depiction, which guaranteed knowledge of the world. The only drawback was that it was impossible to utter the metaphysical truths made manifest by the logic of depiction, which, of course, severely limited the voice of philosophy.

Another drawback, one not initially owned by Wittgenstein, was that by following Hertz too closely he repeated the latter's critical mistake:

> If a fact is to be a picture, it must have something in common with what it depicts. (*T* 2.16)

> There must be something identical in a picture and what it depicts, to enable the one to be a picture of the other at all. (*T* 2.161)

While the two share nothing more than a form, not a content, the condition remains theoretically otiose. Indeed, Wittgenstein works hard at establishing the non-empirical pedigree of pictures; yet the requirement of some shared element haunts him and eventually contributes to his abandonment of the picture theory of meaning. Like Kant, he too goes beyond his own limits. Nevertheless, guided by the spirit, if not the letter, of Kant's constructional method, Wittgenstein makes the linguistic turn. Instead of the forms of sensibility, ordinary language can serve as the repository of pictures or non-empirical schemata of concepts. Just as geometry or algebra construct mathematical concepts, ordinary language constructs all other concepts making knowledge possible. At first, Wittgenstein attributes language's potential as a natural bridge between thought and the world to its logical structure; we refer to this as the picture theory of meaning. Later, when he relinquishes the pre-critical requirement of identity, he recognizes the unmotivated, picture-quality of words themselves. The word "cow" constructs the thing cow; it pictures cow in a non-literal, abstract way—in the sense modern art uses that term. The resulting representation is non-subjective, non-personal, even non-empirical and thus makes knowledge possible.

Philosophy as Clarification

Philosophy is not one of the natural sciences.

(The word 'philosophy' must mean something whose place is above or below the natural sciences, not beside them) (cf. NB pg. 93). (T 4.111)

Philosophy aims at the logical clarification of thoughts.

Philosophy is not a body of doctrine but an activity.

A philosophical work consists essentially of elucidations.

Philosophy does not result in 'philosophical propositions', but rather in the clarification of propositions.

Without philosophy thoughts are, as it were, cloudy and indistinct: its task is to make them clear and to give them sharp boundaries. (T 4.112)

The results of the picture theory for constructing concepts left philosophy in a mess. According to the picture theory, propositions picture reality; they present the existence and non-existence of states of affairs (*T* 4.1). However, not everything that looks like a proposition is one. In particular, philosophical propositions do not picture. They do not present either the existence or non-existence of a state of affairs. On one hand, in their metaphysical guise, they try to articulate what the use of language shows, namely, logical form, or what language and reality have in common. In their ethical garb, they try to talk about the implications of the facts of the world, the aesthetic and moral values implied by the facts being such-and-such. Their attempt to say things that, as Wittgenstein's spatial metaphor situates it, underlie the existence of things or rise above them, respectively logic/metaphysics, on the one hand, or ethics/aesthetics on the other, results in a failed attempt to say what can only be shown or what cannot be expressed at all. To signal their impossibility, Wittgenstein calls these propositions nonsensical pseudo-propositions and devises at least a bipartite, perhaps tri-partite, scale to measure their failure of representation.

To logical propositions, he assigns a unique place (*T* 6.112). While they remain pseudo-propositions, one may utter them without producing regular non-sense (*unsinnig*); instead, one produces sense-less or *sinnlos* propositions. These are pictureless tautologies, e.g., either it is raining or it is not, or contradictions, both A and not A. In Aristotelian fashion, Wittgenstein speaks of logical propositions as privative to sense rather than lacking in sense, to distinguish them from the kinds of philosophical propositions which might have sense, but do not. Logical discourse is then a possible philosophical activity; however, there is not much mileage in mouthing tautologies. Not only are they of limited stimulation, but once said, there is nothing more for philosophy to say. One quickly turns to other matters, as Wittgenstein did. The only alternative is to hang around, haranguing those who utter metaphysics.

Metaphysical propositions are another matter altogether. The best way to think of them is as failed logical propositions; they go too far in saying the unsayable and thus result in straight nonsense or propositions which fail to picture. However, like logic, what these propositions try to say but fail to achieve is shown by the deployment of signs. Language expresses (*ausdruck-en*) more than it says. Showing and saying are language's two forms of expression. Silence in the domain of what can only be shown speaks profusely.

Sometimes, Wittgenstein treats the last category of propositions, ethics and aesthetics or propositions of value, as if they were comparable to metaphysical ones. They try to say what cannot be said. However, sometimes his language makes it seem as if the thoughts contained in these propositions cannot even be uttered; that is, they do not get expressed through being either said or shown because they do not even get into language:

> And so it is impossible for there to be propositions of ethics.
> Propositions can express nothing that is higher. (*T* 6.42)

> It is clear that ethics cannot be put into words [*nicht aussprechen lasst*].

> Ethics is transcendental
>
> (Ethics and aesthetics are one and the same.) (*T* 6.421)

While Wittgenstein speaks of these things as also making themselves manifest in language, he suggests that unlike metaphysics, what is higher is even
more resistant to expression than what is lower. These things never get formulated into words. Nevertheless, whether there are three gradients of
nonsense or two, philosophy alone faces the Sisyphean task of trying to say
what cannot be said. Squeezed by the emptiness of logic's tautologies, the
pseudo-importance of metaphysics, and the doubtful sense of ethics,
Wittgenstein was hard pressed to find a continuing voice for philosophy.

His first solution followed Kant's lead in arguing that philosophy performs a critique; it shows the limits of what can be said or thought. To recall
Kant's position, philosophy, "should be called a critique, not a doctrine, of
pure reason. Its utility, in speculation, ought properly to be only negative,
not to extend, but only clarify our reason, and keep it free from
errors—which is already a very great pain" (*A* 11, *B* 25). For Kant, as for
Wittgenstein, philosophy is an activity:

> Philosophy can never be learned, save only in historical fashion; as
> regards what concerns reason, we can at most learn to *philosophize* (*A*
> 837, *B* 865).

Its main purpose is:

> to expose the illusions of a reason that forgets its limits, and by suffi-
> ciently clarifying our concepts to recall it from its presumptuous
> speculative pursuits to modest but thorough self-knowledge (*A* 735,
> *B* 763).

However, to suit Wittgenstein's ideas and purposes, the concept of critique
would have to be cleansed of its eighteenth-century subjective tones.
Language, unlike Kantian reason, is not omniscient; it cannot serve as an
arbiter of sense. It cannot put us in the position of judge since no part of
us exists outside language, no transcendental ego with which to make
informed choices. A true critique requires a neutral place to stand. Instead
of critique, Wittgenstein turns to clarification. At most, philosophy can
clarify; it can create clear and distinct concepts, as Descartes wanted. More
guide than critic, philosophy shows the limits of what can be said
(thought) significantly, even if this means the death of philosophy as history knows it, that is, as theoretical discourse. Philosophy can help us to see
not what we knew but have forgotten, but what anyone can see once the

obfuscations of language and subjectivity are eliminated. Philosophy can point, if not define.

Changing the object of critique from reason to language—"All philosophy is a 'critique of language'(though not in Mauthner's sense)" (*T* 4.0031)—and as I have suggested, the purpose of critique from judgment to instruction, Wittgenstein echoes Kant's conception of philosophy precisely. As for Kant, philosophy's major function is not to extend knowledge, but to clarify our concepts and expose the illusions of reason. True philosophy, that aimed at the clarification of thoughts, can only stand guard against temptation and aid others to recognize the limits of philosophical discourse.

But Wittgenstein's "clarification" is harder on philosophy than Kant's "critique." Kant left room for transcendental metaphysics while Wittgenstein ruthlessly invokes silence. Like the tapes on the TV show *Mission Impossible*, philosophical propositions of either sort, *unsinnig* or *sinnlos*, ought to self-destruct once they have done their job (*T* 6.54). Philosophy helps us to see the world aright, but no discourse can articulate what that vision is. Language remains, as it was for the Greeks, only a handmaiden to experience. It leads to something that is ultimately not language. From this perspective the key difference of those thinkers who come after the early Wittgenstein, e.g., the later Wittgenstein, Foucault, Derrida, Gadamer, and Habermas, those whom we call "Postmodern," is that for them there truly is nothing beyond language. Like Heidegger, the early Wittgenstein retained a nostalgia, a romanticism for that which was not language. Accordingly, Wittgenstein leaves philosophy to do other things.[11]

Language's limits were logical, not psychological. The limits were part of the deep structure, the underlying "langue" or representational form of language, and there could be no escaping it.[12] He had written the last philosophical text; there was nothing more to say. Moreover, he had written it in such a way that the text itself embodied his teachings about the nature of philosophy. This was the real coup of the *Logisch-philosophische Abhandlung*; that is, his logical-philosophical discussions or transactions. His was not a treatise in the eighteenth-century style on logical philosophy, but rather a transaction or negotiation between language and philosophy. Even in the early work, something was being effected rather than described: a new way of seeing and doing philosophy.

One may summarize Wittgenstein's first philosophical position in four themes: activity, clarification, transformation, silence. First and foremost philosophy is an activity, not a body of doctrine. One *does* philosophy; in Aristotelian or Marxian terms, it is a praxis, not a poesis or a theoria. The very expression "*doing philosophy*" which everyone uses today originates with Wittgenstein. Secondly, what one does is operate, like a surgeon, on other propositions, those of science, math, and ordinary discourse, in order to make their thoughts perspicuous. Philosophy is a meta-activity concerned with *clarifying* what we say about the world:

> If I am not quite sure how I should start a book, this is because I am still unclear about something. For I should like to start with the original data of philosophy, written and spoken sentences, with books as it were… (C*V* pg. 8)

Clarification puts everything in order; it distills the essence of things. Third, the result of doing philosophy, the product, is not some treatise of philosophical propositions, but a *transformation* in the way we see things: "He must transcend these propositions, and then he will see the world aright" (*T* 6.54). Lastly, and as a direct consequence of the preceding themes, once it has done its job, philosophy is reduced to *silence* (*T* 7). Philosophy is not an activity done with language, but through it. In short, philosophy is an activity engaged in the clarification of language aimed at the transformation of our view of the world which ends in silence. With some modifications, these same four themes characterize his later view of philosophy as well.

The Rhetoric of Elucidation

> *My propositions serve as elucidations in the following way: anyone who understands me eventually recognizes them as nonsensical, when **he** has used them—as steps—to climb up beyond them. (**He** must, so to speak, throw away the ladder after **he** has climbed up it.*
>
> ***He** must transcend these propositions, and then **he** will see the world aright. (*T 6.54*)

How does one write a book of elucidations? That is, how does one articulate propositions whose meaning does not depend on their propositional content, but on what they show about the world? More importantly, how do you get people to use propositions as steps, rungs of a ladder, rather than as signs of information? Normally, words are exchanged for their meaning, not their shapes or their weight-bearing possibilities. Not since Plato has anyone faced such a difficult writing assignment. While Plato wrote against Socrates' moral injunction not to write, Wittgenstein used language against its own grain, namely, to reveal the essence of thought and reality—remember that for Wittgenstein, language is not designed to reveal the form beneath it (*T* 4.002).

To bypass the limits of language, Wittgenstein first turns to poetry as a model of philosophical elucidation. He admired poetry and always wished that he could write it. Among the properties of poetry that he aspired to was the fact that, like music, poetry uses the language of information (in music's case, the language of sound) without playing the language-game of giving information:

> The way music speaks. Do not forget that a poem, even though
> it is composed in the language of information, is not used in the lan-
> guage-game of giving information. (*Z* 160)

In philosophical discourse, "slab" and "brick" mean things other than typical interpretations like "bring me a slab." Philosophy is not a normal, everyday form of discourse, as Wittgenstein is quick to note in all his texts, but especially in *On Certainty*:

> So if I say to someone "I *know* that that's a tree", it is as if I told
> **him** "that is a tree; you can absolutely rely on it; there is no doubt
> about it". And a philosopher could only use the statement to show
> that this form of speech is actually used... (*OC* 433)

As Roman Jakobson has argued, poetry is special because its message is a function of both its context and its particular way of being formed.[13] The key factor about poetry is that it contains the unutterable. Discussing a poem by Uhland with Englemann, Wittgenstein says:

> The poem by Uhland is really magnificent. And this is how it is: if
> only you do not try to utter what is unutterable then *nothing* gets
> lost. But the unutterable will be—unutterably—*contained* in what has
> been uttered.[14]

By not trying to say what cannot be said, one preserves it anyway. As is well known, Wittgenstein felt this way about his own work; he tells Engelmann that his work too contains one unuttered sentence more:

> The book's point is an ethical one. I once meant to include in the
> preface a sentence which is not in fact there now but which I will

write out for you here. What I meant to write then was this: My
work consists of two parts: the one presented here plus all that I have
not written. And it is precisely this second part that is the important
one....[15]

Still, one hesitates to identify the prosaic remarks of the *Tractatus* as
poetry. Perhaps Nietzsche's or Wilde's aphorisms provide a closer model for
Wittgenstein's prosaic one-liners. The quasi-poetic devise of the aphorism—the succinct, well-polished, and ambiguous sentence which like the
poetic utterance manages to show more than it says—seemed to appeal to
Wittgenstein. As a devout reader of Karl Kraus, he learned that an aphorism
jumped the border between the sayable and the unsayable:

> An aphorism doesn't need to be true, but it should go beyond truth.
> It should, as it were, go beyond it with one "satz".[16]

Punning on jump and sentence in *satz*, Kraus hinted that the aphorism
jumped the boundary of the unutterable by providing one unuttered sentence more. Accordingly, Wittgenstein hoped that the terse, carefully constructed remarks of the *Tractatus* would supply, as in poetry, an extra "satz"
by showing what they could not say. Once again, while helpful in understanding the character of Wittgenstein's remarks, the simile to an aphorism
is limited. The propositions of the *Tractatus* remain too thin and un-clever
to truly be accepted as aphorisms.

In the end I think elucidations are in a class all their own, not quite
poem, aphorism, or logical equation, they resist categorization. Yet, like the
poem, or the aphorism, Wittgenstein's elucidations use signs in distinctive
ways. They instruct by example, by showing rather than saying:

> The meanings of primitive signs can be explained by means of
> elucidations. Elucidations are propositions that contain the primitive
> signs. So they can only be understood if the meanings of those signs
> are already known. (*T* 3.263)

Names are primitive signs; they are primitive because they cannot be
defined. They are the end-points that connect a picture to a situation. They
instantiate that moment when language makes contact with reality and thus
that moment when language stutters, when it wants to gesticulate at the
object and make it get up and identify itself: "you there, yes you, I'm talking to you." To say that philosophy consists of elucidations (*T* 4. 112) is to
say that it consists of propositions that *use or apply* signs in appropriate ways.

(Here is where the *Tractatus* anticipated the importance of use even though at this point in his thinking Wittgenstein still believed in the greater importance of structure.) An elucidation correctly applies a sign. Since it is already doing it correctly, it must understand the meaning of its primitive signs and anyone who sees that it is doing it correctly must also understand these primitives. The book then, as Wittgenstein tells us, can only be understood by someone who already speaks the language; by someone who has had the thoughts. Philosophy has no special jurisdiction to use language to reveal the form of reality or thought. To do its job, it must resort to tautologies like, to quote that other famous user of elucidations, Gertrude Stein, "A rose is a rose is a rose." Elucidations cannot define or explain the sign, only instruct by example, a kind of ostensive definition. They clarify the use of signs by using them in new and instructive contexts and thus create a new sense of "meta" or "second-order:"

> One might think: if philosophy speaks of the use of the word "phi-
> losophy" there must be a second-order philosophy. But it is not
> so: it is, rather, like the case of orthography, which deals with
> the word "orthography" among others without then being second-
> order. (*PI* 121)

In addition to the difficulties of getting philosophical propositions to speak was the problem of connecting them in a coherent discourse. For this, Wittgenstein used the seventeenth-century philosophical ideal of the geometric method. Following Euclid, another famous elucidator, the numbering system replaced the connectives between propositions. One could see the varieties of dependence through the relative importance of the numbers. The logic or connection of facts which was mirrored in the logic of language, and thus could not be said, could be shown by the attempted proof structure of the numbering system. Like a poetical Aristotelian syllogism, the seven major headings of the *Tractatus* distribute the middle term pushing the thoughts to a deduction:

The world is all that is the case. (*T* 1)

What is the case—a fact—is the existence of states of affairs. (*T* 2)

A logical picture of facts is a thought. (*T* 3)

A thought is a proposition with a sense. (*T* 4)

A proposition is a truth-function of elementary propositions. (*T* 5)

The general form of a truth-function is $[\bar{p}, \bar{\xi}, \eta(\bar{\xi})]$. This is the general form of a proposition. (*T* 6)

What we cannot speak about we must pass over in silence. (*T* 7)

When one adds the next level of commentary, the n.1, 2, etc., the proof is further fleshed. Interestingly, the propositions that truly don't belong, the ones that Wittgenstein is most embarrassed about articulating, are the 2.0 and 3.0. These asides, which speak about the nature of facts or language, especially break the rules of significant philosophical speech. The end is a statement about the general form of a proposition; the rest is silence. All we can say is something about the nature of language.

Certainly, one cannot discuss the style of Wittgenstein's text without noting the unusual printing practice it initiates and which engenders a very particular reading practice. Because Wittgenstein insisted that the German be published along with the English, the typical reader has the unusual experience of reading only half the pages of the book and of being confronted at every moment with a hostile script or notation. I suspect many resist calling this an aspect of his style since it seems such an accident of publication. Yet the accident is anything but accidental. If it hadn't happened accidentally, it would have had to be invented. The two-language system allows each proposition to contain one unuttered, one untranslated sentence more. It nicely hammers home a variety of points from the simple one that language matters to the complex hermeneutic problem raised by the text that one can only know that which one already knows.

As usual, Wittgenstein did not think he was very successful at his attempt at quasi-poetic prose:

> I think I summed up my attitude to philosophy when I said: philosophy ought really to be written only as *poetic composition*. It must, as it seems to me, be possible to gather from this how far my thinking belongs to the present, future or past. For I was thereby revealing myself as someone who cannot quite do what he would like to be able to do. (*CV* pg. 24)

However, the failure of the *Tractatus* has little to do with Wittgenstein's failure as a poet. Rather, inconsistencies between what he wanted philosophy to do, i.e., reveal the essence of the world, and what it could do, i.e., clarify propositions, undermined his efforts. Most embarrassing was his failure to improve on Kant's solution. According to the strict correspondence of the picture theory between what can be said, what can be thought, and what can be known, all talk about propositions showing something more become extremely puzzling. What status can the class of things that cannot be said, but only shown, have? One cannot know more than one can say since the limits of thought and language are identical. Thus, what is shown, but not said is, according to the definitions of the *Tractatus,* not even thinkable. As far as not transgressing limits, Wittgenstein fudges just as much as he claimed Kant fudged. At least for Kant, while we could not *know* God, freedom, or immortality, we could at least *think* them. For Wittgenstein, on the other hand, this was impossible; no wedge could be drawn between thinking and knowing. When he realized his errors, he returned to philosophy to put it right.

*If one tried to advance theses in philosophy, it would never be possible to
debate them, because everyone would agree to them. (PI 128)*

*In philosophy we do not draw conclusions. "But, it must be like this!" is
not a philosophical proposition. Philosophy only states what everyone admits.
(PI 599)*

Moving from the sublime to the ridiculous, Wittgenstein's discursive woes
in the later works stem not so much from the tragic limits of language as
from the comic repetitions of philosophy. According to his new conception
of philosophy, any attempt to say what cannot be said ends not in trans-
gressive metaphysics, but in silly prattle doomed to repeat what everyone
already knows. Moreover, release from philosophical anxiety comes not
from stalwart, silent acknowledgement of that which cannot be said, but
from noisy reiteration of what is all too easily said. The difference is that
instead of hidden, recondite truths (disguised nonsense), what philosophy
still needs to say, the essence of things (*PI* 92), is open to view and always
already known (patent nonsense).[1] A hermeneutic of the commonplace
comprises the new domain of philosophical exchange:

> The aspects of things that are most important for us are hidden
> because of their simplicity and familiarity. (One is unable to notice
> something—because it is always before one's eyes.) The real founda-
> tions of **his** inquiry do not strike a **man** at all. Unless *that* fact has at
> some time struck **him**.—And this means: we fail to be struck by
> what, once seen, is most striking and most powerful. (*PI* 129)

The solution to philosophical problems comes from the exchange of the familiar. Wittgenstein refers to these everyday beliefs as a way of seeing, a world-picture, *Weltbilt,* of a particular *Lebensform,* form of life. Philosophy's new task is to *map* this world-picture which either cures the idling speculations caused by misguided philosophical analysis or points to the need for a new way of seeing:

> Philosophy simply puts everything before us, and neither explains not deduces anything.—Since everything lies open to view there is nothing to explain. For what is hidden, for example, is of no interest to us.
>
> One might also give the name "philosophy" to what is possible *before* all new discoveries and inventions. (*PI* 126)

Philosophy cannot interfere with language, not even to draw a limit; it can only trace the boundaries of concepts as they record themselves in our form of life.

These changes are due to a variety of factors. First, while language is no longer the main culprit, it still disguises thought:

> The power language has to make everything look the same, which is most glaringly evident in the *dictionary* and which makes the personification of *time* possible: something no less remarkable than would have been making divinities of the logical constants. (*CV* pg. 22)

Instead of mystical, however, its obfuscations are now mundane; that is, its forms of expression gloss over differences, tempt us to use one picture where we should use another, seduce us into a one-sided diet of examples, or entangle us in it our own rules. Language is messy and uninterested in making thought precise. To counter its deceptive force, philosophers must patrol the territory exposing infelicitous expressions. They must map forms of life, instead of construct concepts. Mapping concepts is less aggressive and intrusive than constructing them. In constructing, one literally builds thoughts by piling layers of words together. Mapping, on the other hand, passively records a linguistic system. It provides a synoptic view of how both language and concepts lie. A map is a miniaturized projection of how things stand.

Most importantly, maps do not pretend to theory; that is, of thinking that everything can be explained in the same way.[2] Like language, theory conceals differences and overgeneralizes. For example, all of us in this form of life know how a clarinet sounds (*PI* 78), or how coffee smells (*PI* 610), or what a game (*PI* 75) or time is (*PI* 89); yet, when asked, we are unable to give a definition of these things or formulate what we know in the same way we are able to say how high Mt Blanc is (*PI* 78). We know these things, indeed, they are classic examples of the *Weltbild* or system of beliefs that comprise our way of seeing, but we are unable to formulate our knowledge in any significant way. For Wittgenstein, this is no longer a shortcoming of language, but of our expectations of philosophy. Philosophical language is not a special language; it cannot do what other propositions cannot do and thus it cannot explain what resists explanation.

While the dynamic preventing significant philosophical exchange has changed, the question of how philosophy is to speak remains. How does one repeat the obvious without sounding stupid and foolish, e.g., "that's a tree" or "2 plus 2 equals 4?" Given language's continued obfuscations and philosophy's new task, a new rhetorical strategy had to be found to outwit language, (an enormous job if "wit" depends on language). As in the earlier work, speaking and writing philosophy had to be divorced from the language of information, only now, he could no longer rely on language speaking for itself, showing what it could not say. Instead, he had to repeat the obvious—talk tautologies, but in such a way that his saying focused not on the content of what was being said, but on its function. He instructed by example—not just by giving examples, but by being an example. Philosophy became a performance with him reading the lines of his script as if in a play. This fictional frame allowed him to perform the correct way of seeing, rather than describe it, bringing language closer to direct action. In this sense, his propositions still gesture beyond the words, but now they point to a way of seeing, not the logic of a state of affairs.

Using verbal sketches (language-games) to underwrite these scenes of instruction, Wittgenstein plays with language to remind us of the everyday. Stylistically, grammatical, irreducible prosaic remarks, representing incomplete, empirical observations on the use of expressions, replace the earlier logical, quasi-poetic elucidations. Wittgenstein calls them reminders since they serve to remind us of what we already know but have forgotten or have simply failed to articulate. While "reminders" might also remind us of Plato's doctrine of *anamnaesis,* remembrance or recognition is not recollection. Unlike Plato, what we know but cannot say is not learned in another form of life, but in the very one in which we grew. Facing the known, rather than the unknown, philosophy's difficulty, as Augustine knew, is making people see what they have always already seen in a new way:

Here it is easy to get into that dead-end in philosophy, where

one believes that the difficulty of the task consists in our having to describe phenomena that are hard to get hold of, the present experience that slips quickly by, or something of the kind. Where we find ordinary langage too crude, and it looks as if we were having to do, not with the phenomena of every-day, but with ones that "easily elude us, and in their coming to be and passing away, produce those others as an average effect". (Augustine: Manifestissima et usitatissima sunt, et eadem rusus nimis latent, et nova est inventio eorum.)
(*PI* 436)

As words are returned from their metaphysical use to their everyday one, the way of seeing will be brought into view. Clarification now clarifies the way we see things. Ambling back and forth across the conceptual terrain like an itinerant artist or peripatetic philosopher of old, he concentrates on mapping the connections between concepts implying, I believe, that, *contra* Hume, resemblance sometimes needs to be demonstrated. By drawing the physiognomy of concepts, he makes our worldview come alive. Repossessed of the ordinary and free from the fly-bottle, philosophers find peace—until, that is, someone speaks again.

Mapping Forms of Life

If it is asked: "How do sentences manage to represent?"—the answer might be: "Don't you know? You certainly see it, when you use them." For nothing is concealed.

How do sentences do it?—Don't you know? For nothing is hidden.

But given the answer: "But you know how sentences do it, for nothing is concealed" one would like to retort "Yes, but it all goes by so quick, and I should like to see it as it were laid open to view." (PI 435)

The *Investigations* opens with a resounding critique of the picture theory of meaning temporarily displaced as an attack on Augustine's conception of language. The transference allows Wittgenstein, as well as his audience, to see his mistakes by providing a primitive version of the picture theory. Augustine (*PI* 1), like Wittgenstein (*PI* 46), made the crucial mistake of thinking of a proposition as a construction or projection of a situation or a thought(*T* 3.1–3.13). He viewed it as a composition of names or a model of reality. In contrast, Wittgenstein's later approach abandons the idea of language as a projection, externalization, or manifestation of something else. Language is not a representational structure, but a presentational act. It is still comprised of signs, but signs mean by doing for themselves, not pointing to something other. Thus, like other post-structuralists, Wittgenstein comes to appreciate the importance of speech, *parole,* instead of language, *langue.* Language is an action, a tongue whereby sounds achieve meaning:

> But how many kinds of sentence are there? Say assertion, question, command?—There are *countless* kinds: countless different kinds of use of what we call "symbols", "words", "sentences". And this multiplicity is not something fixed, given once for all; but new types of language, new language-games, as we may say, come into existence, and others become obsolete and get forgotten...
>
> Here the term "language-*game*" is meant to bring into prominence the fact that the *speaking* of language is part of an activity, or of a form of life...(cf. *PI* 24). (*PI* 23)

Words are tools or instruments (*PI* 11) with which to do things. To keep that activity as open and non-functional as possible, Wittgenstein lights on the simile of a game. "Game" here does the same work as it does for Gadamer or Derrida. Instead of thinking of language as work, as something towards some end, it focuses on the activity itself as an end in itself. Secondly, game includes the notion of rules; speaking is play according to rules. By separating language from such ends as representation or communication, one can see its dynamic more clearly. (While Wittgenstein often uses the similes of tool and work, they do not conflict with those of game and play because the latter terms incorporate the former. The difference is that in games and play the rules and the point are both flexible.)

Language's connection to action is nicely etched in the idea of calling language a refinement; that is, something that improves upon action:

> The origin and the primitive form of the language game is a reaction; only from this can more complicated forms develop.
>
> Language—I want to say—is a refinement. "In the beginning was the deed." (*PO* pg. 395)

Language polishes, makes action clear. Generally, the more language, the more civilized we consider someone to be; but for Wittgenstein this is because the more language, the more differences are made visible. Philosophy ought not to refine language further, distill it so that nothing is left but the words; rather, it must reverse the process of rarefaction and reconnect language to its roots in action. For Wittgenstein, this is a process of synopsis or synthesis:

> The essence of the language game is a practical method (a way of acting)—not speculation, not chatter. (*PO* pg. 399)

Because only a used language is meaningful, the foreign Latin phrases which first greet readers when they open the *Investigations* emphasizes dramatically Wittgenstein's change of mind about language: it does not quite speak for itself, but needs help:

> "Put a ruler against this body; it does not say that the body is of such-and-such a length. Rather is it in itself—I should like to say— dead, and achieves nothing of what thought achieves."—It is as if we had imagined that the essential thing about a living **man** was the outward form. Then we made a lump of wood in that form, and were abashed to see the stupid block, which hadn't even any similarity to a living being. (*PI* 430)

Language does not mean, that is, sentences do not represent, by modeling objects or thoughts. Rather, language-users must apply language to make it mean:

> We want to say: "When we mean something it's like going up to someone, it's not having a dead picture (of any kind)." We go up to the things we mean (cf. *Z* 233). (*PI* 455)

> Yes: meaning something is like going up to someone. (*PI* 457)

Use brings us near the things we mean. Only in use is language alive. In fact, the reason he cautions us not to think of language as "human"—this connection is prepared for by remark 430—as something fully determined which is then brought to life by the breath of use, is to stress the natural life of language: "Language is not something that is first given a structure and then fitted on to reality" (*PG* pg. 89). On the contrary, only a living language, a used language, is a language; we should not even call a dead-sign system a language—another reason for his starting with Latin. Use is the proper function of language. When language is functioning, it is performing; it is alive.

Of course, words may still refer (go proxy for objects), but reference can no longer account for meaning (MRx). Instead, meaning is a function of use (M=Ux):

> For a *large* class of cases—through not for all—in which we
> employ the word "meaning" it can be defined thus: the meaning of a
> word is its use in the language.
>
> And the *meaning* of a name is sometimes explained by pointing
> to its *bearer*. (*PI* 43)

The cautionary tone guards against theory. He does not want to make a
theoretical statement about use, but an empirical observation, a remark
about language's natural history. Like names, some sentences may still mean
by modeling, but that is because, as his detailed arguments against ostensive
definition make clear, of the way the signs are being used by sign-users and
not because of any transcendental connection of its elements with the elements of states of affairs.

Language represents because it was born to, only it wears its DNA on
its sleeve. That is, it isn't a potential structure actualized by use (Chomsky,
Aristotle), but a virtual machine formed by its use. As my logical formulation (M=Ux) is meant to stress, a word is its functions, nothing else. It isn't
a spatial/temporal structure, but an abstract one. Like the soul, it will not be
found by dissection. The connection, one, like Wittgenstein, would like to
say, between language and the world, is no longer conceived of as internal,
but external. Humans provide the mechanism that makes language work.
However, this is poorly said; the scale internal/external or the corny opposition, "Man and the World," no longer makes sense in Wittgenstein's later
philosophy. Because humans are an integral part of nature, and language an
integral part of being human, one can no longer think of human intervention as external:

> What we are supplying are really remarks on the natural history
> of human beings; we are not contributing curiosities however, but
> observations which no one has doubted, but which have escaped
> remark only because they are always before our eyes. (*PI* 415)

We are a natural part of the universe, a cog through which operations
cycle—a part of the system.

The years Wittgenstein spent teaching schoolchildren reminded him
that language does not spring full-grown from the mouths of babes; rather,
language requires training. One is taught a language, and with that teaching one is born into a form of life, that is, a way of seeing and doing things.[3]
Both the syntax and the semantics of language work to orient us in a world.
(And since language is always changing, one cannot step into the same

world twice.) Language maps a world and a thought at the same time. Yet one cannot choose or readily change the language one learns; it is not an arbitrary system of signs. Before relativism, conventionalism, behaviorism, or pragmatism settle in our minds as the philosophy expounded by Wittgenstein, one *must* remember that language is not a product of art or *techne* for him; it is not a human-made artifact, but a living dimension of existence. "Dimension" is the right word since language is not a thing, either artificial or natural, but a space, like physical space/time. Between arbitrary and intentional, contingent and necessary, exists another nameless dimension that Wittgenstein argues has aspects of both. He likens language to a style of painting (*PI* pg. 230) in that neither do we assume a style of painting at will, nor is how we paint entirely arbitrary. We live in the physical world cradled by its linguistic net with no danger of falling.

Thus, what was of utmost importance in the early work, language as a method of representation, fades into the background as an instrument whose value lies in its use, "Look at the sentence as an instrument, and at its sense as its employment" (*PI* 421). Just as a rule does not automatically tell us which way to go (*PI* 85), grammar must be applied in order for it to make sense. Grammar is no longer necessary and sufficient for meaning. Instead, situations, context, history, and a form of life all play a part. To employ the distinction developed by Saussure, the Swiss linguist, again, the logic of the symbolism, the "langue," gives way to the conventions of linguistic usage, the "parole". Even grammars change, when the river-bed itself shifts, and none of these changes can be justified by appealing to the logical form of reality.

The introduction of language-users, however, brought a new and different set of problems to the fore. First, if some pre-established harmony could not account for language's representing capacities, perhaps the mind, or human psychology, achieved what God could not? Wittgenstein immediately rejects such an option. Meaning is never going to be satisfactorily explained by pointing to the mental, to things like intention. Surely it would not take him long to show that if words did not mean by referring to an object, they certainly could not mean by referring to an idea. Mind cannot do what matter cannot. Use would certainly suffice as an explanation of how words mean. While language's ability to represent was no longer the main issue, its ability to communicate, to speak to any number of different people simultaneously, was. The fact was that language was still a picturing medium and nothing stopped people from associating different pictures with words. Their personal histories and different cultures legislated against their ever being a single–general use for a word. How then did we communicate? Explaining the conditions of synonymy, rather than reference, became the primary puzzle of the later works.

Maintaining his original conception of language as a picturing medium, he discovers that willy–nilly words evoke pictures. Often these pictures clash with the correct application of a word, and one finds oneself torn between two possible pictures. More often, one accepts the picture evoked by the word and cannot make sense of the facts:

> What am I believing in when I believe that **men** have souls?
> What am I believing in, when I believe that this substance contains
> two carbon rings? In both cases there is a picture in the foreground,
> but the sense lies far in the background; that is, the application of the
> picture is not easy to survey. (*PI* 422)

> The picture is *there;* and I do not dispute its *correctness.* But *what*
> is its application? Think of the picture of blindness as a darkness in
> the soul or in the head of the blind **man**. (*PI* 424)

Pictures mask the appropriate application and thus the sense of the word. More generally, language abstracts from the differences in a situation and, for example, speaks of a red patch whether it is there or not (*PI* 446) or suggests that just as it is impossible to hang someone who is not there, it is impossible to look for someone who is not there (*PI* 462). Thus the grammar of language still deceives, only now it is not a question of masking the logical form of reality, but of covering the endless possibilities of "parole":

> We remain unconscious of the prodigious diversity of all the
> everyday language-games, because the clothing of our language
> makes everything alike. (*PI* pg. 224)

Completely reversing his earlier reasoning, Wittgenstein argues that the tendency to assume that language or thought serves one purpose, to describe facts, prevents an understanding of the many uses of language:

> Think of the tools in a tool-box; there is a hammer, pliers, a saw,
> a screw driver, a rule, a glue-pot, glue, nails, screws. The function of
> words are as diverse as the functions of these objects. (And in both
> cases there are similarities.)

Of course, what confuses us is the uniform appearance of words when we hear them spoken or meet them in script and print. For their *application* is not presented to us so clearly. Especially when we are doing philosophy! (*PI* 11)

With the recognition that language and thought serve a variety of functions, Wittgenstein found a more complex ground for mistakes. To violate the ruling grammar or say something completely out of context, for example, produces nonsense:

> My difficulty can also be shewn like this: I am sitting talking to a friend. Suddenly I say: "I knew all along that you were so-and-so." Is that really just a superfluous, though true, remark? I feel as if these words were like "Good Morning" said to someone in the middle of a conversation. (*OC* 464)

Sense and nonsense are determined by a form of life, and that is reflected in the language-games we play. Contexts and situations often make the most grammatical remark nonsensical. To discover the limits of language, one must look beyond the method of representation to the pragmatic considerations which establish a language-game.

One obvious consequence of this new view of language is that it no longer makes sense to speak of *the* limits of language. Language is like a city: it grows, changes, and reinvents itself constantly (*PI* 18). There is no permanent boundary between the sayable and the unsayable. One can decide, that is, a form of life decides, to exclude certain combinations of words from the language and call them nonsense, but not because they violate some boundary:

> To say "This combination of words makes no sense" excludes it from the sphere of language and thereby bounds the domain of language. But when one draws a boundary it may be for various kinds of reason. If I surround an area with a fence or a line or otherwise, the purpose may be to prevent someone from getting in or out; but it may also be part of a game and the players be supposed, say, to jump over the boundary; or it may shew where the property of one **man** ends and that of another begins; and so on. So if I draw a boundary line that is not yet to say what I am drawing it for (cf. 68–71). (*PI* 499)

Concepts are not closed by a frontier; one draws boundaries when one needs to depending on the situation and all the other pragmatic considerations of a language game, but the method is mute. Accordingly, the border between sense and nonsense has become elastic and pliable.

Yet, when we turn to the later work, he is still having trouble expressing himself. In fact, he continues to speak of the limits of language even though his new conception of language vitiates any such idea:

> …Philosophy is a battle against the bewitchment of our intelligence by means of language. (*PI* 109)

> The results of philosophy are the uncovering of one or another piece of plain nonsense and of bumps that the understanding has got by running its head up against the limits of language. These bumps makes us see the value of the discovery. (*PI* 119)

Philosophical discourse remains identified with idling nonsense and Wittgenstein becomes even harder on the discourse of established philosophy. The question is, why is Wittgenstein still having trouble, if philosophy no longer aims at the unsayable?

Philosophy as Performance

> *(As one can sometimes reproduce music only in one's inward ear, and cannot whistle it, because the whistling drowns out the inner voice, so sometimes the voice of a philosophical thought is so soft that the noise of spoken words is enough to drown it and prevent it from being heard, if one is questioned and has to speak.) (Z 453)*

Saying philosophy, literally voicing ideas, overwhelms them; they get lost in the clatter of words. Consequently, to reveal what everyone always already knows, philosophers must use language differently. Instead of a game of information, they must imitate playing a game of information. They must perform the deed or complete it outside the context of the everyday to show how language normally informs. Playing or active bodily motion is essential to philosophical performing. It concentrates attention precisely on the obvious. "Play" means many things. First, philosophers must play *with* language in the sense of "toy," stretching and contracting it, inventing intermediate and fictitious cases, in order to learn how much play exists in an expression. They must study, as John Austin would have said, "what we say when."[4] The philosopher's freedom from any community of ideas and the ability to see aspects comes into play at this juncture. In order to play, one must be free. "Suppose this" and "imagine that" become the "let's pretend" of children's games. Secondly, another sense of "play", invoked by Wittgenstein, is that of playing *at* language. Like children, philosophers must engage in games, pretending to speak as they reteach themselves their mother tongue. The language-games stage utterances, like making tea, rather than say them. Like elucidations, the games, use the expressions in significant ways and thus demonstrate their applicability. Just as teachers of children create verbal games using the word in question to teach language, philosophers engage in verbal play to teach adults a way of seeing and eventually free them from fly-bottles. A language-game is a primitive use of language, one in which the rules are being both rehearsed and invented at the same time.

In a third sense, language must also be seen as a play, a script to be performed. Instead of using words to instruct his readers, Wittgenstein enacts fly-bottles, dramatizing not the structure of a state of affairs, but the dynamics of a linguistic situation. Wittgenstein's words in the later works play at language, rather than use it in the traditional exchange of information. Not knowing that he is playing at, with, and in language, many misunderstand his intentions. Like the unintelligible lion, we fail to understand him (*PI* pg. 223). Engaged in this play, philosophers appear foolish, insisting that this is a tree, that this is my hand. The difficult thing is to not have those who are reading over one's shoulder misinterpret what one is doing. Most importantly, one is not creating theory; indeed, most of the time nothing is even being asserted. One is enacting a game of language in front of one's audience in order to show them something about the world. The measure of success is that all players go on in a different way. Wittgenstein was not playing a game of "simple Simon."

Perspicuity (*übersehen*), or clarity, is the reward of this reenactment. Clarity is still the goal in the later works, but with the concept of play it is achieved not through analysis or a paring away of that which appears superfluous, but through amplification, a multiplication of cases. By letting things grow and expand in all directions, the rough outline of the phenomena comes more clearly into view. Analysis is not the technique of the later work. Instead of smaller units, Wittgenstein strives for larger ones; the piece of the puzzle one is trying to find falls into place when one looks at the whole. Only in context is a unit a unit at all. Indeed, his rejection of analysis is one important way he departs from therapy as the primary simile for his concept of philosophy.

In many ways, the simile of therapy is apt. For example, a therapist is not a theorist, but instead is a practitioner whose main function is to attend the remembrance of the patient and help be an agent of that recuperation. Therapy is all about remembering what one already knows, but has forgotten, only in standard therapy, one would say "repressed" or "denied." Furthermore, it is a little crazy to forget the obvious. Those who do, and at sometime or another we all do, need a special kind of care. In this sense, the medical analogy seems appropriate:"The philosopher's treatment of a question is like the treatment of an illness" (*PI* 255).

While the problems of philosophy are universal in that they emanate from our ordinary everyday dealings with language, those whom we call "philosophers" seem particularly susceptible to language's charms:

> …What we 'are tempted to say' in such a case is, of course, not philosophy but it is its raw material. Thus, for example, what a mathematician is inclined to say about the objectivity and reality of mathematic facts, is not a philosophy of mathematics, but something for philosophical *treatment*. (*PI* 254).

Perhaps this is the case because philosophers are "lovers of wisdom" and sometimes when their desire to explain the essence of things gets out of hand, they become especially forgetful. At these moments, like any lover, they take language on a holiday, distorting the expressions of ordinary language:

> …We mind about the kind of expression we use concerning these things; we do not understand them, however, but misinterpret them. When doing philosophy we are like savages, primitive people, who hear the expressions of civilized **men**, put a false interpretation to them, and then draw the queerest conclusions from it. (*PI* 194; see also *PI* 38, *PI* 132)

In particular, Wittgenstein points to three different kinds of mistakes to which philosophers are prone and which a therapeutic approach might cure.

First, philosophers mistakenly believe that what can be known but not easily said is some kind of special, hidden knowledge. They think that they must improve their knowledge-base to solve the problem. However, like Augustine's problem with time, much of what we ordinarily know eludes definition and succinct expression:

...Something that we know when no one asks us, but no longer
know when we are supposed to give an account of it, is something
that we need to *remind* ourselves of. (And it is obviously something
of which for some reason it is difficult to remind oneself.) (*PI* 89)

Instead of believing that the forgotten is some profound piece of knowledge, Wittgenstein argues that this kind of knowledge is always already
being expressed in ordinary ways:

What does it mean to know what a game is? What does it mean
to know it and not be able to say it? Is this knowledge somehow
equivalent to an unformulated definition? So that if it were formulated I should be able to recognize it as the expression of my knowledge? Isn't my knowledge, my concept of a game, completely
expressed in the explanations that I could give? That is, in my
describing examples of various kinds of game; shewing how all sorts
of other games can be constructed on the analogy of these; saying
that I should scarcely include this or this among games; and so on.
(*PI* 75)

There is nothing special about this knowledge; it gets expressed in all the
examples and distinctions we draw. It is not philosophy's task to somehow formulate this knowledge for the first time, but rather just to point to the cases.
Curing philosophers of their expectations is certainly a task for therapy.

A second mistake is that philosophers try to use what everybody
already knows for special philosophical purposes. Wittgenstein's attack on
Moore best illustrates this kind of mistake:

For when Moore says "I know that that's..." I want to reply,
"you don't *know* anything!"—and yet I would not say that to anyone
who was speaking without philosophical intention. That is, I feel
(rightly?) that these two mean to say something different. (*OC* 407)

(One says the ordinary thing—with the wrong gesture.) (*Z* 451)

The lesson learned from Moore is that when these ordinary beliefs are
taken out of context and used like a hammer to prove, in Moore's case, realism, they lose all meaning and justifiably provoke Wittgenstein's ridicule:

I am sitting with a philosopher in the garden; **he** says again and
again, "I know that that's a tree", pointing to a tree that is near
us. Someone else arrives and hears this, and I tell **him**: "This **fellow**
isn't insane. We are only doing philosophy." (*OC* 467)

Thus, he says of Moore's arguments:

> It is as if "I know" did not tolerate metaphysical emphasis. (*OC* 498)

> "I know" is here a *logical* insight. Only realism can't be proved by means of it. (*OC* 59)

One again, these delusions of grandeur can be treated.

A third mistake occurs when philosophers say the obvious with normal intentions, to inform or exchange information:

> Thus it seems to me that I have known something the whole time, and yet there is no meaning is saying so, in uttering this truth. (*OC* 466)

There is no meaning because the context is lacking. These are the occasions when philosophers sound especially foolish. Also, as I have already discussed, at these moments Wittgenstein begins to wonder about the use of philosophy. If nothing is being said, what is the point of philosophy:

> Plato: "What? he said, *it* be of no use? If wisdom is the knowledge of knowledge and is prior to other knowledges, then it must also be prior to that knowledge which relates to the good and in that way must be of use to us. Does *it* make us healthy, I said, and not medicine? And similarly with the rest of the arts; does *it* direct their business, and not rather each of them its own? Again, have we not long since allowed that it would only be the knowledge of knowledges and ignorances and not of any other matter?—We have indeed...So how can wisdom be useful, if it does not bring us any utility?" (*Z* 454)

While he mocks Plato above, the question troubled him. If philosophy is the repetitive activity of reminding people of what they already know, how can it be useful? Sometimes wishing that philosophy could do more than this, he becomes pessimistic about his chosen career. Other times, he remembers that reminding people of what they know but have forgotten is an important task. Their problems are deep disquietudes, which when understood reveal important issues and questions. The therapy is worth doing and worth experiencing. The trick is to remember that the worth of philosophy is not in what it says, not in the content of its propositions, but in what it does. Philosophy has become pure performance.

But the simile of therapy has its limitations. It evokes much that has nothing to do with Wittgenstein's conception of philosophy. For example, the unconscious plays no role in Wittgenstein's thoughts. He is not suggesting that what we forget has emotional motivations. He does not care at all about the psychology of philosophical problems. Rather, his therapy is nothing more than "playing." Just as clarification improves upon critique in the earlier work, play improves upon therapy in the later work. Wittgenstein uses old models; he picks them up to help situate his thought, but he never simply dons these old clothes. Rather, he constantly tailors the simile to his own distinctive way of seeing. We must follow his poetic sensitivity and seek the right word to name the activity of philosophy. Like many artists of today, I think he is best seen as a performing artist playing language. His remaining problem was that of execution; how does one write or speak so that what one says is not mistaken for having content, but is only used to do something?

The Rhetoric of Reminders

The work of the philosopher consists in assembling reminders for a particular purpose. (PI 127)

[I do philosophy now like an old woman who is always mislaying something and having to look for it again: now her spectacles, now her keys.] (OC 532)

Like Beckett's, Wittgenstein's later style is prosaic to a fault. Words collect on the page without any apparent necessity. A typical sentence for either of them drones on noisily. Having withdrawn all of philosophy's exciting expressions for cleaning, he is left with only those plain clothes that would have made Socrates proud: "Sometimes an expression has to be withdrawn from language and sent for cleaning,—then it can be put back into circulation" (CV pg. 39). Chatty, even dull, not a smidgeon of music sneaks into his expressions or sentences. (He even compares his style to a bad musical composition (CV pg. 39).) Neither rhyme (poetry or rhetoric more generally), nor reason (logic) structures his later sentences. Readers will not need to transcend the propositions of the *Investigations,* since no illegitimate philosophical propositions are uttered. Rather, only the most commonplace and banal observations, things that normally escape notice because they are so banal, pass his lips:

"But being guided is surely a particular experience!"—The answer to this is: you are now *thinking* of a particular experience of being guided. (*PI* 173)

Of course, this effect is completely intentional. Given his new view of philosophy, the *Investigations* is intended as a travesty of our standard conception of a philosophical work. Dressed as an old woman (a guise used often by philosophers, e.g., Diotima) instead of the conquering hero, Wittgenstein pads about the conceptual domain seeking what he mislaid, namely, the pictures that free one from a fly-bottle. Philosophy's task is to remind us of what we forget. Its goal is pure performance in that once it completes its job, to change the way of seeing, it ought to self-destruct. Words ought to dissolve into the attitudes and actions from which they came. They are, in the strictest sense of the word, "deeds":

> In this way I should like to say the words "Oh, *let* **him** come!" are charged with my desire. And words can be wrung from us,—like a cry. Words can be *hard* to say: such, for example, as are used to effect a renunciation, or to confess a weakness. (Words are also deeds.)
> (*PI* 546)

As deeds, words do things. They execute actions and perform functions. Another word for them is "probes"; they hurtle forth, clearing and opening a world of possibilities. Wittgenstein's new use of language does not exist on Jacobson's map. In terms of the latter's definitions, it crosses all categories, for example, it is directed at the self and other simultaneously.

Poetry, even though it is not a discourse of information and thus appropriate for mouthing tautologies—what everybody already knows—no longer appeals. For one thing, it issues in a body of propositions, whereas philosophical propositions ought to completely dissolve. The same applies to logical propositions: its tautologies no longer capture the full sense of what he now means by the obvious, the already known. Besides, logic gives the immpression that philosophers are privy to some private, secret language, e.g.,(x)(y)(fx&Gy). No, for Wittgenstein, philosophical propositions should leave no residue or remainder, no trace of having been articulated. Perhaps Socrates was right in thinking that philosophy ought not to be written. Writing can't be the issue since Wittgenstein doesn't want them spoken either. It is not only the writing, but even the saying, that causes grief. Clearly, he would have to find a way of saying and writing that really wasn't a kind of saying or writing, that is, that didn't declare, question, or importune. He would have to invent a new rhetoric for reminders, a new form philosophical exchange. Indeed, the thing that makes Wittgenstein's later philosophy so difficult to follow is that in trying to find a discourse that captures his new vision for philosophy, he uses language in completely unchartered ways. Monk notes that he once remarked at the beginning of a series of lectures that "'What we say will be easy, but to know why we say it will be very difficult'" (Monk, 338).

To renounce theory, explanation, truth, and persuasion, the one-time goals of rhetoric and logic, Wittgenstein engages in a number of subversive strategies aimed at undermining standard philosophical styles: 1) he talks to himself; 2) he contradicts himself often; 3) he avoids arguments and conclusions, 4) he refuses any orientating structures, e.g., introductions, chapters, footnotes, formal dialogue procedures, etc.

1) Wittgenstein's monologue is different from the more familiar soliloquy in philosophy, the meditation. Most noticeably, meditators talk to God and thus hide a dialogue within a monologue. Wittgenstein talks to no one in particular, not even to himself. This is dramatically made evident by a lack of footnotes and frugal mention of the ideas of others. Of course, sometimes he addresses himself, other philosophers, and sometimes the reader directly. But, most times, he talks to a host of imagined interlocutors who are fragments of himself and others. The boundary between self and other breaks down in Wittgenstein's thinking, and the slippage is reflected in the lack of delineation between speakers in the text and positions. Sometimes Wittgenstein puts quotes around the tempting belief, other times not. He is not consistent about this, making it difficult to discover what he believes or is saying. However, this is his whole point. He isn't saying something; it is nothing that is different from what others say and think. He is just trying to say what he knows and remind everyone else of what they know at the right moment, the moment it will help.

Like someone on stage, he speaks to the pretended empty schoolroom and also to the more distant eavesdropping audience at the same time. We the readers are the distant audience who overhear him thinking. The people in the text are the immediate players. Yes, the text is full of voices, thoughts personified, but without names as they would be in a typical script. Had I been Derek Jarman, I would have had Robin Williams do a many-voiced reading of the text.[5] The world is full of problems and points of view; Wittgenstein wanted to capture this polyphony—to show that there isn't only one view and its antithesis, but a rich profusion of beliefs. Dialogues, monologues, and treatises fail to capture this chaos. He prefers, rather, to reduce everything to a few lines of thought. Not prepared for such confusion, many readers get mad, bored, or frustrated. However, perhaps one can have more patience when this point is appreciated.

2) To help thwart our tendency to comb the text for his beliefs and theories, he nonchalantly contradicts himself often. This strategy is the most unsettling. The remarks battle each other in a conversational and debating tone. They say contradictory things and are never able to say what they want to say in one declaratory sentence. Instead, he must always say two things in an effort to evoke the common sense things that need to be said. For example, in a famous but typical series of remarks (*OC* 400-405) he tries to talk about the fact that in the end knowledge is based on acknowledgment, that there are empirical propositions which serve as foundations for discourse, that there is a difference between knowledge and certainty, and that there is something we have not recognized about "truth." Yet, he is reluctant to simply say these things, to assert them. Instead of accepting them as reminders for the problem at hand, we are all too eager to accept them as theories, as philosophical propositions uttering some new fact about the world. But, for Wittgenstein, the only goal of these remarks is to get us to see the way we see things so we may either support our commitments or change them when necessary.

As I have remarked elsewhere in this work, he often says one thing and then the precise opposite or simply less dramatically qualifies what he recently asserted. For example, he twice takes back his claim that meaning is use (*PI* 43) in the *Investigations*: once when he is talking about sudden knowledge and once when he is discussing experiencing the meaning of a word (pg. 215). There are countless examples. Even Wittgenstein thematizes this point explicitly denying the law of excluded middle, i.e., either it must look like this, or like this (*PI* 352). For him, this law only prohibits a third possibility, something that goes beyond the iron-grasp of the dichotomy. Pushing Gödel one step further, he argues that philosophy can be neither consistent, nor complete. It will always remain unfinished and inconclusive. Philosophers cannot proclaim, only suggest. Their voice is suggestive, suppositional, seeking uncertainties rather than sure bets.

As I already discussed, his reminders are embodied in what he calls "remarks" or "sketches." Both concepts are intended to convey tentativeness and empirical observation. Like notes, they stress the unfinished nature of his thoughts.[6] They replace the aphorisms of the earlier work and loosely explore the use of an expression, noting what we might say, what we wouldn't say, what is said, or what could be said. By free-handing the scene of instruction, Wittgenstein hopes to circumscribe the domain of interpretation without literally inscribing its boundaries. He does not want his remarks to say, for example, what knowledge is, only what we have considered it to be. The latter descriptive version, what we call knowledge, is not meant to replace the normative one of what knowledge should be called; he is not replacing truth for opinion. Rather, the latter describes our way of seeing and thus might release one from a dilemma. In this way, the book becomes an album; as I suggested earlier, a portrait gallery of the concepts of a way of seeing. New information, conclusions, arguments are, thus, conspicuously absent. He does not want to persuade, only nudge.

3) The third strategy of avoiding conclusions goes beyond the failure to conclude any specific argument. The text globally does not conclude. The later texts do not come to any resting place, any sense of closure. Instead, the album works if after visiting it and viewing our history and family, we leave it and continue growing and living as we will, building new rooms on our developing form of life. There is no conclusion; any philosophy text worth its salt must emulate that fact; it must perform, experience itself, the endlessness of thought, language, and the world.

However, Wittgenstein's texts do not completely lack argument. He often amasses reasons to accept one claim rather than another. He argues forcibly, for example, against the view of meaning as reference or against the idea of a private language. Indeed, many Wittgenstein commentators gravitate to these parts of the *Investigations* since they feel the most familiar. However, such readings often lead to disastrous misunderstandings of his work. Yet the arguments remain odd; they never conclude and often disappear into irony, epiphanies, and personal anecdotes. The problem is arguments have only a limited value; they convert only the already converted. When someone does not share a form of life or is captured by a picture, she is useless. Wittgenstein's remarks in *On Certainty* are the most powerful on this subject:

> Supposing we met people who did not regard that [physics] as a telling reason. Now, how do we imagine this? Instead of the physicist, they consult an oracle. (And for that we consider them primitive.) Is it wrong for them to consult an oracle and be guided by it?—If we call this "wrong" aren't we using our language-game as a base from which to *combat* theirs. (*OC* 609)

> When two principles really do meet which cannot be reconciled
> with one another, then each **man** declares the other a fool and
> heretic. (*OC* 611)

His message here is that we must find other ways to convince
Thrasymachus that virtue is not vice and vice-versa. Argument alone only
displaces the fistfight from the streets into the salons, but it doesn't bring
peace, truth, or progress.

4) Wittgenstein drops us in the middle of a discussion or thought with
no clues as to why he is saying what he is saying or where he is going. One
is intentionally disoriented in Wittgenstein's text; he forces you to loose
your way so that you can go through the process of remembering what you
know and thus slay the dragons of skepticism, solipsism, etc. One can begin
at different places in the text depending on one's needs and reflections.
There is no beginning, nor end of either the text or the problems, since the
ramifications of a concept are endless.

Consecutive numbers provide the only ordering system. The numbers
that initiate each remark suggest no order or hierarchy as they did in the
Tractatus; they might continue indefinitely. They arbitrarily distinguish one
remark from another. Yet, there is some order; remarks cluster about a subject and pass onto a connected subject. One knows that had Wittgenstein the
patience and energy to have reshuffled all the later remarks as often as he had
the early ones, the second half of Part I of the *Investigations* (*PI* from roughly 437 on) would be just as organized as the first. But, the randomness of the
indexical system reminds us that there is no one correct order. Seeing things
aright requires a constant redrawing of the connections since both language
and forms of life are alive and therefore constantly changing.

The rhetoric of reminders lets us re-experience ourselves as language
-users in such a way that what is taken for granted becomes special once
again:

> Don't take it as a matter or course, but as a remarkable fact, that
> pictures and fictitious narratives give us pleasure, occupy our minds.
>
> ("Don't take it as a matter of course" means: find it surprising, as
> you do some things which disturb you. Then the puzzling aspect of
> the latter will disappear, by your accepting this fact as you do the
> other.)
>
> ((The transition from patent nonsense to something which is dis-
> guised nonsense.)) (*PI* 524)

((((One can see Wittgenstein's orthographical passion and the levels of philo-sophical comment in his move from no parentheses to two. I could not resist taking things a step further.))) First comes the direct address to make the familiar strange; then, the effect of this is evaluated:

> Nothing is more important for teaching us to undertand the con-cepts we have than constructing fictitious ones. (*CV* pg.74)

Its goal is ultimately to reduce puzzlement. Lastly, the whole process is named for the purposes of identifying philosophical practice. Philosophy can disguise itself as nonsense as long as it recognizes nonsense for nonsense and does not fool itself:

> Don't *for heaven's sake*, be afraid of talking nonsense! But you must pay attention to your nonsense. (*CV* 56)

By playing the clown, it gets the last laugh if its antics free one from a fly-bottle; this is true even if one is last to arrive:

> In philosophy the winner of the race is the one who can run most slowly. Or: the one who gets there last. (*CV* pg. 34)

Philosophy must carry on; it is a game whose "etcetera" is not an abbrevi-ation for continuing in the same manner. Rather, one must generate new values.

Part Three Wittgenstein's Way of Seeing

...We must recognize how language takes care of itself....(cf. NB 27.4.15). (NB 26.4.15)

In fact, all the propositions of our everyday language, just as they stand, are in perfect logical order... (T 5.5563)

Logic must look after itself... (see also NB 22.8.14), (T 5.473)

Am I not getting closer and closer to saying that in the end logic cannot be described? You must look at the practice of language, then you will see it. (OC 501)

...The world has a fixed structure... (NB 17.6.15)

The world is independent of my will.[1] (T 6.373)

Three ideas about reality (actually, three facets of the same idea) run through Wittgenstein's work from beginning to end: the ideas that language, logic, and the world take care of themselves. They are autonomous and as such, self-governing and independent of human control. Consciousness need not intervene on their behalf to make meaning, truth, and sense, respectively, possible; they do it themselves.[2] In their turn, these three ideas lead to three comparable observations about the autonomy of knowledge, namely, that knowledge is possible without experience, without certainty, and without authority. Language's independence obviates experience, while logic's free-play unseats certainty. Authority dissolves when the world is unchained and allowed to change freely. By the time Wittgenstein finishes with both the metaphysics and epistemology of Modern philosophy, he has completely disabused us of its pretensions. Kant, the last great spokesperson for the seventeenth century, is vanquished. Transcendental idealism with its noumena/phenomena divide falls as the synthetic–*a priori* defense of knowledge crumbles. A new world–picture is about to be born.

At first, Wittgenstein uses the Kierkegaardian metaphor of "care;" later, he settles on "speaking for" themselves:

A name has meaning, a proposition has sense in the calculus to which it belongs. The calculus is as it were autonomous.—Language must speak for itself (cf. *PG* I 2). (*PG* II 27)

His move from "cares" to "speaks" reflects his withdrawal from romantic, existential themes. "Speaking for oneself" is more socially directed and less psychologically oriented than caring for oneself. The angst is gone, even if the responsibility remains. "Speaking for onself" also connotes a more agressive policy to self-care; language, for example, stands up for itself, speaking plain enough to outwit all interpreters and would-be explainers. The odds for developing a perspicuous representation are better when language speaks for itself.

In his last remarks in *On Certainty,* he changes metaphors again; this time, however, the change concerns the subject, not the activity. He now speaks of the *practice* as having to speak for itself:

> Not only rules, but also examples are needed for establishing a practice. Our rules leave loop-holes open, and the practice has to speak for itself. (*OC* 139)

This advance is significant since "practice" encompasses the other three and situates them in a living context; language, logic, and the world meet and interact in a practice. Their mutual support systems give greater plausibility to their overall autonomy and also make their self-governance more effective. The concept of a practice circles further and further from dependence on either mind, nature, or God. Eventually, it frees knowledge as well as reality from previous metaphysics.

Abandoning all previous attempts to guarantee truth and also validate the senses and reason as adequate ways of knowing, Wittgenstein acknowledges that, in the end, there are no assurances: "Knowledge in the end is based on acknowledgment" (*OC* 378). Knowledge has no foundations, nor ultimate purposes. Like any other animal on the planet, we struggle to discover the information needed to secure survival. Since the conditions are always changing, knowledge can never stay the same. Philosophy's role in making that knowledge possible is critical, but it can no longer serve as guardian, jumping through hoops to demonstrate the necessity or accuracy of what we know. Plato is wrong about what philosophers, and rulers more generally, can or ought to do. However, neither can philosophy dedicate itself to proving that we know nothing and can never "really" know anything. The absence of foundations is no excuse for skepticism. The skeptic is just a fallen believer and thus always subject to temptation. The only course, then, is to acknowledge that we know. Given any sensible/reasonable definition of what we mean by know, we know many things. Indeed, as the later Wittgenstein admits, we know even more than we can say. Language has no special hold on what can know.

Chapter 5 *Three Ideas about Reality*

...For this is what disputes between Idealists, Solipsists and Realists look like. The one party attack the normal form of expression as if they were attacking a statement; the others defend it, as if they were stating facts recognized by every reasonable human being. (PI 402)

Like leitmotifs in a Wagnerian opera, the themes of the autonomy of language, logic, and the world re-occur throughout Wittgenstein's works, announcing first and foremost his emancipation from all forms of idealism, especially Kant's transcendental idealism. For Wittgenstein, Kant's great compromise between the claims of realism and idealism still subjugates reason as well as the world. The former's domain of operation is restricted, and the latter's territory is occupied by a dividing force. He was determined to free them both. Neither the sense of the world, nor the possibility of either meaning or truth could be enslaved to human consciousness taken in either an internal sense as intention or in an external one as convention. (Obviously, human consciousness and social rules are necessary for meaning, but only as background conditions, not as foreground players.) Consciousness would have to abdicate its throne and be replaced by the impersonal representation of the world.

Realism, on the other hand, is no alternative. For Wittgenstein, the traditional dualisms plaguing philosophy since the time of the Greeks were the problem and could play no part in the solution. Both metaphysics had to be abandoned for a new way of seeing, but one which could not, as I have already discussed, be understood as another metaphysic or *Weltanschauung*. Philosophy would have to develop a new politics which prohibited absolute rulers of all sorts and made hierarchy with its branching dualisms *passé*.

The autonomy of language, for example, dethrones human rule in favor of language's representational system. For Wittgentein, no symbolic practice of any kind requires human assistance:

> I should like to say "What the picture tells me is itself." That is, its telling me something consists in its own structure, in *its* own lines and colours. (What would it mean to say "What this musical theme tells me is itself"?) (*PI* 523)

Art and music, if they tell us something in the conventional sense of "tell," do not do it by pointing to something else. Their signs are their being in which spiritual and physical coincide. Since the very logic of "sign" has always been based on one thing standing for another, Wittgenstein's recommendation to remove the bar separating the signifier from the signifed is truly radical. Language doesn't represent as much as it presents. While not joining Heidegger to proclaim that "language speaks us," Wittgenstein resists the tendency of "constructivists" of all kinds, from Hobbes to Kant, to say *tout court:* "*we* speak language." Consciousness does not operate for Wittgenstein as a hidden ventriloquist breathing life into a wooden language. Severed from a practice, thought is as impotent as public convention to account for meaning. Instead, Wittgenstein argues that in one sense, nothing can account for meaning; that is, as long as one thinks it is necessary to worry about how meaning is possible, no solution will be found. However, if one stops thinking that meaning needs an accounting, i.e., if one stops finding it strange, its functioning will be obvious. Language, like walking, is a natural aspect of human existence. Despite the tendency to see it, or sociality more generally, as a later development in human evolution, almost an artifact or a gift from the Gods, Wittgenstein urges that we acknowledge its original presence.[3]

Russell and Frege provide the immediate context of Wittgenstein's recognition that logic takes care of itself; however, once again, Kant lurks close-by. Transcendental logic, the adjustment Kant made to reason's method of achieving knowledge, had to be exposed for the imposter it was. There is no such thing as transcendental logic, nor do we need it to understand the world. Wittgenstein lacked patience with such fudges. The problem with transcendental logic is that it confuses logic with its application. It anticipates too much, too soon. Instead, Wittgenstein argues that logic itself is transcendental; its tautologies do the talking. While he recognized, even in the early work, that logic cannot anticipate its application, he was unable at that time to truly free logic from human manipulation. Later, however, he shows how synthetic—*a priori* propositions are possible without tampering with logic.

Generally speaking, the autonomy of language, logic, and world become even more significant in the later works when Wittgenstein abandons the naive realism of the *Tractatus* which, like Kant, compromised language's independence by anchoring it safely in the structure of the world, instead of consciousness. The picture theory of meaning undermined Wittgenstein's own best efforts to liberate his triumvirate from a variety of different bosses. In the later works, no such shuffle exists; all three remain autonomous even as language-users are introduced to take the place of the lost "logical form of reality."

As for the world, Wittgenstein apparently renounced all effort in the later works ever to speak of it again. I imagine that the failure of his updated "theory of blending" in the opening sections of the *Tractatus* convinced him never to write about the relations between it and language again. Space and time are forms of objects, not consciousness, but it is as silly to say the one as the other. He would truly pass over the world's relation to language and thought in silence; not because they were mysteriously ineffable, but because they were so obvious it was redundant to say anything. In the *Investigations*, Wittgenstein finally learns how to show the independence of the world without whistling it either.

Thus, using the autonomy of language, logic, and world in pincher fashion, Wittgenstein mounts a three-pronged attack against a metaphysics of idealism. Of course, what is distinctive about Wittgenstein's attack on idealism is that realism topples with it. Neither metaphysic is necessary to explain the phenomena of meaning, truth, or sense. The secret to his success is that rather than attempt to show these theories wrong and risk having a position of his own, he shows them to be irrelevant. In the end, language means, logic proves, and the world turns without us.

Impersonal Solipsism

> ...The representation of the world by means of completely generalized propositions might be called the impersonal representation of the world.
>
> How does the impersonal representation of the world take place?
>
> The proposition is a model of reality as we imagine it. (NB 27.10.14)

The slogan, "language speaks for itself" responds to the question, How is language possible? Exercising his Kantian muscle, Wittgenstein's begins transcendentally, i,e, with an inquiry into the conditions of language's possibility. Without much argument, however, he immediately denies the subjective underpinnings of Kant's analysis, the transcendental ego. From the very beginning, Wittgenstein was an anti-Kantian seeking the structuralist point of view. The impersonal representation of the world eliminates subjects as the builders of their experiential world. For Wittgenstein, logic, not ego, supports language. As he explains, a good modeling theory makes an impersonal representation possible by obviating the need to correlate names with objects:

> We can describe the world completely by means of fully generalized propositions, i.e. without first correlating any name with a particular object... (*T* 5.526)

Effectively, this bars experience or acquaintance as a necessary condition for meaning: "Thus it is possible to devise a picture of the world without saying what is a representation of what" (*NB* 17.10.14). Generalized propositions are not obtained inductively from cases, but rather are drawn from observation of the logic of composition. They are descriptions of syntatical rules for the combination of signs. On this view, the subject enters a world already structured by language, rather than creates one through individual experience. In the final analysis, impersonal solipsism abandons all forms of phenomenalism, including Russell's knowledge by acquaintance.

Wittgenstein's disinterest in identifying simples in the *Tractatus,* for which he has been soundly castigated, emanates from his belief in their ultimate irrelevance.[4] Modeling theory is not concerned with the individual constituents of a fact, but with their forms, i.e., with the network of relations from which the constituents obtain their meaning. Structure or design is the all important concept. Once the design works, values for the variables can always be assigned. Rudolf Carnap makes a similar point while explicating his project of "construction theory:" "generally speaking, construction theory considers individual objects secondary, relative to the network of relations in which they stand."[5] For Carnap, the task of "construction theory," was to "characterize all objects through merely structural properties (i.e., certain formal-logical properties of relation extensions or complexes of relation extensions) and thus transform all scientific statements into purely structural statements."[6] His idea, like Wittgenstein's, was to deduce the individual properties of an object from purely structural descriptions of a construction:

> Let us look at a railroad map of, say, the Eurasian railroad network. We assume that this map is not a precise projection, but that it is distorted as much or more than the customary maps found in ticket offices. It does not then represent the distances, but only the connections within the network; (in the terminology of geometry): it indicates only the topological, not the metrical, properties of the network... We assume now that all stations are marked as points, but the map is not to contain any names nor any entries other than rail lines. The question now is: can we determine the names of the points on the map through an inspection of the actual railroad network? Since it is difficult to observe an actual railroad network, let us use in its stead a second map which contains all the names. Since our (first) map may be distorted more than customary railroad maps, we will gain little by looking for characteristic shapes, for example, the long Siberian railroad. But there is a more promising way: we look up the intersections of highest order, i.e., those in which the largest number of lines meet....But once we have discovered the name for even one point on the map, the others are easily found, since only very few names qualify for the neighboring points.[7]

Carnap reasoned that as long as the object domain is not too limited and the relations have a sufficiently variegated structure, one could derive the empirical world from purely structural descriptions.[8]

Exactly the same reasoning drives Wittgenstein's discussion of *Darstellungsformen*:

> We ought not to forget that any description of the world by means of mechanics will be of the completely general kind. For example, it will never mention *particular* point-masses: it will only talk about *any point-masses whatsoever. (T* 6. 3432)

For both philosophers, the nets used to describe the world are completely general, giving only topological information. Empirical information can be deduced from these maps because of the mirroring relation between the map and the territory.[9] However, Wittgenstein is more cautious than Carnap about the nature of the information obtained. For him, the generalized descriptions only allow deductions about the net and not about the world they describe:

....The possibility of describing a picture like the one mentioned above with a net of a given form tells us *nothing* about the picture. (For that is true of all such pictures.) But what *does* characterize the picture is that it can be described *completely* by a particular net with a *particular* size of mesh.... (*T* 6.342)

Yet, the fact that one net fits better than another reveals an indirect picture of the objects. For Wittgenstein, the nets offer indirect knowledge because they show more than they say:

The laws of physics, with all their logical apparatus, still speak, however, indirectly, about the objects of the world. (*T* 6.3431)

Synthetic–*a priori* truths of a sort are possible, then, namely, those that describe the net, without ever having mentioned consciousness. In both cases, the impersonal representation of the world offers an escape from subjectively based theories of truth and meaning.

Yet both Carnap and Wittgenstein recognized that while consciousness or the subject was not needed to construct the world, it nevertheless played a central epistemic role. Odd as it may seem, solipsism, an extreme form of subjectivism, played a greater role in both their thinking than one would have expected. In fact, Wittgenstein provocatively professes the truth of solipsism:

This remark provides the key to the problem, how much truth there is in solipsism.

For what the solipsist *means* is quite correct; only it cannot be *said*, but makes itself manifest.

The world is *my* world: this is manifest in the fact that the limits of *language* (of that language which I alone understand) mean the limits of *my* world. (*T* 5.62)

To understand this odd twist of ideas, one must untangle a number of riddles in the text.

First, as a point of logic, Wittgenstein reminds us that I can only know the world as I see it: "...What brings the self into philosophy is the fact that the world is my world" (*T* 5.641). As he further explains in the *Notebooks*:

What has history to do with me? Mine is the first and only world! I want to report how *I* found the world.

What others in the world have told me about the world is a very small and incidental part of my experience of the world.

I have to judge the world, to measure things. (*NB* 2.9.16)

It is tautologically or logically true that only I alone can think my thoughts. No information is gained from this statement other than a rule about the use of "my." Thus, the statment can in no way support the claim that I alone exist.

Carnap's similar metamorphosis of the solipsist traditional thesis provides a helpful gloss on Wittgenstein's. Carnap chooses "my elementary experiences" as the basic elements for his constructional system:

> The constructional system shows that all objects can be constructed from "my elementary experiences" as basic elements. In other words (and this is what is meant by the expression "to construct"), all (scientific) statements can be transformed into statements about my experiences (more precisely, into statements about relations between my experiences) where the logical value is retained.[10]

He explains that his choice of the "autopsychological" or "solipsistic base" is guided by its epistemological priority:

> The most important reason for this lies in our intention to have the constructional system reflect not only the logical-constructional order of the objects, but also their epistemic order.[11]

Yet Carnap argues that even though he has chosen the solipsistic base, he is not subscribing to the view that only one subject and its experiences are real, while the others are non-real. Instead he claims that only the form and method of solipsism are being used. He calls his position "methodological solipsism" and explains that his use of this method does not entail the central thesis of solipsism because it does not entail the existence of the self:

> The self does not belong to the original state of affairs...
> Philosophical introspection has led philosophers of various persuasions to the same result, namely, that the original processes of consciousness must not be envisaged as the activities of an acting subject, the "self."[12]

Wittgenstein develops exactly the same idea, arguing for methodological silence; for him too, the subject is not a part of the world:

> There is no such thing as the subject that thinks or entertains ideas.... (*T* 5.631)

> The subject does not belong to the world: rather, it is a limit of the world. (*T* 5.632)

Wittgenstein claims that the self of solipsism shrinks to a point without extension; there is no self or rather it is coterminous with the world:

> I am my world. (The microcosm.) (*T* 5.63)

> Here it can be seen that solipsism, when its implications are followed out strictly, coincides with pure realism. The self of solipsism shrinks to a point without extension, and there remains the reality coordinated with it. (*T* 5.64)

His argument for this disappearing act is rather clever.

To obtain the equation, "I equals world" or its partner, "the world equals life (*T* 5.621)," one must introduce Wittgenstein's reasons for arguing for an unalterable form of the world:

> If the world had no substance, then whether a proposition had sense would depend on whether another proposition was true. (*T* 2.0211)

> In that case we could not sketch out any picture of the world (true or false). (*T* 2.0212)

If sense had to depend on truth, then some empirical correlation between word and object would be required, and the subject's experience would be implicated. Happily, this is not necessary; for Wittgenstein, the world can be described in completely general propositions because form produces structure. Form implies content. Thus, Wittgenstein's notion of substance explains how general propositions or the impersonal representation of the world is possible. Transcendentally speaking, it is obvious that sense cannot depend on truth because we sketch pictures of the world all the time and what already occurs is clearly possible.

Moreover, since all languages manifest logical form, the form of reality, substance also guarantees the translatability of different languages, even an imagined one:

> It is obvious that an imagined world, however different it may be from the real one, must have *something*—a form—in common with it. (*T* 2.022)

Thus, my language and my world are logically equivalent with the limits of language and the world; that is, the world to which I have epistemological access shares with your world, or the world, a form. Since they are formally isomorphic, one transcends subjectivity. Thus, there is no real dispute between the theses of idealism, solipsism, and realism, because "the world

and life are one" (*T* 5.62l), and "I am my world" (*T* 5.63). Carnap's solution is analogous:

> The solution to this problem lies in the fact that, even though the
> *material* of the individual streams of experience is completely differ-
> ent, or rather altogether incomparable, since a comparison of two
> sensations or two feelings of different subjects, as far as their immedi-
> ately given qualities are concerned, is absurd, certain *structural proper-*
> *ties* are analogous for all streams of experience.[13]

The main difference is that Carnap remains a phenomenalist dependent on
knowledge by acquaintance; he did not have Wittgenstein's metaphysics of
substance.

Unfortunately, the thorn in Wittgenstein's approach is that it depends on
the proposition that "Logic pervades the world: the limits of the world are
also its limits" (*T* 5.61). It depends, that is, on the belief that logic is transcendental and shares with the world a common form—something Wittgenstein
could only have known by transcending the limits of logic or, as he later says,
by subliming logic, which he admits is the cardinal error of the *Tractatus:*

> *Unklar im Tractat war mir die Logische Analyse und die hinweisende*
> *Erklärung. Ich dachte damals, dass es eine, 'Verbindung der Sprache mit der*
> *Wirklichkeit,'gibt.* (*WVC* ppg. 209-210)

> (In the Tractatus logical analysis and ostensive definition were unclear
> to me. At that time I thought that there was 'a connexion between
> language and reality.' [*WVC* ppg. 209-210])

Ultimately, then, he compromises his first vision of the autonomy of language
or the impersonal representation of the world by grounding it in the structure of reality.

In the later work, when language-users are introduced as an essential
ingredient in the meaning process, Wittgenstein must fight the battle against
subjectivity and consciousness on another front, i.e., the mental. While language no longer makes contact with reality—by itself the sign system is
dead—he argues that we still need not postulate mental processes operating
behind the scenes to give life to the signs:

> When I think in language, there aren't 'meanings' going through
> my mind in addition to the verbal expressions: the language is itself the
> vehicle of thought. (*PI* 329)

Meaning results from the application of language. Instead of turning to the human mind to explain the functioning of language, Wittgenstein turns to the pragmatics of language, i.e., to all the practices that surround the use of a method of representation which he calls a "language-game." His earlier mistake of grounding the possibility of language in the structure of the world shall not be repeated by now grounding language in the structure of consciousness. Meaning, like intention, is embedded in a situation and requires a recognition of the conventions of use: "Our talk gets its meanings from the rest of our proceedings" (*OC* 229). He removes the subject from the center of the universe and replaces it with systems of signs. The limits of sense and nonsense are a function of the calculus and cannot be attributed to human consciousness. Again and again, Wittgenstein reminds us that it is the system that decides, not us:

> Do not say, "one cannot", but say instead: "it doesn't exist in this game". Not: "one can't castle in draughts" but—"there is no castling in draughts"; and instead of "I can't exhibit my sensation"—"in the use of the word 'sensation', there is no such thing as exhibiting what one has got"; instead of "one cannot enumerate all the cardinal numbers"—"there is no such thing here as enumerating all the members". (*Z* 134)

There isn't something we cannot do, e.g., reach noumena or things in themselves—it is not a matter of physical limitations. Rather, the logic of the system of representation makes some things sayable and other things not. In one colorful passage that makes this point particularly well, Wittgenstein speaks in the voice of Hardy, the Cambridge mathematician:

> Hardy: "That 'the finite cannot understand the infinite' should surely be a theological and not a mathematical war-cry." True, the expression is inept. But what people are using it to try and say is: "We mustn't have any juggling! How comes this leap from the finite to the infinite?" Nor is the expression all that nonsensical—only the 'finite' that can't conceive the infinite is not **'man'** or 'our understanding', but the calculus.... (*Z* 273)

Language and representational systems in general have lives of their own; neither the world, God, nor human consciousness is responsible.

The difference between the early and later works is comparable to that between structuralism and semiotics. While the early work was content with the structure of "langue," i.e., only the rules of a method of representation counted as part of the system, the later work recognizes the need for speakers and the styles of "parole." Now the system includes everything from gestures to silences. Wittgenstein calls it a practice. As he stresses in *On Certainty*, it is the practice and not just the language which speaks for itself. Contexts and purposes must be taken into consideration in order to understand a language-game. Finally the impersonal representation of the world is secured, one that does not depend on human consciousness and is thus not arbitrary, nor on the structure of the world and is therefore not necessary. Language takes care of itself.

Talking Tautologies

It is clear that something about the world must be indicated by the fact that certain combinations of symbols—whose essence involves the possessing of a determinate character—are tautologies. (T 6.124)

Historically speaking, the autonomy of logic is the founding idea of the trilogy. Wittgenstein's very first remarks in his *Notebooks of 1914-16* concern logic's independence. This should not be surprising since Wittgenstein entered philosophy as a logician and in conversation with Russell and Frege. Logic, as the world had known it since Aristotle, had been undergoing dramatic transformations since the middle of the nineteenth century. Both Russell and Frege were leaders of this revolution. Wittgenstein immediately knew his idea about logic's autonomy to be his most important idea and also recognized its upsetting implications for philosophy:

> How is it reconcilable with the task of philosophy, that logic should take care of itself? If for example, we ask: Is such and such a fact of the subject predicate form? we must surely know what we mean by "subject-predicate form".... We may indeed say: We have signs that behave like signs of the subject-predicate form, but does that mean that there really must be facts of this form? That is, when those signs are completely analyzed? And here the question arises again: Does such a complete analysis exist? *And if not*: then what is the task of philosophy?!!?
>
> Then: if *everything* that needs to be shewn is shewn by the existence of subject-predicate SENTENCES etc, the task of philosophy is different from what I originally supposed....

> The obscurity *obviously* resides in the question: what does the logical identity of sign and thing signified really consist in? And this question is (*once more*) a main aspect of the whole philosophical problem. (*NB* 3.9.14)

As for the Greeks, logic revealed the structure of the world; it was designed to talk about simple objects, relations, facts. But if logic can not answer such ontological questions, what is there for philosophy to do? Without logic, philosophy is helpless; it has no method of knowing whether what we call things fits their being (shades of Plato and Socrates). In many ways, however, Wittgenstein found himself disagreeing with his teachers. Neither Russell's theory of types, for example, nor Frege's conception of legitimate or well-formed propositions were on the right track for Wittgenstein. Russell's theory of types appealed to an extra-logical domain to deal with the conundrums of logical symbolism:

> From this observation we turn to Russell's 'theory of types'. It can be seen that Russell must be wrong, because he had to mention the meaning (*bedeutung*) of signs when establishing the rules for them. (*T* 3.331)

And Frege invoked convention:

> Frege says that any legitimately constructed proposition must have sense. And I say that any possible proposition is legitimately constructed, and, if it has no sense, that can only be because we have failed to give a *meaning* to some of its constituents.
>
> (Even if we think that we have done so.)
>
> Thus the reason why 'Socrates is identical' says nothing is that we have *not* given any *adjectival* meaning to the word 'identical'. For when it appears as a sign for identity, it symbolizes in an entirely different way—the signifying relation is a different one—therefore the symbols also are entirely different in the two cases: the two symbols have only the sign in common, and that is an accident. (*T* 5.4733)

Frege's approach requires human interference; it suggests that we establish rules for being well-formed and thus rob logic of its self-determination. To both of them, Wittgenstein replied that the explanation of logical symbolism would have to proceed without anticipating its application. Whether a proposition had sense or was a tautology would have to be visible from the signs themselves:

> Identity of object I express by identity of sign, and not by using a
> sign for identity. Difference of objects I express by difference of signs.
> (*T* 5.53)

The signs have to speak for themselves; logic can not anticipate its application:

> The *application* of logic decides what elementary propositions
> there are.

> What belongs to its application, logic cannot anticipate.
> It is clear that logic must not clash with its application.
> But logic has to be in contact with its application.
> Therefore logic and its application must not overlap. (*T* 5.557)

For Wittgenstein, "we can foresee only what we ourselves construct"
(*T* 5.556), and all that we construct is the notational system. Whether or not
that system can be used in the service of knowledge, i.e., whether it applies
to the world of facts cannot be anticipated. Instead, what logic can or cannot
say will be evident from its application. One cannot explain logic in terms of
its applied domain without compromising its generality. Thus, logic *shows* the
limits of sense and nonsense, that is, the limits of thought, if we do not interfere with its calculus and try to buttress it with either a system of conventional rules or an appeal to extralogical reality. It is possible to state the "truths
of logic" only insofar as we have an adequate notation (*T* 6.1223). The notation (form of representation) and its calculus is everything. We cannot go
beyond logic and talk about the world because the limits of logic are the limits of the world. Thus, there is no way of grounding logic.

Russell and Frege, however, were not the first to confuse logic with its
application, nor were they the worst sinners. Kant's postulation of two log-
ics, one that applies to the things themselves and one that is designed especially for the conditions of experience, *transcendental logic*, is surely the paradigm case of anticipating the application of logic:

> Transcendental philosophy has the peculiarity that besides the rule
> (or rather the universal condition of rules), which is given in the pure
> concept of understanding, it can also specify *a priori* the instance to
> which the rule is to be applied (*A* 136, *B* 175).

For Kant, "general logic, as we have shown, abstracts from all content of
knowledge, that is, from all relation of knowledge to the object, and considers only the logical form in the relation of any knowledge to other

knowledge; that is, it treats of the form of thought in general" (*A* 55, *B* 80). Transcendental logic, on the other hand, "concerns itself with the laws of understanding and of reason solely in so far as they relate *a priori* to objects" (*A* 57, *B* 82). Transcendental logic, then, is specifically constructed by Kant to anticipate the conditions of its employment or, as he otherwise says, to show how the subjective conditions of thought can have objective validity. The prize of such a logic are synthetic–*a priori* truths, that is, informative necessary truths.

Transcendental logic makes synthetic–*a priori* judgments possible by offering an interpreted calculus calculated to deal with the conditions of its employment. Instead of the propositional form, "fx", Kant converts x to x_1, where x_1 equals the object intuited under the conditions of sensibility, and f to f_1, where f_1 equals the categories of thought schematized. Since a schematized category is nothing but a category viewed under the conditions of sensibility, transcendental logic succeeds in showing how f necessarily applies to x. For Wittgenstein, however, there can be no such thing as transcendental logic, that is, no anticipation of logic's application. Logic can have nothing to do with its employment. The stipulation of values for a variable must proceed independently of the variables themselves. The distinction between syntax and semantics must be maintained at all costs. Thus, there can be no such thing as synthetic–*a priori* propositions for Wittgenstein:

> This is connected with the fact that no part of our experience
> is at the same time *a priori*.
> Whatever we see could be other than it is.
> Whatever we can describe at all could be other than it is.
> There is no *a priori* order of things. (*T* 5.634)

Knowledge that a thought was necessarily true would be possible only if its truth were recognizable from the thought itself (without anything to compare it with.) Since the truth of any proposition depends upon a comparison with a state of affairs, no proposition can be true *a priori*. The fact that logical propositions were true *a priori,* then, led to only one conclusion, logical statements are not propositions. Logic is not one form of representation among others, it is the essence of form. Logical expressions are really rules for the combination of signs, not finished combinations themselves. Logic is a second-order language, and thus not really a language:

It is the peculiar mark of logical propositions that one can recognize that they are true from the symbol alone, and this fact contains in itself the whole philosophy of logic. And so too it is a very important fact that the truth or falsity of non-logical propositions *cannot* be recognized from the propositions alone. (*T* 6.113)

Yet Wittgenstein was sensitive to Kant's dilemma; while logic must not clash with its application, it must be in contact with it. But, how can logic with all its peculiar crotchets of human contrivances yield information about the world?:

And anyway, is it really possible that in logic I should have to deal with forms that I can invent? What I have to deal with must be that which makes it possible for me to invent them. (*T* 5.555)

Thus, the question that bothered Kant so much, "How are synthetic–*a priori* judgements possible?, reappears for Wittgenstein as the question, How is logic possible?, that is, "If there would be a logic even if there were no world, how then could there be a logic given that there is a world?" (*T* 5.5521).[14] The connection between their two projects is evident from Wittgenstein's assertion that, "The theory of tautologies will throw light on Kant's question, "'how is pure mathematics possible?'" (*NB* 19.10.14) From this perspective, the discovery that logic takes care of itself shows how logic is possible without the illegitimate appeal to transcendental logic, i.e. without having logic anticipate its application.

Wittgenstein's alternative to Kant is to claim that logic, Kant's general logic, is itself transcendental:

Logic is not a body of doctrine, but a mirror-image of the world Logic is transcendental. (*T* 6.13)

This claim amounts to the belief that logical form and the form of reality are the same. And, if this is true, one can easily see how logic manages to be in contact with its application. Indeed, reality can not possibly elude its net. Stripped of its trimmings, his argument for the transcendentality of logic contains two steps. The first argues that logical propositions are tautologies and the second claims that tautologies show the formal properties of language and the world:

The propositions of logic are tautologies. (*T* 6.1)

The fact that the propositions of logic are tautologies *shows* the formal-logical properties of language and the world.

The fact that a tautology is yielded by *this particular way* of connecting its constituents characterizes the logic of its constituents.

If propositions are to yield a tautology when they are connected in a certain way, they must have certain structural properties. So their yielding a tautology when combined *in this way* shows that they possess these structural properties. (*T* 6.12)

The propositions of logic describe the scaffolding of the world, or rather they represent it. They have no 'subject-matter'. They presuppose that names have meaning and elementary propositions sense; and that is their connexion with the world. It is clear that something about the world must be indicated by the fact that certain combinations of symbols—whose essence involves the possession of a determinate character—are tautologies. This contains the decisive point. We have said that some things are arbitrary in the symbols that we use and that some things are not. In logic it is only the latter that express: but that means that logic is not a field in which *we* express what we wish with the help of signs, but rather one in which the nature of the natural and inevitable signs speaks for itself. If we know the logical syntax of any sign-language, then we have already been given all the propositions of logic. (*T* 6.124)

Step one seems unproblematic: to say that logic is comprised of tautologies is to say that logic is the body of analytic propositions subject to the law, *Simplex sigillum veri* (*T* 5.4541). However, according to the picture-theory's conditions for sense, logical propositions say nothing:

Propositions show what they say: tautologies and contradictions show that they say nothing.

A tautology has no truth-conditions, since it is unconditionally true: and a contradiction is true on no conditions.

Tautologies and contradictions lack sense.

(Like a point from which two arrows go out in opposite directions to one another.)

(For example, I know nothing about the weather when I know that it is either raining or not raining.) (*T* 4.461)

The rest of the description of tautologies (*T* 4.461–N 4.4661) continues to explain why it is that tautologies fail to picture reality. These passages show that tautologies and contradictions represent the limiting cases of sign combination; that is, in logical propositions signs are combined in such a way as to show the upper and lower limits of sign combination. As Wittgenstein concludes: "Tautologies and contradictions are the limiting cases—indeed the disintegration of the combination of signs" (*T* 4.466). Thus, the uttering of such propositions is nonsensical; "either it is raining or not raining" takes us in circles and gives no information. Obviously the question is, how does it come about that Wittgenstein invests the classic nonsense of logical propositions with so much weight?

Step two, which says that the fact that the propositions of logic are tautologies shows the formal-logical-properties of language and the world, begins to make this perspicuous. What the first part of step two accomplishes is that while tautologies are nonsense, they show the logical properties of language:

> The propositions of logic demonstrate the logical properties of propositions by combining them so as to form propositions that say nothing.

> This method could also be called a zero-method. In a logical proposition, propositions the state of equilibrium then indicate what the logical constitution of the propositions must be. (*T* 6.121)

Thus, we do not technically need logical propositions because their function is to show the logical properties of language; they are an attempt to reiterate those properties in explicit form. So, they are part of the symbolism of language, just as 0 is part of the symbolism of arithmetic, even though it adds to nothing (*T* 4.4611). In showing the logical properties of language, however, one has shown a very important thing according to Wittgenstein's definitions: one shows that propositions contain *structural properties*. The decisive point is that language has certain structural properties; the existence of tautologies can only show something about the world as well as language because what it primarily shows is that language has structural properties. To fully appreciate this point, one must briefly consider Wittgenstein's opening discussion on the logic of the depiction.

According to the analysis of pictures, a structural or internal property (*T* 4.122) is a necessary feature of a fact. Thus, the possibility of combining signs together in such a way as to say nothing, i.e., to bring them into equilibrium, is not something we arbitrarily do with signs, but something that emanates naturally and inevitably from the nature of the signs themselves. Language, if you will, by containing the possibility of tautologies, expresses itself. And since nothing in logic is accidental, the structural properties of language, its logical properties, are a necessary feature of language. Since we can only construct propositions by way of experiment, we cannot be responsible for the miracle of analytic propositions. Therefore, it cannot be for us to postulate the truths of logic; rather, they show themselves.

Secondly, structural or internal properties of language are reflective of the structural or internal properties of states of affairs:

> The existence of an internal property of a possible situation is not expressed by means of a proposition: rather, *it expresses itself in the proposition representing the situation, by means of an internal property of that proposition.* (*T* 4.124, emphasis mine.)

> The existence of an internal relation between possible situations expresses itself in language by means of an internal relation between the propositions representing them. (*T* 4.125)

The logical properties of language reflect, mirror, those of the world. Indeed, to call logic a mirror rather than a picture is to indicate that it presents the structure of the world in reverse or up-side down. Yet it is one with it. Ultimately, of course, the reflective properties of language must be derived from Wittgenstein's definition of pictorial form:

> The fact that the elements of a picture are related to one another in a determinate way represents that things are related to one another in the same way.
> Let us call this connection of its elements the structure of the picture, and let us call the possibility of this structure the pictorial form of the picture. (*T* 2.15)

> Pictorial form is the possibility that things are related to one another in the same way as the elements of the picture. (*T* 2.151)

While "pictorial form" only guarantees the possibility of correspondence, "logical form" makes it actual because logical form is the form of reality. Thus, Wittgenstein concludes that the propositions of logic reveal the formal logical properties of language and the world. Just as tautologies show the limiting cases of the possible combination of signs, they show the limiting cases of the possible combination of objects. Tautologies and contradictions, without our help, i.e., without the postulation of consciousness, show what is certain, possible, and impossible about the world. What is reflected in the mirror of logic are the limits of the world.

Despite the strong differences in their arguments, Wittgenstein's appeal to the transcendentality of logic accomplishes the same task as Kant's appeal to transcendental logic. With only one important exception, Wittgenstein means the same thing by transcendental knowledge as Kant means when he says:

> I entitle *transcendental* all knowledge which is occupied not so much with objects as with the mode of our knowledge of objects in so far as this mode of knowledge is to be possible *a priori* (*A* 12, *B* 26).

Just as Kant's *a priori* synthetic judgements are transcendental, in that they describe the necessary conditions for there to be experience, Wittgenstein's tautologies are transcendental in that they reflect the necessary conditions for there to be a language. Unlike Kant, however, our mode of knowing objects can only speak indirectly about the world, in what logic shows rather than in what it says. Nevertheless, they can speak about the world and not the appearance of a world:

> Although the spots in our picture are geometrical figures, never-theless geometry can obviously say nothing at all about their actual form and position. The network, however, is *purely* geometrical; all its properties can be given *a priori*.
>
> Laws like the principles of sufficient reason, etc. are about the net and not about what the net describes. (*T* 6.35)

Technically, then, according to Wittgenstein, we cannot use information about logic for interpreting the world. This inference was possible for Kant because of transcendental logic. Without this invention, Wittgenstein is forced to make the linguistic turn. All philosophy is a critique of lan-guage. With logic as its tool, philosophy can only talk about the symbolism and not about the world:

> All theories that make a proposition of logic appear to have con-tent are false.... Indeed, the logical proposition acquires all the char-acteristics of a proposition of natural science and this is the sure sign that it has been construed wrongly. (*T* 6.111)

Unlike science, a philosophical theory has its source in linguistic fact and is ultimately about those facts. The world, for philosophy, must be bracketed, lit-erally, put in quotes. Now it should be clear why Wittgenstein's recognition of these limits to philosophical inquiry raise the question: "How is it reconcilable with the task of philosophy that logic should take care of itself?" Questions about the world, which Wittgenstein had once thought essential to philosophy, e.g., "Whether 'A is good' is a subject-predicate proposition" or "Are there subject-predicate facts?" or "Is a point in our visual field a *simple object*, a *thing*?" seem absolutely beyond the reach of logical inquiry. Strictly speaking, one cannot conclude anything about the world from the structure of logic. Yet, as Wittgenstein must have encouraged himself, there *must* be some way out of this dilemma; an analysis of logic must show something about the world. Instead of taking the Kantian turn, he postulates a pre-given correspondence between language and reality; they share logical form. Without this pre-critical assumption, the conditions necessary for there to be language would reveal nothing about the world: the logical mirror would be mute. To recognize the assumption for what it is, i.e., an assumption, is to shake the foundations of the *Tractatus*. Such recognition came to Wittgenstein in the 1930s. The crystalline purity of logic's mirror was shattered. When he began again, the belief in a connection between language and reality was abandoned. But then, everything had to be reconsidered. All the problems that had initially motivated the *Tractatus* reassert themselves: questions about the foundations of logic and language, about the relationship between language and reality, about the possibility of knowledge, and about the task of philosophy.

In the *Investigations*, Wittgenstein rejects his sublimation of logic and moves to a more conventional approach to logic's autonomy. He comments that, "The *preconceived* idea of crystalline purity can only be removed by turning our whole examination around. (One might say: the axis of reference of our examination must be rotated, but about the fixed point of our real need") (*PI* 108). And that point, as the *Remarks on The Foundations of Mathematics* indicate, is the need for a convention:

> It is as if this expressed the essence of form.—I say, however: if you talk about *essence*—you are merely noting a convention. But here one would like to retort: there is no greater difference than that between a proposition about the depth of essence and one about a mere convention. But what if I reply: to the *depth* that we see in the essence there corresponds the *deep* need for the convention. (*RFM* I, 74)

Perhaps the best passage which contrasts his early and late views is the following:

> Isn't it like this: so long as one thinks it can't be otherwise, one draws logical conclusions. This presumably means: *so long as such-and-such is not brought in question at all.*

The steps which are not brought in question are logical inferences. But the reason why they are not brought in question is not that they 'certainly correspond to the truth'—or something of the sort,—no, it is just this that is called 'thinking', 'speaking', 'inferring', 'arguing'. There is not any question at all here of some correspondence between what is said and reality; rather is logic *antecedent* to any such correspondence; in the same sense, that is, as that in which the establishment of a method of measurement is *antecedent* to the correctness or incorrectness of a statement of length. (*RFM* I, 155)

Note that logic is *a priori* or antecedent; however, now it obtains this position not because it mirrors reality, but because it *defines* what we mean by rationality. Methods of measurement make measuring possible not because they are true, but rather because they define what is meant by measuring. They show what we call "measuring:"

The laws of logic are indeed the expression of 'thinking habits' but also of the habit of *thinking*. That is to say they can be said to shew [sic]: how human beings think, and also *what* human beings call "thinking". (*RFM* I, 131)

Thus, logic conceived of as the rules of inference provide the standard or paradigm for what is meant by thinking. In the later works, all such standards are considered to be part of the grammar of language and define our conceptual situation:

The connexion which is not supposed to be a causal, experiential one, but much stricter and harder, so rigid even, that the one thing somehow already *is* the other, is always a connection of grammar. (*RFM* I, 128)

To call them part of the grammar, however, emphasizes the fact that they are neither true nor false. In addition, it reminds us that the rules can change, since grammar changes. This relativization of logic has some disturbing effects. Often, Wittgenstein wonders if logic can have its rigor bargained away like this. However, these worries are a function of not fully rotating the axis; that is, logic appears to be something less than we hoped for only when we compare it against the ideal. To some extent, Wittgenstein continues doing this in the *Investigations*, although he is aware that one needs a whole new picture:

If language is to be a means of communication there must be agreement not only in definitions but also (queer as this may sound) in judgments. This seems to abolish logic, but does not do so. It is one thing to describe methods of measurement, and another to obtain and state results of measurement. But what we call "measuring" is partly determined by a certain constancy in result of measurement. (*PI* 242)

Here he recognizes that not even the rules are rigid; one must also apply the rules in a certain way. More and more, Wittgenstein is coming to realize that there is no great difference between logical propositions and empirical ones. Ultimately, instead of looking for synthetic–*a priori* propositions, logic is able to take care of itself by using plain old empirical propositions in analytic ways. The reason why the later works get closer and closer to saying that logic cannot be described is because, in one sense, there is no longer anything special to describe. The breakdown of the analytic/synthetic distinction is the recognition that propositions are *not* inherently one or the other; this enables him and us to see that logic needs neither conventional (formal), nor ontological underpinnings: "Is it that rule and empirical proposition merge into one another?" (*OC* 309)

Logic takes care of itself because there is nothing to take care of. It describes the world because it is part of the world, part of the language we use to describe the world. Logic makes contact with its application because there is no divide between the calculus and its application:

> The *application* of the calculation must take care of itself and that is what is correct about 'formalism'.
>
> The reduction of arithmetic to symbolic logic is supposed to shew the point of application of arithmetic, as it were the attachment by means of which it is plugged in to its application. As if someone were shewn, first a trumpet without the mouthpiece—and then the mouthpiece, which shews how a trumpet is used, brought into contact with the human body. But the attachment which Russell gives us is on the one hand too narrow, on the other too wide; too general and too special. The calculation takes care of its own application. (*RFM* II, 4)

He has come a long way from insisting that logic cannot anticipate its application, as far as asserting that the calculation takes care of its own application. Finally, he has appreciated the advantages of a good modeling theory.

Wise Objects

If I know an object I also know all its possible occurrences in state of
affairs. (Every one of these possibilities must be part of the nature of the object.)
A new possibility cannot be discovered later. (T 2.0123)

Starting from what can only be described as an instinctual aversion to the
idea that we are nature's keeper, Wittgenstein begins the *Tractatus* with a discussion of the world, and not, as one might expect from his statement "My
work has extended from the foundation of logic to the nature of world"
(NB 2.8.16), with a discussion of logic or language. Textually, this beginning announces his intention to ground language in the structure of reality and not, as was current among his neo-Kantian contemporaries, e.g.,
Ernst Cassirer, in the structure of the mind. Again and again, Wittgenstein
confronts the reader of his early work with his pre-critical faith that the
world possesses a fixed order independent of human consciousness:

> It does not go against our feeling, that *we* cannot analyse
> PROPOSITIONS so far as to mention the elements by name; no, we
> feel that the WORLD must consist of elements. And it appears as if
> that were identical with the proposition that the world must be what
> it is, it must be definite. Or in other words, what vacillates is our
> determinations, not the world. It looks as if to deny things were as
> much as to say that the world can, as it were, be indefinite in some
> such sense as that in which our knowledge is uncertain and indefi-
> nite. The world has a fixed structure. (*NB* 17.6.15)

He sought to reduce the role of consciousness to that of silent spectator
contemplating the world from the appreciative, but distant perspective of
sub specie aeterni. Looking ahead to the *Investigations,* his ultimate goal was to
exempt the world from philosophic psuedo-scientific intervention. If philosophy is to worry about "What is the case," it must do so without turning ontology into a servant of epistemology. Whatever our epistemological
needs, he might say to Kant, one cannot force nature to play an unnatural
role. Of course, both the idealists and realists are guilty of this crime, however, given the boasts of transcendental idealism, one can easily understand
how Kant came to be identified as the prime target:

> By *transcendental idealism* I mean the doctrine that appearances are to
> be regarded as being, one and all, representations only, not things in

themselves, and that time and space are therefore only sensible forms of our intuition, not determinations given as existing by themselves, nor conditions of objects viewed as things in themselves (*A* 369).

As if in direct imitation of Kant, the ontology described in the opening sections of the *Tractatus* retraces Kant's architectural split between phenomena and noumena: "The world is the totality of facts, not of things" (*T* 1.1). Facts (phenomena), not things (noumena), constitute the world. Indeed, "The facts in logical space are the world" (*T* 1.13). Things, or objects, on the other hand, "make up the substance of the world" (*T* 2.021). Like noumena, substance exists independently of what is the case" (*T* 2.024). Objects make up the unalterable form of the world (*T* 2.023). Facts, on the other hand, stand for their changing configurations (*T* 2.0271) and are produced by the configuration of objects (*T* 2.0272). Moreover, as in Kant's distinction, facts represent what can be experienced, or, more appropriately for Wittgenstein, what is sayable in language, and substance, what cannot be experienced or described:

> Only facts can express a sense, a set of names cannot. (*T* 3.142)

> Objects can only be *named*. Signs are their representatives. I can only speak *about* them: I cannot *put them into words*. Propositions can only say *how* things are, not *what* they are. (*T* 3.221)

Throughout the *Tractatus,* Wittgenstein's emphasis on a fixed division between objects and facts is unmistakable:

> Even if the world is infinitely complex, so that every fact consists of infinitely many states of affairs and every state of affairs is composed of indefinitely many objects, there would still have to be objects and states of affairs. (*T* 4.2211)

Yet after invoking Kant's noumena/phenomena distinction, Wittgenstein rejects it. Where Kant says that appearances or phenomena are to be regarded as *representations* (*Vorstellungen*) only, not things in themselves, Wittgenstein calls these representations, *presentations* (*Darstellungen*), i.e. facts, and insists that they are all we have: "The world is all that is the case" (*T* 1). Indeed, the world divides into facts, not into noumena and phenomena (*T* 1.2). In other words, while he speaks of objects and facts, they do not comprise two separate realms; the world is one. His argument for collapsing Kant's two separable realms is ingeniously simple. Since objects or substances contain the possibility of all situations (*T* 2.014), reality is defined as the existence *and* non-existence of states of affairs (*T* 2.06). Reality thus includes the negation of all that is. Against this, the world is defined as the totality of existing states of affairs only (*T* 2.04). Since we can also call the existence of states of affairs a positive fact, and their non-existence a negative fact (*T* 2.06), we can say when we add them together that "The sum total of reality is the world" (*T* 2.063). The addition of negative facts to positive facts adds 0 to a column of figures; it adds nothing to the world. Thus, he no longer need worry about what is not the case. The world takes care of itself. Autonomously, it determines its finite and fixed structure: "It is form and content" (*T* 2.025).

In making this argument, Wittgenstein has carefully not grounded his faint distinction between objects and facts epistemologically, i.e., as contingent upon what can and cannot be experienced. The distinction, that is, is not forced upon the world by the character of human consciousness. On the contrary, it applies to the world, regardless of human will:

> ...The world is *given* me, i.e. my will enters into the world completely from the outside as into something that is already there. (*NB* 8.7.16)

or thought would have:

> Space, time, and colour (being coloured) are forms of objects. (*T* 2.0251)

In direct contrast to Kant, Wittgenstein argues that space and time are forms of the objects themselves, and not, as Kant would have it, of intuition. This difference is of utmost importance since it returns to reality the responsibility of world-making.

Whether or not Wittgenstein had Kant explicitly in mind when he argued that space and time were forms of objects themselves is an historical question, which, given Wittgenstein's lack of references, will remain forever uncertain. However, there is one suggestive passage which demonstrates Wittgenstein's acquaintance with Kant:

> From the fact that I *see* that one spot is to the left of another, or that one colour is darker than another, it seems to follow that it *is* so; and if so, this can only be if there is an *internal* relation between the two; and we might express this by saying that the form of the latter is part of the *form* of the former. We might thus give a sense to the

assertion that logical laws are *forms* of thought and space and time *forms* of intuition. (*NB* pg. 117)

He even extends himself in trying to understand how one might be led into a doctrine of the transcendental ideality of space and time. Instead of following Kant's route, however, Wittgenstein opts for making the forms of perception or intuition forms of the facts. However, he does not deny an "internal relation" between language (thought) and reality.

Thus, objects, not human beings, supply the form which render states of affairs, content, possible:

> The substance of the world *can* only determine a form, and not any material properties. For it is only by means of propositions that material properties are represented—only by the configuration of objects that they are produced.[15] (*T* 2.0231)

The representations which Kant had thought a function of consciousness are for Wittgenstein produced by the *blending* of objects to form states of affairs. The world presents itself to us in facts. Since space and time are conditions of objects as they appear in states of affairs, Wittgenstein can dispense with Kant's doctrine of the transcendental ideality of space and time.[16] Indeed, for Wittgenstein, between its two aspects, objects and states of affairs or form and content, the world is complete and takes care of itself.

His specific arguments for *how* the world takes care of itself are made most perspicuous when compared to Plato's theory of blending. In the *Sophist* Plato argues for the following two claims: a)if objects do not exhibit some blending, discourse would be impossible; b)if objects blended randomly, discourse would be nonsensical.[17] In short, for Plato, there is a *logos* or order to the world. Wittgenstein echoes this reasoning precisely when he argues that objects must combine with one another to form states of affairs: "It is essential to things that they should be possible constituents of states of affairs" (*T* 2.011). His primary argument for this conclusion depends on the consideration that "nothing in logic is accidental":

> It would seem to be a sort of accident, if it turned out that a situation would fit a thing that could already exist entirely on its own.
>
> If things can occur in states of affairs, this possibility must be in them from the beginning.
>
> (Nothing in the province of logic can be merely possible. Logic deals with every possibility and all possibilities are its facts.)

Just as we are quite unable to imagine spatial objects outside space or temporal objects outside time, so too there is *no* object that we can imagine excluded from the possibility of combining with others.

If I can imagine objects combined in states of affairs, I cannot imagine them excluded from the *possibility* of such combinations. (*T* 2.0121)

Thus, if it is possible for objects to blend, it is impossible for them not to combine. This otherwise faulty inference from what is possible to what is necessary is justified only on the assumption that nothing in logic can be merely possible or accidental:

In logic nothing is accidental: if a thing *can* occur in a state of affairs, the possibility of the state of affairs must be written into the thing itself. (*T* 2.012)

To propose that an object could exist on its own and also fit a state of affairs would make the connection between a state of affairs and its objects purely contingent. In that case, the world would not be logical, nor would it be susceptible to logical characterization since logic deals with what is necessary. Thus, objects cannot exist both on their own and in states of affairs:

Things are independent in so far as they can occur in all *possible* situations, but this form of independence is a form of connection with states of affairs, a form of dependence. (It is impossible for words to appear in two different roles: by themselves, and in propositions.) (*T* 2.0122)

While his appeal to "words" in the above passage is indicative of his linguistic model, he might as well have said "It is impossible for objects to appear in two different roles: by themselves, and in states of affairs." Thus, arguing from a different route, objects cannot be thought of as constituting a separable, noumenal realm behind the world of facts.

Sometimes, as in the latter half of *T* 2.0121 and in the following passage, his argument for the claim that there must be blending appears to derive from epistemological considerations, i.e., on what can and cannot be imagined (thought):

Each thing is, as it were, in a space of possible states of affairs. This space I can imagine empty, but I cannot imagine the thing without the space. (*T* 2.013)

One must remember that, for Wittgenstein, thinking is simply a form of picturing. As such, there cannot be illogical thought. Thus, what can be imagined is also possible:

> A thought contains the possibility of the situation of which it is the thought. What is thinkable is possible too. (*T* 3.02)

Consequently, what can or cannot be imagined serves as a criterion only on condition that it is reflective of what can be the case. It is not an independent criterion, but one that assumes that, like the world and language, thought too is logical.

Perhaps more reminiscent of Aristotle's theory of predication, which formalized Plato's unique, but powerful idea of blending, Wittgenstein argues that to be an object *means* to be a possible constituent of some state of affairs or other and thus describable in language. Evidence for this reading comes from Wittgenstein's remark that: "In a manner of speaking, objects are colourless" (*T* 2.0232). That is, in their role as substance, objects lack characterization. They are not the kind of things that can be thought of as either colored or uncolored. They are privative to color or, for that matter, any predicate. However, since their independence from states of affairs is only theoretical and never actual, no object is privative to all predicates:

> A spatial object must be situated in infinite space. (A spatial point is an argument-place.)
>
> A speck in the visual field, though it need not be red, must have some colour: it is, so to speak, surrounded by colour-space. Notes must have *some* pitch, objects of the sense of touch *some* degree of hardness, and so on. (*T* 2.0131)

Thus, there is no object such that it is incapable of some characterization. Objects exist in logical space, the space of facts, and blend to produce states of affairs:

> The substance of the world *can* only determine a form, and not any material properties. For it is only by means of propositions that material properties are represented—only by the configuration of objects that they are produced. (*T* 2.0231, see also, *T* 2.0272)

As for the second part of Plato's claim, i.e., that objects must blend in a determinate way, Wittgenstein's definitions provide an elegant method for establishing structure. He calls the possibility of its occurring in states of affairs, the *form* of an object (*T* 2.0141), and "The determinate way in which objects are connected in a state of affairs is the structure of the state of affairs" (*T* 2.032). Since, "Form is the possibility of structure" (*T* 2.033), the very possibility of its occurring in a state of affairs insures the structure of the state of affairs. Where there is form there is structure (content). Thus objects do not blend randomly; they display structure:

> There cannot be an orderly or a disorderly world, so that one could say that our world is orderly. In every possible world there is an order even if it is a complicated one, just as in space too there are not orderly and disorderly distributions of points, but every distribution of points is orderly. (*NB* 19.9.16)

Moreover, as if in anticipation of the criticism that might be leveled at either Plato or Aristotle by someone like Leibniz, namely, that it is a wise object that knows with what other objects to blend, Wittgenstein argues that objects contain from the beginning the possibilities for the particular state of affairs that they can enter (*T* 2.012).

On the whole, the model is strikingly efficient and sensitive to the questions that fascinated philosophers from the beginning. One can, for example, reconstruct an answer to the Pre-Socratic problem of change or the problem of the one and the many from the fragments of the *Tractatus*:

> Objects are what is unalterable and subsistent; their configuration is what is changing and unstable. (*T* 2.0271)

That is, once we see the stuff, the substance, of the universe in terms of "form", we will not feel the need to invent some cataclysmic device or occurrence to explain the presence of structure; form implies structure. As for truth, that is a matter of comparing the facts of language with the facts of states of affairs. Logical form, which is shared by both language and the world, establishes the needed method of comparison. Leibniz's problem about other possible worlds is answered by making the form of the world unalterable. That is, objects which constitute the unalterable form of the world contain the possibility of all situations (*T* 2014). To say that a speck in the visual field must have color is not yet to say what color it is. Since its specific color is contingent, it is possible for material situations to be other than they are. That is, objects can combine in such a way as to produce a world different from the one we know, but it cannot be totally alien since it must share a form with this world:

> It is obvious that an imagined world, however different it may be
> from the real one, must have *something*—a form—in common with it.
> (*T* 2.022)

In fact, about the only question the model cannot answer is the question,
"Why is there blending?" or, as it has been otherwise asked, "Why is there
something rather than nothing?" The question has no answer, "It is not *how*
things are in the world that is mystical, but that it exists" (*T* 6.44).

Unfortunately, in the early work, Wittgenstein did not comprehend the
significance of his theory of blending; in an obvious overreaction to Kant,
he compromises its autonomy by confusing his pre-critical and essentially
ineffable faith in an autonomous world with an argument for realism. Of
course, as he himself later realizes, there was an enormous gap between his
intentions and his results. Instead of realism, the *Tractatus,* by projecting its
analysis of the structure of language onto the world, ends up with a variation of transcendental idealism which might be called linguistic idealism.[18]
As Arthur Danto notes, for Wittgenstein, "Nature is frozen language and
language is liquid world."[19] Danto compares Wittgenstein's belief that the
world divides into facts, not things, with Galileo's belief that the world is
essentially mathematical, or Descartes' belief that the world is made up of
primary qualities, and concludes: "In all these cases, the ontology one adopts
is but a projection of one's language on the surface of reality, which is then
peeled back and set up as a discovery of how the world must be if we are
to speak of it as we do."[20] Wittgenstein comes to this same realization when
he decides to return to philosophy in the 1930s.

In the later work, the autonomy of the world is finally separated from
the context of an argument for realism and assumes its proper role as an
argument for a foundationless epistemology. If the world is autonomous,
not only can it not be reduced or seen as a function of language, but language, or knowledge, cannot be made to depend on it. As we shall see, while
he never changes his mind about the world having a structure independent
from consciousness in the later works, he no longer speaks very much about
the world or its relation to language. In part, this has to do with the fact
that it is difficult to say anything about the relation between language and
reality without sounding metaphysical, indeed, perhaps, without being
metaphysical; however, he has a more important reason for his silence,
namely, he has discovered that the world is irrelevant. He need not mention
the facts of nature in order to address the problems of meaning and knowl-

edge. Ontology is simply irrelevant. One need not fall back on the facts of nature to understand how meaning is possible. Since one can do without it and since it is risky, not only in the sense of being misinterpreted, but in the sense of deceiving oneself, the best thing to do is allow the object, or facts of nature, to drop out of consideration as irrelevant. Ultimately, then, Wittgenstein's belief that the world takes care of itself issues in a new attitude towards the role of ontology in philosophy, namely, that it is entirely beside the point and, along with it, is the longstanding conflict between idealism and realism. If the problems of knowledge or meaning can be treated without mentioning the structure of the world, then, as Ockham would say, "by all means eliminate unnecessary variables." The connection between language and the world, however, is still there:

> One ought to ask, not what images are or what happens when one images anything, but how the word "imagination" is used. But that does not mean that I want to talk only about words. For the question as to the nature of the imagination is as much about the word "imagination" as my question is…. (*PI* 370)

Only now, one must truly be silent about it.

Chapter 6   *Three Ideas about Knowledge*

One is often bewitched by a word. For example, by the word "know".
(OC 435)

Wittgenstein's ideas about the autonomy of language, logic, and world spawn three corollary ideas about the autonomy of knowledge; namely and in reverse order, knowledge is possible without experience, without certainty, and without authority. Recognition of language's autonomy gives rise to his rejection of authority; logic's autonomy rejects Cartesianism or rationalism, and the autonomy of the world denies empiricism. By refusing both empiricism and rationalism, Wittgenstein signals his departure from Modern philosophy's grand theorizing. For him, neither theory adequately describes the grammar of knowledge as it is embodied in our way of seeing. His more devastating and forward-looking critique, however, concerns his challenge to authority or convention. By rejecting rulers of all sorts, Wittgenstein frees knowledge from more primitive and popular attempts to ground knowledge in either extraordinary authority, God, or ordinary control, e.g., history, language, opinion, law. Appeals to a "who" precede both ontogenically and phylogenically Greek and Modern appeals to a "how." Medieval philosophy embodies appeals to authority. So do myth and religion; yet Hegel and his nineteenth- and twentieth-century successors return in more sophisticated ways to this same foundation. In fact, Wittgenstein's own early appeal to language as the arbiter of what can be known is a perfect example of a conventional compromise of knowledge's independence. Given this personal context, and the historical proximity of authoritarian arguments, his battle against the tyranny of convention, so magnificently dramatized in the later works, is the most significant for him and us.

In Wittgenstein's terms, the battle against authority boils down to the question, whether one can know more than one can say. Can we, do we, know more than we can say or does language's boundary circumscribe that of knowledge exactly? Like Augustine's puzzle about time, the conundrum of the limits of the sayable tormented him. Indeed, it is the founding problem of his work and the one that dogged him till the end:

> The whole sense of the book might be summed up in the following words: what can be said at all can be said clearly, and what we cannot talk about we must passover in silence. (*T* pg. 3)

On one hand, he *knew* that he knew more than he could say; on the other, he *knew* that he couldn't know more. Theoretically, thought could not surpass language. Kant's shuffle separating thinking from knowing with its concomitant division of the world into noumena and phenomena made a mockery, not a critique of reason. Wittgenstein had to be more severe, denying what he knew in order to preserve logic's rigor. Of course, he failed. One cannot just say "no" to these temptations since they are the deep well-springs of philosophy. Even as he wrote the *Tractatus*, he knew that his distinction between showing and saying provided knowledge with a loop-hole similar to Kant's. Frank Ramsey's penetrating criticism forced him to acknowledge his mistakes, i.e., if you can't say it, you can't whistle it either. Accordingly, Wittgenstein returns to philosophy to renegotiate the boundaries between the knowable and the sayable.

Finally, a kind of peace comes to him in the later work through the idea that knowledge is based on acknowledgment. To say that knowledge is based on acknowledgement effectively undermines all previous foundations. Knowing is not "based on" anything other than one's grudging admission that one knows what one thinks one knows even though it cannot be articulated. Following his intuitions, rather than his early theories, he concedes that we know more than we can say. About some things, however, knowledge must be wrenched from us like a tooth aching to be pulled. We have been protecting the rotten belief that all knowledge must be demonstrated for to long.

The ramifications of Wittgenstein's liberation of knowledge are endless. Consider just a few! If knowledge is possible without experience, we no longer need to suffer in order to know. Like the lifting of a biblical curse—"**Man** shall only know by the sweat of **his** brow"—we may know without the pain of having to suffer events. And if knowledge is possible without certainty, one can know and still be wrong, or as I like to argue, one can play faultlessly and still lose.[1] Losing is no criterion for having played badly. One can be wrong without blame. Mistakes and errors are possible, indeed often unavoidable. Knowledge is free from the moral aura created by the demand for certainty. Lastly, if knowledge is possible without authority, one has license to be free. One can finally trust one's own ability to know and learn and once more do so without substituting the crutches of experience or reason for authority. One can know, indeed, even know oneself.

Essentially, Wittgenstein's ideas dismantle the apparatus of knowledge as true belief, dominant in epistemology since Plato. Knowledge without experience eliminates the truth condition; knowledge without certainty frees knowers from being true believers; and knowledge without authority makes being in a position to know a humble, manageable feat. Ultimately, instead of focusing on the truth status of propositions or the mental state of knowers, Wittgenstein turns to acts and their circumstances. Knowing something is not a simple relationship between a mind and a fact, but a complex one involving many variables. Above all, one must move in order to know, not contemplate. And to do that, one must acknowledge that one already knows something:

> I want to say: propositions of the form of empirical propositions, and not only propositions of logic, form the foundation of all operating with thoughts (with language).—This observation is not of the form "I know... ". "I know... " states what *I* know, and that is not of logical interest. (*OC* 401)

> In this remark the expression "propositions of the form of empirical propositions" is itself thoroughly bad; the statements in question are statements about material objects. And they do not serve as foundations in the same way as hypotheses which, if they turn out to be false, are replaced by others.
> … und schreib getrost
> "Im anfang war die Tat." (*OC* 402)

Knowledge without Experience

You learned the concept 'pain' when you learned a language. (PI 384)

How do I know that this colour is red? It would be an answer to say: 'I have learnt English'. (PI 381)

When properly taught, these remarks are meant to shock and disturb. Students almost all object, "What! we learned about pain and color by learning a language? Surely, these are things we experience and moreover things which we learn by experiencing them. We *feel* pains and *see* colors." While they are right to insist that they feel pains and see colors, they are wrong to confuse this point with a second, namely, that one learns about colors and pains through experience. In the popular mind, i.e., according to the unexamined way of seeing found in ordinary language, experience is the best, perhaps, the only teacher; language only lazily adds labels to what is sensed. To think differently about both language's and experience's roles is to upset this popular picture and proclaim a new relationship between language and experience.

Jumping on the one hedge in the above remarks, students remove the sting from Wittgenstein's claims by arguing that he is not really saying that one feels pains by learning a language; rather, he is only claiming that one learns to identify one's experiences *as* pain by learning a language. Since this move confines language to a system of labeling, they are mollified. The sting is removed from Wittgenstein's claim. Yet more ground is allowed than they realize. If one agrees that knowledge of pain or color depends on language, then, one is getting closer to acknowledging a critical role for language in the actual experiencing of them. After all, what kind of experience comes unlabeled, even if the label is "vague," or "sharp?" Learning is part of the knowledge game, not the experiencing one. To learn pain is not just to have it, but to know it and for this one needs language. Nevertheless, Wittgenstein is as reluctant as anyone to make mastery of a technique a necessary condition of experience:

> The substratum of this experience is the mastery of a technique.
>
> But how queer for this to be the logical condition of someone's having such-and-such an *experience*. (*PI* pg. 208)

It goes against the grain to think that experience requires knowledge. Yet, in some sense, mastery of language is a condition of human experience. The trick is to see language's role *without* making the idealist's mistake of arguing that language is a necessary condition of experience, nor the realist mistake of arguing that language doesn't matter at all. The goal is to slip between the either/or of language and experience and see their interaction.

To negotiate these difficult straits, Wittgenstein begins his attack with the other horn of the dilemma, namely, the belief that experience is a necessary condition for language. In fact, his main point was never one of making language a condition of experience, but of denying experience's claim on knowledge. The issue is one of knowledge or being able to articulate what it is I have when I have a pain or see a color and the point of Wittgenstein's remarks is that one need not experience pain or color in order to know what pain or color is. What people take most for granted is that experience is a necessary condition for *having* language. The picture that knowledge, in this case knowledge of language, is dependent on acquaintance is the more insidious of the two pictures and the one that would have to be undone first. Once one grants the possibility of knowing without an experiential anchor, one will be able to see the extent to which language conditions experience.

His arguments against private language, especially his "beetle-in-the-box" remark, contain his most succinct attack on experiential requirements:

> If I say of myself that it is only from my own case that I know what the word "pain" means—must I not say the same of other people too? And how can I generalize the *one* case so irresponsibly?
>
> Now someone tells me that **he** knows what pain is only from **his** own case! Suppose everyone had a box with something in it: we call it a "beetle". No one can look into anyone else's box, and everyone says **he** knows what a beetle is only by looking at **his** beetle.—Here it would be quite possible for everyone to have something different in **his** box. One might even imagine such a thing constantly changing.—But suppose the word "beetle" had a use in these people's language? If so it would not be used as the name of a thing. The thing in the box has no place in the language-game at all; not even as a *something*: for the box might even be empty.—No, one can 'divide through' by the thing in the box; it cancels out, whatever it is.
>
> That is to say: if we construe the grammar of the expression of sensation on the model of 'object and designation' the object drops out of consideration as irrelevant. (*PI* 293)

As with every remark in the *Investigations,* this one is directed at a number of different, though related, points. Most immediately, it culminates, as does this whole section, on sensation, his sustained argument against a copy theory of meaning.[2] Words do not mean by referring to either objects or ideas. Reference or denotation is irrelevant for determining meaning. Rather, meaning is a function of a) a word's place in the language and b) its use by speakers. Thus, to show that not even sensation words mean by referring is to clinch the more general argument about how words mean. For my current purposes, however, the primary thrust of this remark is to show that the experience of beetles is unnecessary for the correct use of the word "beetle."

The steps of the argument are twofold. First, the private character of experience must be acknowledged, i.e., only I can have my experiences. The privacy of experience is an analytic truth like "one plays patience by oneself" (*PI* 248). Logically, it cannot be otherwise, given the definitions of "patience" and "sensations." Secondly, we need to agree that what we mean by language is something that is public, i.e., language is used to communicate with one another. Like rules, it requires a practice, a mastery of a technique:

> Is what we call "obeying a rule" something that it would be possible for only *one* **man** to do, and to do only *once* in **his** life?—This is of course a note on the grammar of the expression "to obey a rule."
>
> It is not possible that there should have been only one occasion on which someone obeyed a rule. It is not possible that there should have been only one occasion on which a report was made, an order given, or understood; and so on.—To obey a rule, to make a report, to give an order, to play a game of chess, are *customs* (uses, institutions).
>
> To understand a sentence means to understand a language. To understand a language means to be master of a technique. (cf. *PI* 202) (*PI* 199)

Private language, which is defined as, "And sounds which no one else understands but which I '*appear to understand*' ...." (*PI* 269), fails as a language because of the logical requirement that what we mean by language is a shared, public system of rules. Private language is not a physical impossibility; one can, and many do, develop private codes. It is a logical impossibility since we cannot call these private codes "language."

So if experience is private and language is public, the question is, How do they connect? How does a general tool developed in the public arena come to serve private ends? The answer is, if knowledge about how a word is used, e.g., the word "beetle" depends upon having certain experiences, then the word would not exist. Language would be impossible. As the argument demonstrates, each of us might have a different image or experience of a beetle; some might never have had any experiences of beetles at all and so the box might be empty. Clearly, experience alone cannot teach us its many names. But since, by hypothesis, these people use the word "beetle" in intelligible ways, their ability to do so cannot depend on experience. Language is learned from the top down, rather than from the bottom up. Arguing in transcendental fashion, Wittgenstein shows that the conditions under which language is possible exclude the possibility that it depends on experience.

On the other hand, while experience does not cause language in a simple one-to-one linear way, the concepts we have depend in a loose way on certain general facts of nature; e.g., the fact that if we did not experience pains, if no one experienced them, there would not be pain related games in our language:

> It is only in normal cases that the use of a word is clearly prescribed; we know, are in no doubt, what to say in this or that case. The more abnormal the case, the more doubtful it becomes what we are to say. And if things were quite different from what they actually are—if there were for instance no characteristic expression of pain, of fear, of joy; if rule became exception and exception rule; or if both became phenomena of roughly equal frequency—this would make our normal language-games lose their point.— The procedure of putting a lump of cheese on a balance and fixing the price by the turn of the scale would lose its point if it frequently happened for such lumps to suddenly grow or shrink for no obvious reason. This remark will become clearer when we discuss such things as the relation of expression to feeling, and similar topics. (*PI* 142)

The absence of pain-experiences would eliminate the language-games surrounding pain; they would lose their point. In this sense, experience is necessary for language, for the development of the game, not for particular statements within the game. The trouble for those who want proof is that once inside a culture, once shaped by a language, there is no way of deciding whether any one individual has or has not experienced pain. Culture can just as easily fill the gap, making it impossible to distinguish between nature and nurture. Daily, people use the concept pain successfully and there is no way of telling whether they have experienced it or not. What criterion for "experience" shall we use?:

> Could someone understand the word "pain", who had *never* felt pain?—Is experience to teach me whether this is so or not?—And if we say "A **man** could not imagine pain without having sometime felt it"—how do we know? How can it be decided whether it is true? (*PI* 315)

The question is undecidable.

Wittgenstein makes the same point with regard to the ambiguities of ostensive definition:

> … Doubtless the ostensive teaching helped to bring this about; but only together with a particular training. With different training the same ostensive teaching of these words would have effected a quite different understanding.
>
> "I set the brake up by connecting up rod and lever."—Yes, given the whole of the rest of the mechanism. Only in conjunction with that is it a brake-lever, and separated from its support it is not even a lever; it may be anything, or nothing. (*PI* 6)

What something is, in the sense of what we call that thing, depends on the context, the system, and the form of life. What it is outside of the context is irrelevant. Thus, since we do communicate with each other, no matter how varied our experiences, we can conclude that our knowledge of the use of words like "beetle," "pain," "red," which incidently includes such existential tasks as distinguishing beetles from groundhogs, cannot depend on experiencing any of these things.[3] Once again, the object and the experience drop out of consideration as irrelevant.

Almost imperceptively, Wittgenstein has disabused us of one of our most cherished idols, namely, that *true* knowledge and understanding require experience. As the many consequences of the thought slowly penetrate, various objections surface. The most notorious one claims that, "communication is only an illusion anyway. In fact, each of us really means a different thing by 'beetle' and most definitely by 'pain'." Like nineteenth-century romantics, some insist that we never truly understand one another, but only hobble along with the most rudimentary of understandings. Wittgenstein's response to this objection is swift because it denies the data in favor of some wild hypothesis. What could calling our obvious and daily acts of communication illusionary mean here? We learn the word "illusion" in a context of non–illusionary phenomena. This romantic objection wipes out the difference between illusion and non–illusion and so undercuts its own claim. Moreover, what ideal of communication could the objectors have in mind. Surely, we are being asked to achieve something we might call "holy communication," i.e., one without gaps. In contrast, Wittgenstein notes that in objective tests, i.e., everyday behavior, we manage to make comparable discriminations, agreeing on a variety of phenomena despite some oddities and many gaps. Nor do these gaps make skepticism more respectable. No one is claiming that communication always takes place or that it is easy. Thus, the objection that we "really do not communicate" becomes an idling speculation which need not be taken seriously. In fact, the intricacies of private experience need not be mentioned at all. The argument can be made using public phenomena. Designers, for example, have drastically varied our expectations of the looks of a chair. Yet, we have little trouble distinguishing chairs from tables. This ability rests on the fact that we have been taught a language, not invented one. Language is public. While we can invent languages if we want to; they will not share a number of important features that constitute language. His remarks, however, do not outlaw inventiveness or variations on the status quo.[4] Rather, like Vygotsky[5] and against Piaget[6], Wittgenstein argues that the first learning stages of language must be public and taught; variations come later:

> Just as in writing we learn a particular basic form of letters and then vary it later, so we learn first the stability of things as the norm, which is then subject to alterations. (*OC* 473)

Deviations from the norm occur daily; however, they require a mastery of a technique:

> The child, I should like to say, learns to react in such-and-such a way; and in so reacting it doesn't so far know anything. Knowing only begins at a later level. (*OC* 538)

Imaginative variations, like the propositions for which we claim knowledge, occur at a later level.

Once over the "we never communicate" hurdle, a second and more important objection begins to take shape: "So, language teaches me about concepts and makes me articulate about what is happening in my body and how I perceive the world. As I said in the beginning, this is nothing more than labeling. The really important thing is my having these experiences; without this all language would be much ado about nothing." This objection tries to take advantage of the distinction made earlier between identifying experience *as* pain and *having* an experience. If language or knowledge is possible without experience, then the argument would like to run, experience is possible without language. We don't really need language to have experience. To some extent, Wittgenstein agrees; however, not fully. Language's labeling role in teaching someone how to identify their pains has important consequences for, if not actually *having* (*sensing*) the pains, then the *experiencing* of them. Experience, unlike the mere having or suffering of pain, cannot be separated from language, but is always already inflected by language:

> I want to say: an education quite different from ours might also be the foundation for quite different concepts. (*Z* 387)

> For here life would run on differently.—What interests us would not interest *them*. Here different concepts would no longer be unimaginable. In fact, this is the only way in which *essentially* different concepts are imaginable. (*Z* 388)

Language shapes us and gives not only form, but content to our otherwise non-descript experiences. "Grammar," as the remark goes, "tells us what kind of object anything is (theology as grammar)" (*PI* 373). Language's grammatical conventions, the ones we bump against, teach us to identify pain *as* "pain"; they teach us how to apply the word and thus direct our existential discriminations in the world. Learning how to use language delimits the conceptual realm which in turn outlines the existential one. The connection is there prior to learning a language.

Theoretically, for Wittgenstein, there is no limit to language's classificatory power; it can do as it pleases:

> One is tempted to justify the rules of grammar by sentences like "but there really are four primary colours". And the saying that the rules of grammar are arbitrary is directed against the possibility of this justification, which is constructed on the model of justifying a sentence by pointing to what verifies it.

> Yet can't it after all be said that in some sense or other the grammar of colour-words characterizes the world as it actually is? One would like to say: May I not really look in vain for a fifth primary colour? Doesn't one put the primary colours together because there is a similarity among them, or at least put *colours* together contrasting them with e.g. shapes or notes, because there is a similarity among

them? Or, when I set this up as the right way of dividing up the world, have I a pre-conceived idea in my head as a paradigm? Of which in that case I can only say: "Yes, that is the kind of way we look at things" or "We just do want to form this sort of picture." For if I say "there is a particular similarity among the primary colours"—whence do I derive the idea of this similarity? Just as the idea 'primary colour' is nothing else but 'blue or red or green or yellow'—is not the idea of that similarity too given simply by the four colours? Indeed aren't they the same? "Then might one also take red, green and similar together?"—Why not [cf. *Z* 350]?! (*Z* 331)

However, as Wittgenstein insisted, the theoretical perspective is suspect since it distorts a form of life and makes ordinary language-games lose their point. The theoretical temptation must be resisted as much as the dogmatic one, the one that tries to ground the rules of language. One must steer a course between these two extremes; neither "necessary" nor "arbitrary" correctly describes the situation:

If the formation of concepts can be explained by facts of nature, should we not be interested, not in grammar, but rather in that in nature which is the basis of grammar?—Our interest certainly includes the correspondence between concepts and very general facts of nature. (Such facts as mostly do not strike us because on their generality.) But our interest does not fall back upon these possible causes of the formation of concepts; we are not doing natural science; nor yet natural history—since we can also invent fictitious natural history for our purposes.

I am not saying: if such-and-such facts of nature were different people would have different concepts (in the sense of a hypothesis). But: if anyone believes that certain concepts are absolutely the correct ones, and that having different ones would mean not realizing something that we realize—then let **him** imagine certain very general facts of nature to be different from what we are used to, and the formation of concepts different from the usual ones will become intelligible to **him**.

Compare a concept with a style of painting. For is even our style of painting arbitrary? Can we choose one at pleasure? (The Egyptian, for instance.) Is it a mere question of pleasing and ugly? (*PI* pg. 230)

The relation between language and reality eludes both the realist's attempt to speak of causal necessity and the idealist's attempt to speak of arbitrary determination. Like styles of painting they are neither directed by the facts, nor by subjective will. This either/or is the philosophical dilemma that creates a fly-bottle; to solve it one must reject the question and come at the problem in a different way.

Wittgenstein's solution is to agree that, of course, facts of nature, general facts that usually escape our notice, are of consequence for the formation of concepts, e.g., mice do not regenerate from a bunch of rags, and, for our purposes, live creatures experience pain:

> What we have to mention in order to explain the significance, I mean the importance, of a concept, are often extremely general facts of nature: such facts as are hardly ever mentioned because of their great generality. (*PI* pg. 56)

Still, one cannot assert this observation in the form of a hypothesis. The relation between how the world is and how we think about it is too open and too complex for any theory. There is no such thing as tallying with the facts:

> Well, if everything speaks for an hypothesis and nothing against it—is it then certainly true? One may designate it as such.—But does it certainly agree with reality, with the facts?—With this question you are already going round in a circle. (*OC* 191)

> The reason why the use of the expression "true or false" has something misleading about it is that it is like saying "it tallies with the facts or it doesn't", and the very thing that is in question is what "tallying" is here. (*OC* 199)

Indeed, one can even invent a fictitious natural history because there is no strict causal connection between the facts of nature and the conceptual ones. To parody Wittgenstein; a drop of nature equals a cloud of concepts (*PI* pg. 222). The conceptual domain is elastic and utterly pliable. Variations abound. Thus, for all practical purposes, "Essence is expressed by grammar" or learning how to use a word teaches us what something is. Yet one must recognize that a totally different world, different in basics not details, would probably mean different concepts:

> If we imagine the facts otherwise than as they are, certain language-games lose some of their importance, while others become

important. And in this way there is an alteration—a gradual one—in the use of the vocabulary of a language. (*OC* 63)

> When language-games change, then there is a change in concepts, and with the concepts the meanings of words change. (*OC* 65)

So while the conceptual domain cannot be seen as a function of the experiential one, the two remain related.

The world is autonomous; it is independent and cares nothing for our theories. In the later work, the substance and logic of the world become irrelevant. He need not fall back upon them to explain how language is meaningful. Irrelevance is Wittgenstein's version of Ocham's razor: If one need not appeal to certain entities to explain language, then, don't.

The implications of this position are often misunderstood. Wittgenstein is not a behaviorist; he is not saying that inner processes do not take place, or that they are insignificant; he is only saying that they are not necessary for knowledge:

> "But you surely cannot deny that, for example, in remembering, an inner process takes place."—What gives the impression that we want to deny anything? When one says, "Still, an inner process does take place here"—one wants to go on: "After all, you *see* it." And it is this inner process that one means by the word "remembering."—The impression that we wanted to deny something arises from our setting our faces against the picture of the 'inner process.' What we deny is that the picture of the inner process gives us the correct idea of the use of the word "to remember." We say this picture with its ramifications stands in the way of our seeing the use of the word as it is.
> (*PI* 305)

The picture of the private experience of "pain" or "remembering" make it seem as if acquaintance is a necessary condition for knowledge and, moreover, that one is always in the position of judging from one's own case. Both these assumptions create the philosophical problems that haunted Wittgenstein's time in England. To deny the assumptions, as Wittgenstein says, is to deny the problems and make them disappear.

The third and final objection raised by Wittgenstein himself to further clarify the character and extent of his claim brings us back from these metaphysical issues to the rough ground, indeed, to the rough ground of Plato's road to Larissa:

"But you will surely admit that there is a difference between pain-behavior accompanied by pain and pain-behavior without any pain?"—Admit it? What greater difference could there be?—"And yet you again and again reach the conclusion that the sensation itself is a *nothing*."—Not at all. It is not a *something*, but not a *nothing* either! The conclusion was only that a nothing would serve just as well as a something about which nothing could be said. We have only rejected the grammar which tries to force itself on us here.

The paradox disappears only if we make a radical break with the idea that language always functions in one way, always serves the same purpose: to convey thought—which may be about houses, pains, good and evil, or anything else you please. (*PI* 304)

Unquestionably, the knowledge of those who have experienced pain differs from that of those who have not. They make different discriminations and usually have a more complete knowledge of the subject. As Plato noted, they will be able to give better directions. Yet the knowledge obtained from language and culture, from Pain 101 for example, might be so effective as to undermine any attempt to differentiate it from the real thing. Lack of experiencing does not disqualify someone from claiming knowledge. Secondly, we must resist the temptation to call experiential knowledge, "true knowledge," or "first-hand knowledge," and the later "not-quite true-knowledge" or "second-hand knowledge." Both are cases of knowledge, despite the differences. Rather than grade them, the goal is to recognize the differences and appeal to the appropriate one in appropriate circumstances. "I am certain that," for example, more likely requires experience; but "I know," as Wittgenstein uses it in *On Certainty,* does not. It rests on conceptual grounds for knowing.

The blessings of this view, correct or incorrect, are bountiful. First, it finally makes use of the fact that we are linguistic animals. Culture, as everyone know, makes it possible for human beings to learn without having to re-invent the wheel. While we have always paid lip-service to this idea, Wittgenstein finally offers an epistemology which makes this belief more than a wish. Knowledge is possible without first-hand experience. We learn and grow by acquiring a language. Contrary to popular myth, which holds that one "really" does not understand until one has experienced the exact same phenomenon, it is possible to have an understanding without this "really." Moreover, one doesn't need psychological empathy as a foundation for this possibility. We share a form of life, a language, and that ensures a degree of understanding. Wittgenstein's insight ends the revenge system. One need not experience poverty in order to know what poverty is. Nor need one be black in order to understand the problems of being black in America, nor female to know about sexism. Examples abound! Once again, being poor or black enhances and provides dramatic witness to our knowledge; but one is not ignorant without experience. In addition, recognition of this claim might give to formal education, i.e., classroom and book learning, the respect it deserves. Instead of thinking of books as poor, vicarious substitutes for the real thing, i.e., being out in the world experiencing things for oneself, people might come to see that not only is much learned through books, but that only books provide the correction to experience's often narrow education. Language is a teacher as much as experience and in many cases a better teacher. Wittgenstein's conclusion is *not* that experience fails to teach, only that its success in teaching depends upon a linguistic training. It depends, that is, on a form of life. Experience teaches in context. And this context is as much a function of language as it is of experience.

Knowledge without Certainty

—For "I know" seems to describe a state of affairs which guarantees what is known, guarantees it as a fact. One always forgets the expression "I thought I knew". (OC 12)

This section can equally be called, "Knowledge Without Descartes," since it was he who made certainty or indubitability a condition of knowledge. For Descartes, we know something only when all doubt and error are expunged and, moreover, when they are shown to be impossible. Both mathematics and religion, the two world-pictures that nurtured Descartes, contributed heavily to this picture. Ironically, certainty's hold became even stronger during the seventeenth century when it vied with science for control of our paradigm of knowledge. Since then, the two models have been in heated contention.

By "free from doubt," Descartes means both psychologically and objectively free; that is, the claim had to be both indubitable in the sense that the inquirer is making no mistake and necessarily true, i.e., no mistake is possible in the circumstances. If one such truth existed, deduction could do the rest. Of course, the truth had to be more than analytic; in Kant's language, it has to be synthetic, i.e., capable of expanding our knowledge of matters of fact. Only if all propositions could be grounded in at least one such necessary, but empirical truth, could indubitable, apodictic, certain knowledge be possible.

Cogito Ergo Sum, I think, therefore I am, was Descartes's famous choice for the archimedean point of all knowledge. It was an indubitable proposition and therefore *a priori*, yet empirical and thus synthetic. Besides the synthetic–*a priori* nature of the claim, the telling thing about the *Cogito* concerns its broader picture of knowledge and thinking. It claims that everything can be deduced from the act of one subject thinking. Thinking is mental, private, anti-social, and perceptual or immediate. This conception of thought, even more than the conception of knowledge to which it was linked, disturbed Wittgenstein greatly. These conceptions laid the groundwork for all idealisms of the next two decades. More than any of the other pictures that hold us captive, Wittgenstein worked hard in his later years to undermine every aspect of these conceptions of knowledge and thought.

He first challenges Descartes' picture of doubt itself and thus the merits of Descartes' method, "methodological doubt." We cannot doubt at will (*OC* 221), he argues, nor can we doubt everything (*OC* 115). Like Peirce, he argues that doubt must have a context and that it follows trust and certainty, rather than precedes them (*OC* 122, 150, 160).[7] "Free from doubt," on the other hand, cannot be a mark of knowledge since while one cannot doubt everything, anything can be doubted. There are no special propositions exempt for all times from doubt. Generally speaking, Wittgenstein concludes that skepticism is not the best stance for philosophy.

Most importantly, he wanted to show that knowing is not seeing: knowing does not make direct contact with a fact guaranteeing truth and making error impossible:

> "I know" has a primitive meaning similar to and related to "I see" ("*wissen*," "*videre*"). And "I know **he** was in the room, but **he** wasn't in the room" is like "I saw **him** in the room, but **he** wasn't there." "I know" is supposed to express a relation, not between me and the sense of a proposition (like "I believe") but between me and a fact. So that the *fact* is taken into my consciousness. (Here is the reason why one wants to say that nothing that goes on in the outer world is really known, but only what happens in the domain of what are called sense-data.) This would give us a picture of knowing as the perception of an outer event through visual rays which project it as is

into the eye and the consciousness. Only then the question at once arises whether one can be *certain* of this projection. And this picture does indeed show how our *imagination* presents knowledge, but not what lies at the bottom of the presentation. (*OC* 90)

There is no revelation nor intuition that makes contact with facts. Knowing is a more discursive process than this picture allows.

Indeed, Wittgenstein does not simply contradict Descartes by arguing that knowledge is possible where both doubt (subjective criteria) and falsity or error (objective criteria) are possible, but that, "technically speaking," knowledge is *only* possible in such circumstances:

> Can one say: "Where there is no doubt there is no knowledge either"? (*OC* 121)

> Moore's view really comes down to this: the concept 'know' is analogous to the concepts 'believe', 'surmise', 'doubt', 'be convinced' in that the statement "I know…" can't be a mistake. And if that *is* so, then there can be an inference from such an utterance to the truth of an assertion. And here the form "I thought I knew" is being overlooked…. (*OC* 21)

While knowing is not like seeing, it is not like believing either. Both comparisons from different angles, the former objective, the latter subjective, attempt to eliminate error. They both pretend that knowledge can be a sure thing. Knowing is not like belief because it is subject to doubt, and it is not like seeing because error is possible.

The most radical implication of Wittgenstein's challenge to Descartes, however, is his questioning of the long-standing belief that I know that p implies p or the truth of the proposition in question. Poor comparisons with seeing and believing confuse knowing with certainty. Unlike "I am certain that," "I know that" does not imply p. Knowing implies neither being free from doubt, nor truth. Many remarks suggest this radical revision in our conception of knowledge:

> It would be wrong to say that I can only say "I know that there is a chair there" when there is a chair there. Of course it isn't *true* unless there is, but I have a right to say this if I am *sure* there is a chair there, even if I am wrong.

> Pretensions are a mortgage which burdens a philosopher's capacity to think. (*OC* 549)

With respect to some of the things we know—and the context determines these beliefs—we need not withdraw claims to knowledge even though p is false since it is always possible for it to turn out that we only thought we knew what we claimed to know. Science regularly denies past claims to knowledge, e.g., "the earth is flat," "humans have never been very far from the earth's surface," etc. Knowledge should not be restricted to cases where p is true. However, he is reluctant to simply say that knowledge does not imply truth. The problem is that knowing is a tangled, confused concept with many facets. Renovations and clarifications are difficult without sounding theoretical and without confusing one point with another. Wittgenstein often gets overwhelmed as he tries to tease apart all the different relations among the concepts central to the language-game of knowledge: doubt/trust, belief/certainty, ignorance/knowledge, truth/falsity, right/wrong, mistake or error/insanity or other, not to mention experience/reason, evidence/judgment, assumption or presupposition/hypothesis, etc. The avenues of description truly get congested as all these concepts tumble round each other, mixing in different ways and bearing old pictures with the new indiscriminately.

Nevertheless, Wittgenstein is committed to changing the picture of knowledge as guaranteeing truth:

> It would not be surmise and I might tell it to someone else with complete certainty, as something there is no doubt about. But does that mean that it is unconditionally the truth? May not the thing that I recognize with complete certainty as the tree that I have seen here my whole life long—may this not be disclosed as something different? May it not confound me?
>
> And nevertheless it was right, in the circumstances that give this sentence meaning, to say "I know (I do not merely surmise) that that's a tree." To say that in strict truth I only believe it would be wrong. It would be completely *misleading* to say: "I believe my name is L.W." And this too is right: I cannot be making a *mistake* about it. But that does not mean that I am infallible about it. (*OC* 425)

One may be certain, not mistaken, but wrong, fallible; yet it would not be right to switch to belief, since one was sure. "Know" has a place in this context, although it may be better expressed by "I am certain that...."

A crucial step in Wittgenstein's argument blurs the analytic/synthetic distinction. Watching Moore, he noticed that claims to certainty occur in the presence of certain kinds of propositions, ones that, for Wittgenstein, characterize a way of seeing and stand fast, e.g., "2+2=4," "This is my hand," "My name is…." All these propositions are part of the *Weltbild;* they belong to logic, or to the river-bed of thought. Thus, they function as norms of description, even though they are ordinary, empirical propositions:

> We know, with the same certainty with which we believe *any* mathematical proposition, how the letters A and B are pronounced, what the colour of human blood is called, that other human beings have blood and call it "blood"'. (*OC* 340)

> Compare with this 12 x 12 = 144. Here too we don't say "perhaps". For, in so far as this proposition rests on our not miscounting or miscalculating and on our senses not deceiving us as we calculate, both propositions, the arithmetical and the physical one, are on the same level.
>
> I want to say; The physical game is just as certain as the arithmetical. But this can be misunderstood. My remark is a logical not a psychological one. (*OC* 447)

Ordinary empirical propositions, those Kant would have called "synthetic," are as certain as arithmetical ones; but they are certain not because they are unequivocally true—no proposition is exempt from doubt—but because we treat them as true. They have become fossilized, river-bed propositions providing a framework for all further truth determinations. Thus, there is no clear boundary between analytic and synthetic propositions, logical versus empirical propositions. Everything turns on how they are treated and used:

> But if someone were to say "So logic too is an empirical science" **he** would be wrong. Yet, this is right: the same proposition may get treated at one time as something to test by experience, at another as a rule of testing (cf. *OC* 167, 309, 331, 401). (*OC* 98)

If treated as a rule, it becomes part of the logic, i.e., part of the mechanics for describing a language-game. Logical propositions describe the conceptual situation (*OC* 51, 56, 628). If treated as an empirical proposition, its truth remains to be considered.

Moore's propositions stand fast for us. We cannot doubt them without overturning our whole *Bezugsystem*. Consequently, for Wittgenstein, they are neither true nor false and for the same reason that the standard meter of the *Investigations* is neither true nor false:

> But on the other hand: how do I *know* that it is my hand? Do I
> even here know exactly what it means to say it is my hand?—When
> I say "how do I know?' I do not mean that I have the least *doubt* of
> it. What we have here is a foundation for all my action. But it seems
> to me that is wrongly expressed by the words "I know". (*OC* 414)

All the propositions Moore discusses require an unconscious decision to be
treated as true:

> To say of **man**, in Moore's sense, that **he** *knows* something: that
> what **he** says is therefore unconditionally the truth, seems wrong to
> me.—It is the truth only inasmuch as it is an unmoving foundation
> of **his** language-games. (*OC* 403)

Any attempt to try to prove them true or false enters into a metaphysical
battle for which there is no outcome. In fact, to convince someone of the
truth of these propositions requires a transformation of one's way of
seeing. Thus, in one important sense, we ought not to consider these
propositions as part of the knowledge system. Rather, they belong to
the mythology of the way we see things. In these cases, certainty implies
neither knowledge, nor truth. However, since Wittgenstein is not reform-
ing language, he wants to be able to use "know" as we ordinarily
do, even though there is an important grammatical difference between
the two.

From a technical point of view, knowledge ought to be restricted to
those cases where a mistake is tolerated and where argument and proof hold
sway, for example, in cases where one is dealing with an hypothesis about
the height of Mt. Blanc. However, even here, Wittgenstein suggests that the
most important thing about knowledge is not that it guarantees the truth
of p, but that the claim has grounds. For Wittgenstein, "being in a position
to know" is the primary criterion for knowledge:

> We say we know that water boils when it is put over fire. How
> do we know? Experience has taught us.—I say "I know that I had
> breakfast this morning"; experience hasn't taught me that. One also
> says "I know that **he** is in pain." The language-game is different every
> time, we are *sure* every time, and people will agree with us that we
> are *in a position* to know every time. And that is why the propositions
> of physics are found in textbooks for everyone.
>
> If someone says **he** *knows* something, it must be something that,
> by general consent, **he** is in a position to know. (*OC* 555)

One doesn't say: **he** is in a position to believe that. But one does say: "It is reasonable to assume that in this situation" (or "to believe that"). (*OC* 556)

Claims to knowledge are most in place when one is in a position to know, i.e., has good reasons:

If someone believes something, we needn't always be able to answer the question 'why **he** believes it'; but if **he** knows something, then, the question, "how does **he** know?" must be capable of being answered. (*OC* 550)

And if one does answer this question, one must do so according to generally accepted axioms. *This* is how something of this sort may be known. (*OC* 551)

Because knowledge depends most of all on "being in a position to know," it can occur in the presence of error and the absence of truth. Of the three conditions traditionally associated with the analysis of knowledge as true belief, Wittgenstein is most in sympathy with the belief that knowledge requires a context for the knower.

A third strategy Wittgenstein uses to topple Descartes's view of knowledge evaluates the different kinds of mistakes people make:

"**He** told me about it today—I can't be making a mistake about that."—But what if it does turn out to be wrong?!—Mustn't one make a distinction between the ways in which something 'turns out wrong'?—How *can* it *be shewn* that my statement was wrong. Here evidence is facing evidence, and it must be *decided* which is to give way. (*OC* 641)

A mistake that was not possible is one for which no place has been prepared for in the game:

There is a difference between a mistake for which, as it were, a place is prepared in the game, and a complete irregularity that happens as an exception. (*OC* 647)

When the latter kind of mistake occurs, it is unclear whether to classify it as a mental disturbance or as a mistake:

If my friend were to imagine one day that **he** had been living for a long time past in such and such a place, etc, etc., I should not call this a *mistake*, but rather a mental disturbance, perhaps a transient one. (*OC* 71)

Not every false belief of this sort is a mistake. (*OC* 72)

But what is the difference between mistake and mental disturbance? Or what is the difference between my treating it as a mistake and my treating it as mental disturbance? (*OC* 73)

When we treat it as a mental disturbance and the person isn't disturbed, the disagreement concerns a bed-rock belief; beliefs that one is unwilling to relinquish. Before allowing our opponents to be right, we would rather commit them to an institution or send them back to space:

"I can't be making a mistake; and if the worst comes to the worst I shall make my proposition into a norm." (*OC* 634)

"I can't be making a mistake; but if after all something *should* appear to speak against my proposition I shall stick to it, despite this appearance." (*OC* 636)

"I can't etc." shows my assertion its place in the game. But it relates essentially to *me*, not to the game in general.

If I am wrong in my assertion that doesn't detract from the usefulness of the language-game. (*OC* 637)

This way of going wrong should not be called a mistake since it suggests that the game as a whole is being played wrongly:

If I were to say "I have never been on the moon—but I may be mistaken", that would be idiotic.

For even the thought that I might have been transported there, by unknown means, in my sleep, *would not give me the right* to speak of a possible mistake here. I play the game *wrong* if I do. (*OC* 662)

Again, one cannot say that the game as a whole is being played wrongly since no criterion for wrong or right exists in this case:

This is a similar case to that of shewing that it has no meaning to say that a game has always been played wrong. (*OC* 496)

Rather, one needs to say that she or he is playing a different game.

In the *Investigations*, he makes the same distinction by differentiating between a random mistake and a systematic one (*PI* 143). Only the later challenges the game as a whole. Rather than call these kinds of errors "mistakes," Wittgenstein wants to call them "misunderstandings:" we thought we were playing one game and find that we are playing another with different rules. Confronted with a situation of clashing world-views, one can only turn to persuasion, to converting someone to your way of seeing. Even where a mistake of the usual kind is impossible, one may still go wrong, only it is hard to say what wrong means here:

> Here one must realize that complete absence of doubt at some
> point, even where we would say that 'legitimate' doubt can exist,
> need not falsify a language-game. For there is also something like
> *another* arithmetic.
>
> I believe that this admission must underlie any understanding of
> logic. (*OC* 375)

The *Weltbild* can change; what we call knowledge one day can change on another. When this happens it is difficult to compare the two games and say one is right and the other is wrong. If one can, however, for whatever reasons (e.g., the alternative view is more useful, has better predictive power, etc.), one has a right to say, "'I can't be making a mistake about this' even if I am in error" (*OC* 663). With regular mistakes, falsity plays a role in what we thought we knew; but in systematic mistakes, true and false do not enter the picture. Not every mistake says something untrue. One can play faultlessly, make no mistakes, and still lose since one may be playing the "wrong" game.

This reversal in many of modern epistemology's essential beliefs is of tremendous consequence. Freed from mathematical imperialism, science's conception of knowledge, or the one where knowledge is the product of experimentation, finally comes into its own. One has knowledge even if one is in a state of uncertainty, has made a mistake, or is wrong about p. No longer need Hamlet fret and strut upon the stage since knowledge is possible even where doubt creeps in. Indeed, perhaps a picture of knowledge without certainty will make us less ethnocentric and more open to other points of view and other ways of living. Jacob Bronowski, in the episode called "Knowledge and Certainty," of his old television series "The Ascent of **Man**," makes this point dramatically. Standing ankle deep in a concentration camp pool, he lets the ashes of millions of dead Jews sift through his fingers as he pleads with us to become less sure about what we know. When it comes to knowledge, humility is the best policy. Certainty, indubitability, necessity, were all requirements for being more than human and always gave way before the clever skeptic (*OC* 436). Now all skeptics are robbed of their chief arguments. Knowledge has found more humble foundations:

> If "I know etc." is conceived as a grammatical proposition, of course the "I" cannot be important. And it properly means "There is no such thing as a doubt in this case" or "The expression 'I do not know' makes no sense in this case." And of course it follows from this that "I *know*" makes no sense either. (*OC* 58)

Skepticism, if you will, has become an essential ingredient of knowing rather than its arch enemy. Paradoxically, for Wittgenstein, knowing is at the same time a not-knowing. One need not believe in what one knows; one can be, indeed is better off being, uncertain.

Knowledge without Authority

> *Knowledge is in the end based on acknowledgement. (OC 378)*

If neither experience (the world), nor certainty (logic), provide a ground for knowledge, what does? "Nothing!" answers Wittgenstein proudly; knowledge is groundless: "The difficulty is to realize the groundlessness of our believing" (cf. *OC* 253) (*OC* 166). Knowledge is not, therefore, helpless; like language, logic, and the world, it "authors" itself. Before one can truly make this claim, one must consider a third possibility: authority, God, or the laws, etc. Appeal to the Gods or other secular authorities to ground knowledge characterize earlier, but not forgotten, periods in the history of thought. External authority, external, that is, to what either our senses or reason reveal, has always served knowledge as a primitive line of defense, e.g., Question: "How do you know *p*?" Answer: "My mother told me!" Wittgenstein's job in convincing us of the groundlessness of belief would not be complete without tackling authority, both ecclesiastical and lay.

To eliminate the Gods, Wittgenstein turns, with some irony, to acknowledgement. "Acknowledgement" has a strange and complex grammar. The word derives from the Middle English word for admit or confess and so has a religious setting: the recognition that there is a God or, more specifically for Christianity, that Jesus Christ is the one true God. To acknowledge something is to own it as one's own, as in to own one's obligations or one's children or parents. It is to avow or assent to something as knowledge, to recognize it for what it is, despite, as the tone suggests, an initial impulse to disown it:

> And don't I know that there is no stairway in this house going six
> floors deep into the earth, even though I have never thought about it?
> (*OC* 398)
>
> But doesn't my drawing the consequences only show that I accept
> this hypothesis? (*OC* 399)

Own, it insists, what the theoretical skeptic asks you to doubt, but which you would never have thought of doubting!

While close to "belief" or "faith," "acknowledge" removes their blindfolds. "Faith" accepts a ground: the testimony of authority, even though it cannot prove it, and belief unwittingly champions one master or another. "Acknowledgement," on the other hand, indicates that while we have no certainty, we nevertheless know. Unlike the other states, acknowledgement is wrung from one like an apology at gunpoint. To disentangle himself from the grammar of faith, Wittgenstein uses "trust" instead of "faith":

> I really want to say that a language-game is only possible if one
> trusts something (I did not say "can trust something"). (*OC* 509)

In order to ask questions, one must accept something, trust something. However, this accepting is not based on testimony of any kind; it is not a decision, but something done without thought. He does not say "can trust something" because the question about whether one can trust something would raise an inappropriate investigation. One simply trusts:

> If I say "Of course I know that that's a towel" I am making an *utterance*. I have no thought of a verification. For me it is an immediate
> utterance.
>
> I don't think of past or future. (And of course it's the same for
> Moore, too.)
>
> It is just like directly taking hold of something, as I take hold of my
> towel without having doubts. (*OC* 510)

> And yet this direct taking-hold corresponds to a *sureness* not to a
> knowing.
>
> But don't I take hold of a thing's name like that, too? (*OC* 511)

Actions and assertions show that we are sure about something, not in the sense that we have tested it, but in the sense that we don't question it: "My *life* consists in my being content to accept many things" (*OC* 344). The first step is to acknowledge or trust this sureness, but not blindly.

Acknowledgement serves Wittgenstein not only as a psychological description of our mental attitude, but as a logical or grammatical point about the language-game involving knowledge:

> … I want to say: The physical game is just as certain as the arithmetical. But this can be misunderstood. My remark is a logical one, not a psychological one. (*OC* 447)

The certainty resides in the nature of the game (*OC* 457); knowledge does not rest on certainty as the last section argued, but rather presupposes it:

> But why *am* I so certain that this is my hand? Doesn't the whole language-game rest on this kind of certainty?
> Or: isn't this 'certainty' already presupposed in the language-game? Namely, by virtue of the fact that one is not playing the game, or is playing it wrong, if one does not recognize objects with certainty. (*OC* 446)

In order to play chess, for example, or even ask questions about chess, one must recognize chess as chess. The game does not rest on sureness as a ground, but presupposes it. As discussed earlier, the grammar of presupposition differs from that of ground in that there is nothing solid or firm about a presupposition. In fact, the playing of the game produces the certainty, rather than rests on it:

> I have arrived at the rock bottom of my convictions. And one might almost say that these foundation-walls are carried by the whole house (cf. *OC* 144). (*OC* 248)

If not a ground, something that underlies and supports, a presupposition that surrounds and squeezes: "Our talk gets its meaning from the rest of our proceedings" (*OC* 229). The context implies that to know one thing is to know another; one can't just know one thing: "I want to say: We use judgements as principles of judgement" (*OC* 124). Our beliefs form a system which once acknowledged make knowledge possible.

Philosophical recognition of this context and its function in making knowledge possible is owned by Wittgenstein when he argues that description must replace explanation: "At some point one has to pass from explanation to mere description" (*OC* 189). Mere description works because it makes the context of the disputed proposition perspicuous. To accept a description is to acknowledge that we know something. Explanation seeks what is hidden and assumes that we don't know what we think we know.

In undermining authority as a ground for knowledge, Wittgenstein finally undoes his earlier edict that one can only know what one can say. Like Augustine, whose name, interestingly, means authority, Wittgenstein was mesmerized by the hermeneutical dimensions of knowing, i.e., the facts that one knows more than one can say, that one needs to know something in order to know something else, and that one seems to know, but is not able to express, the things closest to one, like time and knowledge:

> Behind our thoughts, true and false, there is always to be found a dark background, which we are only later able to bring into the light and express as a thought. (*NB* 8.12.14)

> The proposition *expresses* what we do not know; but what I must know in order to be able to say it at all, I *shew in it*. (*NB* 24.10.14)

> …One has already to know (or be able to do) something in order to be capable of asking a thing's name. But what does one have to know? (*PI* 30)

> … We may say: only someone who already knows how to do something with it can significantly ask a name. (*PI* 31)

Language learning is particularly mysterious. How in the world do young children manage it?:

> … To understand a sentence means to understand language. To understand a language means to be master of a technique. (*PI* 199)

It is as if one already understands language before one learns it. This suggests that we do not build language from learning individual sentences or words, but in precisely the reverse manner. We have the whole, if you will, and then figure out the meaning of the components. No matter how much Wittgenstein wanted to disagree with Augustine about learning language, he too was struck by the fact that one seems already to know a language as one learns one:

> …And now, I think we can say: Augustine describes the learning of human language as if the child came into a strange country and did not understand the language of the country; that is, as if it already had a language, only not this one. Or again: as if the child could

already *think*, only not yet speak. And "think" would here mean something like "talk to itself." (*PI* 32)

In making this comment about Augustine, he is, of course, attacking Augustine's ostensive definition of language learning. However, for Wittgenstein too, one must presuppose something in order to begin to learn the language:

> Thus it seems to me that I have known something the whole time, and yet there is no meaning in saying so, in uttering this truth. (*OC* 466)

Like Meno, Wittgenstein questions how one ever learns anything new.

While Wittgenstein feels sure that one knows more than one can say, he has trouble in the early work justifying the phenomenon. As everyone knows, according to the *Tractatus,* what can be said can be thought; there is no gap between thinking and saying, and thus no room for knowing more than one can say. On the other hand, there must be a gap if we are going to accommodate the data to which Augustine, later in Wittgenstein's life, gives such elegant voice:

> …Augustine says in the *Confessions* "quid est ergo tempus? si nemo ex me quaerat scio; si quaerenti explicare velim, nescio". [What, there-fore, is time? If no one asks me, I know; if someone asks me to explain, I do not know.]—This could not be said about a question of natural science ("What is the specific gravity of hydrogen?" for instance). Something that we know when no one asks us, but no longer know when we are supposed to give an account of it, is something that we need to *remind* ourselves of. (And it is obviously something of which for some reason it is difficult to remind oneself.) (*PI* 89)

The claim that language shows more than it says offered Wittgenstein a way out. Unfortunately, one must know in silence:"What we cannot speak about we must pass over in silence" (*T* 7). In time, this solution becomes less than satisfactory; the problem was that the picture theory was illegitimate in the context of the arguments of the *Tractatus*. It really is logically impossible for language to show more than it can say. Besides, this was not the kind of answer Wittgenstein's new method of philosophizing desired. It explained the mysteries of knowing, rather than dissolved them.

The *Investigations'* approach, utilizing the ideas of family resemblance and the openness of concepts, creates a better atmosphere for tacit knowledge:

What does it mean to know what a game is? What does it mean, to know it and not be able to say it? Is this knowledge somehow equivalent to an unformulated definition? So that if it were formulated I should be able to recognize it as the expression of my knowledge? Isn't my knowledge, my concept of a game, completely expressed in the explanations that I could give? That is, in my describing examples of various kinds of game; shewing how all sorts of other games can be constructed on the analogy of these; saying that I should scarcely include this or this among games; and so on. (*PI* 75)

What I know and cannot formulate is not lacking formulation; rather, there is no concise formulation of certain concepts, and that includes more concepts than we know:

Compare *knowing* and *saying*:
> how many feet high Mont Blanc is—
> how the word "game" is used—
> how a clarinet sounds.

If you are surprised that one can know something and not be able to say it, you are perhaps thinking of a case like the first. Certainly not of one like the third. (*PI* 78)

In the first case, one can ultimately say what one knows; it just slipped one's mind. The second and third cases are different; there one's knowledge is more like Freud's unconscious knowledge which is demonstrated through action, but is never brought to consciousness. Definitional articulation is logically impossible in such cases, although not poetically so. One can point to what one knows using examples, go around the bush, but never, as Wittgenstein hoped, hit the nail on the head:

Describe the aroma of coffee.—Why can't it be done? Do we lack the words? And *for what* are words lacking?—But how do we get the idea that such a description must after all be possible? Have you ever felt the lack of such a description? Have you tried to describe the aroma and not succeeded?

I should like to say: "These notes say something glorious, but I do not know what. These notes are a powerful gesture, but I cannot put anything side by side with it that will serve as an explanation. A grave nod. James: "Our vocabulary is inadequate." Then why don't we introduce a new one? What would have to be the case for us to be able to? (*PI* 610)

The grave nod is satiric; it mocks the solemnity with which we greet failure. Our vocabulary is not inadequate, nor are such descriptions impossible. Rather, we know something in this case which does not have a linguistic expression. Not that it lacks one, we just know it a different way. Saying isn't the only criterion for knowing.[8] His style in the *Investigations,* as I have already discussed, reflects his recognition that almost everything important to philosophy is not susceptible to concise formulation. Thus, I take Wittgenstein's remark that in the end knowledge is based on acknowledgment as his own personal acknowledgment that we know more than we can say.

Wittgenstein's approach demystifies the hermeneutic circle. What I know amounts to what I have been taught:

Something must be taught us as a foundation. (*OC* 449)

What we are taught as children is the beginning; it cannot be explained further. As a child, one accepts with trust and sureness and does not question. It is what one treats as the unmoving foundation of a language-game and it is held in place by everything it makes possible. Nevertheless, some marvels remain.

The residue is most visible in Wittgenstein's wonderful remark about the teaching of "etcetera":

Then am I defining "order" and "rule" by means of "regularity"?—How do I explain the meaning of "regular", "uniform", "same" to anyone?—I shall explain these words to someone who, say, only speaks French by means of the corresponding French words. But if a person has not yet got the *concepts,* I shall teach **him** to use the words by means of *examples* and by *practice.*—And when I do this I do not communicate less to **him** than I know myself.

In the course of this teaching I shall shew **him** the same colours, the same lengths, the same shapes, I shall make **him** find them and produce them, and so on. I shall, for instance, get **him** to continue an ornamental pattern uniformly when told to do so.—And also to continue progressions. And so, for example, when given: ... to go on: ....
....

I do it, **he** does it after me; and I influence **him** by expressions of agreement, rejection, expectation, encouragement. I let **him** go his way, or hold **him** back; and so on.

Imagine witnessing such teaching. None of the words would be explained by means of itself; there would be no logical circle.

The expressions "and so on", "and so on ad infinitum" are also explained in this teaching. A gesture, among other things, might serve this purpose. The gesture that means "go on like this", or "and so on" has a function comparable to that of pointing to an object or a place.

We should distinguish between the "and so on" which is, and the "and so on" which is not an abbreviated notation. "And so on ad inf." is *not* such an abbreviation. The fact that we cannot write down all the digits of π is not a human shortcoming, as mathematicians sometimes think.

Teaching which is not meant to apply to anything but the examples given is different from that which '*points beyond*' them. (*PI* 208)

What can be more baffling than the learning of "etc.," especially distinguishing between two different "etceteras"? The one which is an abbreviation implies that one is to continue in the next case, as indicated; it has an end. The one which is not an abbreviation continues indefinitely; one must go on and on with no end. How do we learn this fine difference? "Etcetera" is essential to teaching; no teacher could exist without it. One teaches piecemeal and yet produces something more, something that points beyond the examples. Just as one gets people to continue in a certain fashion, one gets them to begin and to end. Indeed, if Wittgenstein were Bertrand Russell, he might have called "etcetera" the only mystery.

The complexities of learning easily lead to a doctrine of innate ideas or anamnesis or, as it is more currently known, to deep structure or genetic coding. The promise of Wittgenstein's approach is that it makes such scientific myths unnecessary. We can learn because we are never at the beginning. We must acknowledge the ways in which life forms us and how our ways of seeing teach us. There is no explaining how we are able to be taught; it is a bootstrap operation. One must resist the temptation to ask why or one will miss the ways in which it actually happens. Not only do we get people to understand "etc.," but we get them to distinguish between the "etc." that means *ad infinitum* of the same and the one that means *ad infinitum* of the different. One must acknowledge that we use judgments as principles of judgments, that we cannot just know one thing, that in the end there is no ground: not God, not consciousness, not science. One need not choose between Plato's blank tablet or science/religion's formed template; rather, one must seek new options.

Thus, I take Wittgenstein's remark that in the end knowledge is based on acknowledgment as his own acknowledgment that we know things we cannot say and that ultimately there is no way of explaining this. All we can look to is the knowledge embedded in a form of life or way of seeing: "What has to be accepted, the given, is—so one could say—*forms of life*" (*PI* pg. 226). To trust, to acknowledge, dissolves philosophical problems and frees us from debilitating ways of seeing. Trust is not an argument for the status quo, nor does it mean that things will never change or ought not to change. It is the path to change. With philosophical investigation, now and then the foundation walls come into view as a corrective to wild theorizing; on the other hand, now and then our form of life requires some renovating. Despite the difficulties of changing a way of seeing, it can be done, has been done, and will be done. Wittgenstein was committed to change, only it had to be done from within to be successful. One could not create change by fiat; one first had to clear a path for change. Only in this way could one ensure a transformation of one's vision. Otherwise, philosophy was an idling game.

For Wittgenstein, nothing authorizes knowledge other than our acknowledgment that it is knowledge. The task of the philosopher, the lover of wisdom, is to recognize that she knows more than she thinks she knows. Suspicion breeds theory and the dangers of theory should be obvious; witness Plato's appeal to transmigration of souls: we know what we know because we learned it in another form of life, or Kant's appeal to consciousness: we know what we know because of the structure of our minds. Philosophers have no business fashioning such cock-a-mamie, pseudo-scientific stories; they fool no one, not even themselves, even through they may temporarily gather followers. Instead, philosophers must illuminate the tangled pathways of a way of seeing so as to make perspicuous the what and the how of knowing. Only then can one truly know thyself, etc.

Notes

Preface

1. Stephen Hilmy notes that this remark was made six weeks before Wittgenstein's death *(The Later Wittgenstein: The Emergence of a New Philosophical Method* [Oxford: Basil Blackwell, 1987], 15). Taking "notes" very seriously, Hilmy sees this remark as Wittgenstein's indirect invitation to study his Nachlass in order to understand his work, a task Hilmy conveniently undertakes. While this interpretation is unnecessary and perhaps self-serving, it is harmless. Basically, I agree with Hilmy that reading the Nachlass is beneficial for understanding Wittgenstein; one can't go wrong. In this case, for example, Hilmy uses the Nachlass to quote two further expressions of Wittgenstein's tendency to work the same point over and over again: "paint the same face again and again" or "puzzle again and again over the same things" (9).

2. Rush Rhees, ed. *Ludwig Wittgenstein: Personal Recollections,* (New Jersey: Roman and Littlefield, 1981), pg. 186.

3. At first I was reluctant to use the word "obsess" even though it seemed the perfect concept. Wittgenstein, the man, already attracts too much attention away from his work. But Alice Ambrose's free use of the concept in her notes from the 1934–35 lectures encouraged me to believe that there was no better substitute. Philosophy puzzles in the same way as philosophical problems (*WLAA* 98, 107–109). Obsessions can be intellectual and social, rather than just psychosexual.

4. As is well known, Wittgenstein counselled his students to leave philosophy and "do something useful."

5. "Conversations with Wittgenstein," M.O'C. Drury, *Ludwig Wittgenstein: Personal Recollections*, ed. Rush Rhees, pp. 125–26.

6. Hilmy argues adamantly against the importance of Wittgenstein's style. For him, Wittgenstein's style is "incidental" to the latter's method or results (1987, pp. 15–16). I shall argue that Hilmy is wrong on this point. Only a philosopher's continuing distrust of rhetoric could account for such an egregious error in such an otherwise splendid book. Indeed, mastering Wittgenstein's style is even more important for understanding his work than reading the *Nachlass.* (Wittgenstein literally invented two different styles: one for the early work and one for the later. However, since only his later work embodies his final vision for philosophy, I shall speak of his style in the singular.)

7. Hilmy gives much depth to Wittgenstein's "struggle" with science

and philosophy. His was an active, passionate crusade, not a neutral or merely theoretical one (*The Later Wittgenstein*, 190 ff).

8. K.T. Fann, *Wittgenstein's Conception of Philosophy* (Berkeley: Univ. of California Press, 1969) and James F. Peterman, *Philosophy as Therapy* (New York: SUNY Press, 1992) are the two monographs on Wittgenstein's conception of philosophy. Peter Hacker's *Insight and Illusion* (Oxford: Oxford Univ. Press, 1972) is, as he himself says, only secondarily about Wittgenstein's conception of philosophy. Additionally, Morris Lazerowitz has written on the subject: "Wittgenstein on the Nature of Philosophy," *Ludwig Wittgenstein: The Man and His Philosophy*, ed. K.T. Fann (New York: Dell Publishing, 1967), pp. 131–48; and Morris Lazerowitz and Alice Ambrose, *Essays on the Unknown Wittgenstein* (Buffalo: Prometheus Books, 1984) as well as Anthony Kenny, "Wittgenstein on the Nature of Philosophy," *The Legacy of Wittgenstein* (Oxford: Basil Blackwell, 1984). See also, Cora Diamond, *The Realistic Spirit* (Cambridge: MIT Press, 1991); Stephen Hilmy, *The Later Wittgenstein: The Emergence of a New Philosophical Method* (Oxford: Basil Blackwell, 1987), and B.R. Tilghman, *Wittgenstein, Ethics and Aesthetics*, (Albany: SUNY Press, 1991).

9. Hilmy offers another image of crowding from the *Nachlass*; "(My ideas shove themselves pell-mell, the one drives out the other, pushes itself forward, etc. like so many crabs in a basin)" (*The Later Wittgenstein*, 146).

Introduction

1. Friedrich Waismann, "How I See Philosophy." *Logical Positivism*, ed. A. J. Ayer (New York: The Free Press, 1959), pp. 374–75.

2. He had a similar experience with the *Tractatus*; positivists claimed him as their own because they misunderstood his

stance against metaphysics, ethics, and philosophy.

3. Unfortunately, I can no longer find the reference to Rorty's use of this expression.

4. See my "Map of the *Philosophical Investigations*," *Philosophical Investigations* I, 1 (Winter, 1978).

5. As a rule, Wittgenstein distinguishes philosophical theories from scientific ones. In the following passage, however, he speaks as if even scientific theories are best seen in terms of a way of seeing: "What a Copernican or a Darwin really achieved was not the discovery of a true theory but of a fertile new point of view," (*C V*, pg.18). And there are other such remarks. Since there are so few passages that collapse the distinction he usually maintained between science and philosophy, it would be rash to conclude that even science was essentially about new ways of seeing for Wittgenstein. Yet the issue is controversial.

6. For an odd discussion of these remarks, see Andres Kemmerling, "The Visual Room," *Wittgenstein's Philosophical Investigations: Text and Context*, eds. Robert L. Arrington and Hans-Johann Glock, (London: Routledge, 1991), pp. 150–75.

7. J.C. Nyíri, "Wittgenstein's Later Work in relation to Conservatism," *Wittgenstein and his Times*, ed. Brian McGuinness (Chicago: Univ. of Chicago Press, 1982), pp. 44–69. While other aspects of Wittgenstein's thought might be interpreted as conservative, I do not think that this passage adds any fuel to that interpretation.

8. Thomas Kuhn, *The Structure of Scientific Revolutions* (Chicago: Chicago Univ. Press, 1962).

9. Waismann began his major work, *Principles of Linguistic Philosophy* (New York, 1965), originally called *Logik, Sprache, Philosophie*, in the late 1920s. It was intended as a popular exposition of the *Tractatus*. Under pressure from Wittgenstein, who by that time had become dissatisfied with his early work,

Waismann withdrew the book on the eve of publication. He continued to work on the manuscript, again collaborating with Wittgenstein, hoping to disseminate the later ideas. This plan also failed and Waismann abandoned his project of negotiating the world for Wittgenstein. The final version of Waismann's book, published posthumously, contains his own thoughts on many of the problems that he had first considered as a student of Wittgenstein. For a more complete chronicle of their difficult relationship see, *Ludwig Wittgenstein and the Vienna Circle*, ed. B.F. McGuinness (Oxford: Basil Blackwell, 1979), pg. 11–31.

10. As usual, the roots of Wittgenstein's later thought begins in the earlier work. In his belief that "The world of the happy man is a different one from that of the unhappy man" (*T* 6.43), we can see the beginnings of his ideas about the importance of a way of seeing.

11. In the *Apology*, Socrates is referred to as a "gad-fly" or, in some translations, as a "stinging fly," Μύωπότ Τϊνος." Given Wittgenstein's general attack on Socratic positions in the *Investigations*, it is plausible to claim that Socrates is Wittgen-stein's paradigm fly caught in a fly-bottle. In fact the root meaning of Μύωψ is short-sighted. Perhaps Wittgenstein, like Plato, is faulting Socrates for his myopia. Monk also reports Wittgenstein as saying, "that his method could be summed up by saying that it was the exact opposite of that of Socrates." (Ludwig Wittgenstein: *The Duty of Genius* [New York; Macmillan, 1990] pg. 339.)

12. *Ludwig Wittgenstein: Personal Recollections*, ed. Rush Rhees, (Roman and Littlefield, 1981), pg. 131.

13. Richard Rorty also notes Wittgenstein's penchant for satire and irony; *see Philosophy and the Mirror of Nature* (New Jersey: Princeton Univ. Press, 1979), pg. 369, and *Consequences of Pragmatism*

(Minneapolis: Univ. of Minnesota Press, 1982), pg. 34.

14. Rhees, *Ludwig Wittgenstein: Personal Recollections,* pg. 173.

15. Cora Diamond, in her work *The Realistic Spirit: Wittgenstein, Philosophy, and the Mind* (Cambridge: MIT Press, 1991), argues strongly for Wittgenstein's continuing commitment to realism. She correctly shows that his rejection of the *Tractatus* did not entail a similar rejection of realism; however, to disassociate Wittgenstein from standard "theories" of realism, she speaks carefully throughout of a "realistic spirit."

16. Stanley Cavell, *Must We Mean What We Say* (Cambridge: Cambridge Univ. Press, 1978), pg. 86.

17. M. O'C Drury quotes another passage in this vein: "But remember that Christianity is not a matter of saying a lot of prayers; in fact we are told not to do that. If you and I are to live religious lives, it mustn't be that we talk a lot about religion, but that our manner of life is different. It is my belief that only if you try to be helpful to other people will you in the end find you way to God" (*Ludwig Wittgenstein: Personal Recollections*, pg. 129).

18. Gertrude Stein, "Composition as Explanation," *Gertrude Stein: Writings and Lectures 1909-1945*, ed. Patricia Meyerowitz (Penguin, 1967), pg. 21. The essay was first delivered as a lecture in Cambridge and Oxford in 1926. I find many correspondences between the two "Steins": Gertrude spoke in tautologies as well and more generally stretched language to its limits. Both liked to answer a question with another question even more perplexing:

> When the answer cannot be put into words, neither can the question be put into words.
>
> The riddle does not exist....
>
> (*T* 6.5)

Also Stein, like Wittgenstein, realized that description and arrangement can function as an explanation. Nothing more is needed.

19. Ray Monk, in his superb biography *Ludwig Wittgenstein: The Duty of Genius* (New York: Macmillan, 1990), agrees with me: "Wittgenstein's remark about philosophy—that it 'leaves everything as it is'—is often quoted. But it is less often realized that, in seeking to change nothing but the way we look at things, Wittgenstein was attempting to change *everything*," (pg. 533).

Part One: A Way of Seeing
Chapter 1: Commanding a Clear View

1. Other translations are "synoptic view" (*Z* 464), "bird's-eye-view" (*PR* I, 1), and "surveyable" (*RFM* II, 43). No English words translate the German well.

2. Monk believes that Wittgentstein borrowed the concept of an *Übersehen* from Goethe (*Ludwig Wittgenstein: The Duty of Genius*, pp. 510–12). He gives an interesting context for the development of this idea.

3. Martin Heidegger, *An Introduction to Metaphysics*, (New York, Doubleday, 1959).

4. Ray Monk traces Wittgenstein's desire for this Spinozist view of the whole to Schopenhauer who stresses the non-representational character of its gaze (*Ludwig Wittgenstein: The Duty of Genius*, 143).

5. The passage where Wittgenstein compares the view from eternity to an artistic one says that "thought" can give such a view. The remark was written in 1930 and suggests that Wittgenstein had changed his mind about the ability of thinking to attain such a view. I think he did. When he finally made it possible to know more than one can say, thought had more freedom than it did in the *Tractatus*.

6. "I have therefore found it necessary to deny knowledge to make room for *faith*" (*Critique of Pure Reason*, trans. Norman Kemp Smith (London: Macmillan, 1933), pg. 29).

7. In his book *Wittgenstein and Metaphor* (Washington: Univ. Press of America, 1981), Jerry Gill notes that spatial, visual, and static metaphors dominate the *Tractatus* and are replaced by dynamic, kinesthetic ones in the *Investigations* (pp. 150–55).

8. Norman Malcolm, in his book *Nothing is Hidden* (New York: Basil Blackwell, 1986), uses the inner/outer conflict to elaborate Wittgenstein's criticisms of his earlier work.

9. *See* Frank Cioffi, "Wittgenstein and the Fire-festivals," *Perspectives on the Philosophy of Wittgenstein* (Cambridge: MIT Press, 1981), pp. 212–38.

10. Monk traces Wittgenstein's idea that philosophy ought to dissolve problems to Heinrich Hertz (*Ludwig Wittgenstien: The Duty of Genius*, pg. 446).

11. Clifford Geertz sees no opposition between the two: "There is no opposition between general theoretical understanding and circumstantial understanding, between synoptic vision and a fine eye for detail. It is, in fact, by its power to draw general propositions out of particular phenomena that a scientific theory—indeed, science itself-is to be judged" (*Interpretation of Cultures*, (Basic Books, 1977), pg. 51).

12. *See* Rush Rhees, "Wittgenstein on Language and Ritual," *Wittgenstein and his Times* ed. Brian McGuinness, (Chicago: Univ. of Chicago Press, 1982), pp. 69–108.

13. I take the concept of a form of life to be synonymous with a *Weltbild*. The latter provides a more subjective way of speaking of what the former hopes to name more objectively. Yet, the dimension "subjective/objective" is a poor way of trying to name their difference. For all practical purposes, they are interchangable.

Chapter 2: Don't Think, Look!

1. In one remark made in 1946, he speaks of *die Denkweise* :

   Getting hold of the difficulty deep down is what is hard.

Because if it is grasped near the surface it simply remains the difficulty it was. It has to be pulled out by the roots; and that involves our beginning to think about these things in a new way. The change is as decisive as, for example, that from the alchemical to the chemical way of thinking. The new way of thinking (Denkweise) is what is so hard to establish.

Once the new way of thinking has been established, the old problems vanish; indeed they become hard to recapture. For they go with our way of expressing ourselves and, if we clothe ourselves in a new form of expression the old problems are discarded along with the old garment. (*CV* pg. 48)

Also, while other specific remarks do not immediately come to mind, I remember him sometimes speaking of a way of thinking. Yet I still think that there is an important and interesting distinction to be made. In the great majority of remarks, he speaks of a way of seeing, especially in the *Investigations* (*PI* 597 is an exception) and he very consciously switches to "a way of acting" in *On Certainty*. Accordingly, I was surprised to see Stephen Hilmy constantly referring to Wittgenstein's new way of thinking and generally conflating "a new method of doing philosophy" with "a new method of thinking" (*The Later Wittgenstien*, pg. 6). Indeed, Hilmy makes no mention at all of "a way of seeing" even though Wittgenstein carefully writes, "*die Art, wie wir dies Dinge sehen*" (*PI* 122). Even if Hilmy were to subsequently show that Wittgenstein was not consistent in his "form of expression," I think the distinction worth noting because of the handle it provides for exploring Wittgenstein's ideas on the relation between seeing, thinking, and acting. And if he did not manage to always fully clothe himself in the appropriate form of expression, I

think it is because the temptation to speak of thinking goes deep, even for Wittgenstein.

2. Wittgenstein once told M. O'C Drury that he thought of using King Lear's reprimand, "I'll teach you differences," as a motto for the *Investigations* (Rhees, *Ludwig Wittgenstien: Personal Recordings*, pg. 171). Monk repeats this comment and remarks on Wittgenstein's concern with differences: "His concern was to stress life's irreducible variety. The pleasure he derived from walking in the Zoological Gardens had much to do with his admiration for the immense variety of flowers, shrubs and trees and the multitude of different species of birds, reptiles and animals. A theory which attempted to impose a single scheme upon all this diversity was, predictably, anathema to him. Darwin had to be wrong: his theory 'hasn't the necessary multiplicity'" (*Ludwig Wittgenstien: The Duty of Genius*, pg. 537). Monk also relates Wittgenstein's desire to use Butler's phrase: "'Everything is what it is, and not another thing' as a motto for *Philosophical Investigations*" (pg. 451).

3. I believe things changed for Wittgenstein as he worked with kids in the years 1921–1929. His reading of *Sprache theorie* (1934), by Charlotte and Karl Bühler, which contained the ideas of Lev Vygotsky, also helped reorient him.

4. *See* my, "Wittgenstein and Caligari," *Philosophical Forum*, Boston 4 (Winter 1972–73), pp. 186–98 which details Wittgenstein's involvement with finding *Das Wesen* or the inner being of things.

Part Two: Changing a Way of Seeing
Chapter 3: Saying the Impossible

1. Rush Rhees, *Ludwig Wittgenstein: Personal Recollections*, pg. 173.
2. Paul Englemann in his *Letters from Ludwig Wittgenstein with a Memoir*, trans. L. Furtmüller, ed. B.F. McGuinness

(Oxford: Basil Blackwell, 1967) tells how during Wittgenstein's first stay in Olmutz, he suffered from a minor speech defect: "he used to struggle for words, especially when he was trying hard to formulate a proposition" (14). Others who knew him in England are always telling of his painful attempts to express himself. Transcripts of his classes also confirm his personal problems with expression.

3. See my "The Significance of Style," *The Journal of Aesthetics and Art Criticism,* xxxviii 3 (Spring, 1979), pg. 315–324 where I argue that style is primarily a function of the interweaving of the what and the how. Style occurs when one's prose enacts one's thoughts. See also the works of Berel Lang who pioneered the exploration of style in philosophy, e.g., *Philosophical Style: An Anthology about the Writing and Reading of Philosophy* (Chicago: Nelson-Hall, 1980).

4. Wittgenstein is not the only one to take this step. Derrida, Heidegger, and all of twentieth-century philosophy affirms its connections to writing and literature. Moreover, most of these thinkers also try to embody their beliefs in their prose style. Yet, because Wittgenstein has been claimed by those who would still like to maintain a distinction between logic and rhetoric, his contributions to the debate and the importance of his own philosophical styles have been missed.

5. Gershon Weiler claims that Wittgenstein arrived at the idea of a "critique of language" as well as the metaphor of a language ladder which must be destroyed once we have climbed it from Mauthner ("On Fritz Mauthner's Critique of Language," *Mind,* LXVII (1958), pp. 80–87. *See also* Gershon Weiler, *Mauthner's Critique of Language,* (Cambridge: Cambridge University Press, 1979). Wittgenstein's dedication to Kraus is well-known. He was never without a copy of *Die Fackel,* the magazine Kraus edited for most of his life. In a letter of October 25, 1918,

Wittgenstein wrote of his attempt to have the *Tractatus* published in *Die Fackel:* "But I would dearly like to know what Kraus said about it…. Perhaps Loos knows something about it" (Paul Englemann, *Letters from Ludwig Wittgenstein With a Memoir,* pg. 15).

6. Unlike most contemporary linguists, Wittgenstein considers language a "pictorial" mode of expression (see section *T* 4.01–4.016). I shall say more about this important point later.

7. Immanuel Kant, *Critique of Pure Reason,* trans. Norman Kemp Smith (London: MacMillan, 1933). All further references to this text will appear in my text as indicated.

8. Jaakko Hintikka, "Kant on the Mathematical Method," *Kant's Philosophy of Mathemtatics,* ed. Carl J. Posy (The Netherlands: Kluwer Academic Publishers, 1992), pp. 28–29. I was fascinated to recently read these pieces by Hintikka on Kant's method (*See also* Kant's Transcendental Method and his Theory of Mathematics in the same volume, pp. 341–59. The one place where I disagree with Hintikka's reading of Kant is in his belief that Kant confines knowledge of individuals to perception (or acquaintance): "To think of all knowledge of individual objects as being due to perception is to succumb to a temptation which for Kant may have been very real but which it is important to get rid of" (pg. 39). I think recognizing that non-empirical intuitions come from schemata of the imagination helps to see how Kant avoids this error. The form of perception is not itself a perception. I believe Hintikka makes the same mistake with Wittgenstein since he thinks that Wittgenstein shared with Russell an ultimate belief in knowledge by acquaintance ("Wittgenstein's Picture Theory," *Artifacts, Representation and Social Practice,* eds., C.C. Gould and R.S. Cohen (Netherlands: Kluwer Academic Publishers, 1994), pg. 246.

9 Plato, "Republic," *The Collected Dialogues of Plato*, eds. Edith Hamilton and Huntington Cairns. (New York: Random House, 1961), Book VI, pp. 509–11.

10. Heinrich Hertz, *The Principles of Mechanics* (New York: Macmillan, 1956), pg. 1.

11. After finishing the *Tractatus* in the trenches of World War I, Wittgenstein abandons philosophy and spends the next ten years being a schoolteacher, gardener, and would-be monk. He had said all that philosophy could say; there was nothing left but silence.

12. The distinction between "langue" and "parole" comes from Ferdinand de Saussure, *Course in General Linguistics*, ed. Charles Bally, et al., trans. Wade Basken (New York, McGraw-Hill, 1966), pp. 7–11. For Saussure, "langue" signifies the underlying structure, "a system of distinct signs corresponding to distinct ideas" (pg. 10), while "parole" means human speech in all its physiological and psychological trappings.

13. Roman Jakobson, "Linguistics and Poetics," *The Structuralists from Marx to Lévi-Strauss*, eds. Richard and Ferdinand De George (New York: Anchor Books, 1972), pp. 85–122.

14. Engelmann, *Letters from Wittgenstein*, pg. 7. Engelmann's own reaction to Uhland's poem is instructive: "Uhland's poem came to play a part in my life. What I had learned before as a reader of Karl Kraus was here for the first time brought home to me by direct experience: the fact that poetry can produce a profound artistic effect *beyond* (but never without) the immediate effect of its language" (pg. 84). Englemann also indirectly speaks of Wittgenstein's fascination with poetry when he notes that the latter never wrote a poem, "not even at the age when nearly all intellectualy interested young people of his generation tended to try their hand at it" (pg. 89).

15. Engelmann, *Letters to Wittgenstein*, 143.

16. Wilma Abeles Iggers, *Karl Kraus:*

A Viennese Critic of the Twentieth Century (The Hague, 1967), pg. 25. Quoted from Karl Kraus, *Sprücke und Widersprücke* (1909).

Chapter 4: Saying the Obvious

1. Derrida is famous for the expression "always already." Yet it is appropriate to distinguish Wittgenstein from others in his generation who had come upon the hermeneutical problem. Knowing more than one can say is no mystery, no hermeneutic conundrum, but an ordinary, everyday experience, like not being able to pick up more than one can hold. In learning a language, one learns more than one can say.

2. Cora Diamond speaks passionately against philosophy as theory or the laying down of any requirements. She takes this to be Wittgenstein's central message (1991, p. 28).

3. Just as Wittgenstein distinguished himself from behaviorism and pragmatism, it is important to distinguish him from linguistic relativism like that expressed by Benjamin Lee Whorf. As usual, the difference is subtle. While Wittgenstein would agree with the basic sentiment expressed by Whorf, namely, that language constructs how we see things, he would not agree with the way Whorf says it or his intentions in saying such things. Whorf, like Moore, has a philosophical hobby-horse to ride. For Wittgenstein the connection between language and the world is so tight that we can not isolate the two variables in order to have a theory.

4. J. L. Austin, *How to do Things with Words*, ed. J. O. Urmson (New York: Oxford Univ. Press, 1970).

5. Jarman did a film on Wittgenstein for the BBC. *Wittgenstein: The Terry Eagleton Script, The Derek Jarman Film* (London: British Film Institute, 1993) contains a record of the scripts and the making of the film.

6. I read somewhere that Wittgenstein

hated his students to take notes while he was talking, but I can no longer find the reference. Like remarks, notes were not for remembering, but for working through something.

Part Three: Wittgenstein's Way of Seeing
Chapter 5: Three Ideas about Reality

1. While Wittgenstein never actually says that the world takes care of itself, I have taken the liberty of extending his notion of self-care to the world since everything he says about the world implies its autonomy.

2. It is difficult to find the proper concept here. Meaning is a product of language and truth one of logic; but what does the world produce? "Sense" is the closest product, although it collapses too many different notions. I am thinking of sense in terms of ordered whole, structure, value, not the meaning of an individual proposition, but the meaning of the whole. The "Why is there something, rather than nothing?" question again. Since philosophy has long been the discourse that tried to explain the sense of the world, one might even add philosophy to the list of things that the autonomy of the world produces.

3. Hintikka in "Wittgenstein's Picture Theory," *Artifacts, Representations and Social Practice,* eds. C. C. Gould and R. S. Cohen. (Kluwer Academic Publishers-Netherlands, 1994) makes this same point while explaining the theses which underlie the picture theory of meaning:

    The thesis that each simple name shares the same form as the object it represents presupposes a more general idea. It presupposes that a language with its objects is a part of the world. More-over, each simple name is a member of the same facet of the world as its object (233).

4. The *Tractatus* is often criticized for failing to identify any simples, any objects; however, once one understands the picture theory or its *raison d'etre,* such a criticism self-destructs.

5. *The Logical Structure of the World,* trans. Rolf A. George (Berkeley: University of California Press, 1969), pg. 99. Although Carnap did not publish this work until 1928, he wrote it between 1922 and 1925, closer to the time of Wittgenstein's *Tractatus.*

6. Carnap, *The Logical Structure of the World,* pg. 11.

7. Carnap, *The Logical Structure of the World,* pg. 25.

8. Douglas Hofstadter's, *Godel Escher Bach* (New York: Vintage Books, 1980) depends on this same line of reasoning. Formalism, in general, hopes that all can be deduced from syntax.

9. Hintikka makes a nice distinction between mirroring and picturing: "When Wittgenstein is concerned with the way one single proposition represents a state of affairs by means of its form he speaks of a picture and of picturing distinction between mirroring and picturing *Bild* or (*abbildung*) and *abbilden.* When he is concerned with the way the totality of possible elementary propositions reflects the totality of possible combinations of objects, he typically speaks of a mirror and of mirroring, *Spiegel* or (*spiegelbild*) and *gespiegeln*…."("Wittgenstein's Picture Theory," *Artifacts, Representation and Social Practice,* pg. 231).

10. Carnap, *Logical Structure of the World,* pg. 255.

11. Carnap, *Logical Structure of the World,* pg. 101.

12. Carnap, *Logical Structure of the World,* pg. 261.

13. Carnap, *Logical Structure of the World,* pg. 107.

14. In response to a comment by M. O'C. Drury, to the effect that Wittgenstein was concerned with Kant's problem of how synthetic *a priori* positions are possible, he says:

Yes, you could say that. I am concerned with the synthetic a priori. When you have thought for some time about a problem of your own, you may come to see that is is closely related to what has been discussed before, only you will want to present the problem in a different way… (pg. 133).

15. Wittgenstein's comment in *T* 2.025 "It substance is form and content," seems to contradict the claim that substance can only determine a form. Since form is defined as the possibility of structure (*T* 2.033), he is only anticipating the fact that where there is form there is content, structure. Theoretically, he can say, substance is form and content.

16. Peter Hacker in *Insight and Illusion* (Oxford, 1972) maintains that Wittgenstein's equations between the world and life, humans and the microcosm, I and my world, commit him to a doctrine of the transcendental ideality of space and time (pg. 76). I hope that my explanation of these equations shows that Wittgenstein manages these reductions without the apparatus of Transcendental Idealism.

17. *Plato: Collected Dialogues,* eds. Hamilton and Cairns (Princeton: Random House), pg. 251d–262d.

18. In my dissertation, I wrote about Wittgenstein's linguistic idealism and compared him to Cassirer.

19. Arthur Danto, *Analytic Philosophy of Knowledge,* (Cambridge: Harvard University Press, 1968), pg. 242.

20. Arthur Danto, *Analytic Philosophy of Knowledge,* pg. 240.

Chapter 6: Three Ideas about Knowledge

1. I elaborated at greater length on the idea of losing a faultlessly played game in an unpublished paper, "Can One Play a Faultless Game?"

2. See my "Map of the *Philosophical Investigations.*"

3. Knowing the use of a word does not just mean knowing its syntactic use, but its semantic use as well.

4. See Nyíri, "Wittgenstein;s later Work."

5. Lev Vygotsky, *Thought and Language,* trans. and ed. Alex Kozulin, (Cambridge: MIT Press, 1986).

6. *See* Piaget, *The Language and Thought of the Child,* (Harcourt, Brace, and Co., 1926).

7. Charles Sanders Peirce, *Philosophical Writings of Charles Sanders Peirce,* ed. Justus Buchler, (New York: Dover, 1955).

8. I was especially relieved to learn that it is possible to know more than one can say. Leo Kraft would insist, in his sight-singing classes, that if you knew the tune you could sing it. I couldn't; it seemed to me I could hear it perfectly, but because of the terrors of public singing, I could not produce it.

Bibliography

Albritton, Rogers. "On Wittgenstein's Use of the Term *Criterion*," *Wittgenstein: The Philosophical Investigations*. Ed. George Pitcher. Garden City, NY: Anchor-Doubleday, 1966. 231–50.

Anscombe, G. E. M. *An Introduction to Wittgenstein's Tractatus*. 1959. London: Hutchinson University Library, 1967.

—. *Intention*. 2nd ed. Oxford: Basil Blackwell, 1963.

Apel, Karl-Otto. *Analytic Philosophy of Language and the Geisteswissenschaften*. Dordrecht, Neth: Reidel, 1967.

Ayer, A. J., ed. *The Revolution in Philosophy*. London: Macmillan, 1956.

—, ed. *Logical Positivism*. 1959. New York: Free Press, 1966.

—. *Wittgenstein*. New York: Random House, 1985.

Arrington, Robert T. and Hans-Johann Glock, eds. *Wittgenstein's Philosophical Investigations*. London: Routledge, 1991.

Bartley, William Warren III. *Wittgenstein*. Philadelphia: Lippincott, 1973.

Black, Max. *A Companion to Wittgenstein's Tractatus*. Ithaca, NY: Cornell Univ. Press, 1964.

—. "Language and Reality." *The Linguistic Turn*. Ed. Richard Rorty. Chicago: Univ. of Chicago Press, 1967. 331–39.

Block, Irving, ed. *Perspectives on the Philosophy of Wittgenstein*. Cambridge: MIT, 1981.

Bloor, David. *Wittgenstein: A Social Theory of Knowledge*. New York: Columbia Univ. Press, 1983.

Brand, Gerd. *The Essential Wittgenstein*. 1975. Trans. Robert E. Innis. New York: Basic, 1979.

Britton, Karl. "Recollections of Ludwig Wittgenstein." *Cambridge Journal* 7 (1954): 707–715.

Canfield, John V. *Wittgenstein: Language and World*. Amherst: Univ. of Massachusetts Press, 1981.

Canfield, John V., and Stuart G. Shanker, eds. *Wittgenstein's Intentions*. New York: Garland, 1993.

Carnap, Rudolf. *The Logical Structure of the World & Pseudoproblems in Philosophy*. Trans. Rolf A. George. Berkeley: Univ. of California Press, 1969.

Cassirer, Ernst. *Language and Myth*. 1946. Trans. Susanne K. Langer. New York: Dover, 1953.

—. *Philosophy of Symbolic Forms*. Trans. Ralph Manheim. 3 vols. New Haven: Yale Univ. Press, 1953-57.

—. *The Logic of the Humanities*. 1942. Trans. Clarence Smith Howe. New Haven: Yale Univ. Press, 1961.

Cavell, Stanley. "Existentialism and Analytic

Philosophy." *Daedalus* 93 (Summer 1964): 946–74.

—. "The Availability of Wittgenstein's Later Philosophy." *Wittgenstein: The Philosophical Investigations*. Ed. George Pitcher. Garden City, NY: Anchor-Doubleday, 1966. 151–185.

—. "Austin at Criticism." *The Linguistic Turn*. Ed. Richard Rorty. Chicago: Univ. of Chicago Press, 1967. 250-260.

—. *Must We Mean What We Say?* 1969. New York: Cambridge Univ. Press, 1976.

—. *The Claim of Reason: Wittgenstein, Skepticism, Morality, and Tragedy*. 1979. Oxford: Oxford Univ. Press, 1982.

Conway, Gertrude D. *Wittgenstein on Foundations*. Atlantic Highlands, NJ: Humanities, 1989.

Coope, Christopher, et al. *A Wittgenstein Workbook*. Berkeley: Univ. of California Press, 1970.

Copi, I. M., and R. W. Beard, eds. *Essays on Wittgenstein's Tractatus*. New York: Macmillan, 1966.

Cornman, James W. "Language and Ontology." *The Linguistic Turn*. Ed. Richard Rorty. Chicago: Univ. of Chicago Press, 1967. 160-167.

Danto, Arthur. *Analytical Philosophy of Knowledge*. London: Cambridge Univ. Press, 1968.

De George, Richard T. and Fernande M. De George, eds. *The Structuralists: From Marx to Lévi-Strauss*. Garden City, NY: Anchor-Doubleday, 1972.

De Mauro, Tullio. *Ludwig Wittgenstein: His Place in the Development of Semantics*. Dordrecht, Holland: Reidel Publishing, 1967.

Diamond, Cora. *The Realistic Spirit: Wittgenstien, Philosophy, and the Mind*. Cambridge: MIT, 1991.

Dummett, Michael. "Wittgenstein's Philosophy of Mathematics." *Wittgenstein: The Philosophical Investigations*. Ed. George Pitcher. Garden City, NY: Anchor-

Doubleday, 1966. 420–47.

Engel, S. Morris. *Wittgenstein's Doctrine of the Tyranny of Language*. The Hague: Martinus Nijhoff, 1971.

Engelmann, Paul. *Letters from Wittgenstein: With a Memoir*. Trans. L. Furtmüller. Oxford: Basil Blackwell, 1967.

Fann, K. T., ed. *Ludwig Wittgenstein: The Man and His Philosophy*. New York: Delta-Dell, 1967.

—. *Wittgenstein's Conception of Philosophy*. Berkeley: Univ. of California Press, 1969.

Favrholdt, David. *An Interpretation and Critique of Wittgenstein's Tractatus*. Copenhagen: Munkagaard, 1964.

Field, Frank. *The Last Days of Mankind: Karl Kraus and His Vienna*. London: Macmillan, 1967.

Findlay, J. N. *Wittgenstein: A Critique*. Ed. Ted Honderich. London: Routledge & Kegan Paul, 1984.

Frege, Gottlob. "The Thought: A Logical Inquiry." *Mind* LXV 259 (July 1956): 289–311.

Gawronsky, Dimitry. "Cassirer: His Life and His Work." *The Philosophy of Ernst Cassirer*. Ed. Paul A. Schlipp. New York: Tudor, 1958. 3–37.

Gellner, Ernst. *Words and Things*. 1959. Baltimore: Pelican-Penguin, 1968.

Genova, Judith. "Wittgenstein and Caligari." *Philosophical Forum* IV #2 (Winter 1972–73): 186–98.

—. "A Map of the *Philosophical Investigations*." *Philosophical Investigations* I #1 (Winter 1978): 41–56.

—. "Philosophy and the Consideration of Other-Worldly Possibilities." *Proceedings of the Second International Wittgenstein Symposium*. Ed. Hübner. (*Wein* 1978): 398–402.

—. "The Significance of Style." *Journal of Aesthetics and Art Criticism* 37 #3 (Spring 1979): 315–324.

—. "Propositions Again." *Philosophical Investigations* II #4 (Fall 1979): 76–77.

—. "Wittgenstein's Later Picture Theory of Meaning." *Philosophical Investigations* 2 #4 (Winter 1979): 9-23.

—. "Wittgenstein: A Way of Seeing." *Metaphilosophy* 24 #4 (October 1993): 326–343.

—. "Wittgenstein on Thinking: Words or Pictures?" *Philosophy and the Cognitive Sciences*. Eds. Roberto Casati, and Graham White. Vol. 1, Band 1. Kirchberg Am Wechsel, Aus.: Austrian Ludwig Society, 1993. 163–269.

Gill, Jerry H. "Wittgenstein's Concept of Truth." *International Philosophical Quarterly* VI (1966): 71–80.

—. *Wittgenstein and Metaphor*. Washington: Univ. Press of America, 1981.

Gier, Nicholas F. *Wittgenstein and Phenomenology*. Albany: SUNY, 1981.

Griffin, James. *Wittgenstein's Logical Atomism*. 1964. Seattle: Univ. of Washington Press, 1969.

Griffiths, A. Phillips, ed. *Wittgenstein Centenary Essays*. New York: Cambridge Univ. Press, 1991.

Hacker, P. M. S. *Insight and Illusion: Wittgenstein on Philosophy and the Metaphysics of Experience*. London: Oxford Univ. Press, 1972.

Haller, Rudolph. *Questions on Wittgenstein*. Lincoln: Univ. of Nebraska Press, 1988.

Hamburg, Carl H. "Whereof One Cannot Speak." *Journal of Philosophy* 50 (1953): 662–64.

—. *Symbol and Reality*. The Hague: Martinus Nijhoff, 1956.

Hartnack, Justus. *Wittgenstein and Modern Philosophy*. 1962. Garden City, NY: Anchor-Doubleday, 1965.

Heller, Erich. *The Disinherited Mind*. Cambridge, Eng.: Bowes & Bowes, 1952.

—. "Wittgenstein: Unphilosophical Notes." *Encounter* 13 #3 (1959): 40–48.

—, et al. "A Symposium: Assessments of the Man and the Philosopher." *Ludwig Wittgenstein: The Man and His Philosophy*.

Ed. K. T. Fann. New York: Delta-Dell 1967. 64–78.

Hertz, Heinrich. *Principles of Mechanics*. New York: Macmillan, 1956.

Hilmy, S. Stephen. *The Later Wittgenstein: The Emergence of a New Philosophical Method*. Oxford: Basil Blackwell, 1987.

Hintikka, Jaakko. "The Paradox of Transcendental Knowledge." *An Intimate Relation*. Eds. J. R. Brown and J. Mittelstrass. Netherlands: Kluwer Academic, 1989. 243–57.

—. "Kant on the Mathematical Method." *Kant's Philosophy of Mathematics*. Ed. Carl J. Posy. Netherlands: Kluwer Academic, 1992. 21–42.

—. "Kant's Transcendental Method and His Theory of Mathematics." *Kant's Philosophy of Mathematics*. Ed. Carl J. Posy. Netherlands: Kluwer Academic, 1992. 341–59.

—. "An Anatomy of Wittgenstein's Picture Theory." *Artifacts, Representations and Social Practice*. Eds. C. C. Gould, and R. S. Cohen. Netherlands: Kluwer Academic, 1994. 223–56.

Holtzman, Steven H., and Christopher M. Leich, ed. *Wittgenstein: to Follow a Rule*. London: Routledge & Kegan Paul, 1981.

Hunnings, Gordon. *The World and Language in Wittgenstein's Philosophy*. Albany: SUNY, 1988.

Iggers, Wilma Abeles. *Karl Kraus: A Viennese Critic of the Twentieth Century*. The Hague: Martinus Nijhoff, 1967.

Janik, Alan, and Stephen Toulman. *Wittgenstein's Vienna*. New York: Simon & Schuster, 1973.

Kandinsky, Wassily. *Concerning the Spiritual in Art*. 1912. New York: Wittenborn, 1947.

Kant, Immanuel. *Prolegomena To Any Future Metaphysics*. 1783. Indianapolis: Liberal Arts Press, 1950.

Kant, Immanuel. *Critique of Pure Reason*. 1929. Trans. Norman Kemp Smith. New York: St. Martin's Press, 1970.

Kenny, Anthony. *Wittgenstein*. Cambridge: Harvard Univ. Press, 1973.

—. *The Legacy of Wittgenstein*. Oxford: Basil Blackwell, 1984.

Kerr, Fergus. *Theology after Wittgenstein*. Oxford: Basil Blackwell, 1986.

Klemke, E. D., ed. *Essays on Wittgenstein*. Urbana: Univ. of Illinois Press, 1971.

Kolenda, Konstantin. "Wittgenstein's *Weltanschauung*." *Rice University Studies* (Winter 1964): 23–37.

Kripe, Saul A. *Naming and Necessity*, Cambridge: Harvard Univ. Press, 1972.

—. *Wittgenstein on Rules and Private Language*. Cambridge: Harvard Univ. Press, 1982.

Lang, Berel, ed. *Philosophical Style: An Anthology about the Writing and Reading of Philosophy*. Chicago: Nelson-Hall, 1980.

Lazerowitz, Alice Ambrose, "Linguistic Approaches to Philosophical Problems." *The Linguistic Turn*. Ed. Richard Rorty. Chicago: Univ. of Chicago Press, 1967. 147-155.

Lazerowitz, Morris and Alice Ambrose. *Essays in the Unknown Wittgenstein*. Buffalo, NY: Prometheus, 1984.

Levi, Albert William. "Wittgenstein as Dialectician." *Journal of Philosophy* LXI (1964): 127–39.

Malcolm, Norman. "Wittgenstein's Philosophical Investigations." *The Philosophy of Mind*. Ed. V. C. Chappell. Englewood Cliffs, NJ: Prentice-Hall, 1962.

—. *Ludwig Wittgenstein: A Memoir*. 1958. London: Oxford Univ. Press, 1966.

—. "Wittgenstein's *Philosophische Bemerkungen*." *Philosophical Review* 76 (April 1967): 220–29.

McGuinness, Brian, ed. *Wittgenstein and his Times*. Chicago: Univ. of Chicago Press, 1982.

—. *Wittgenstein: Nothing is Hidden*. Oxford: Basil Blackwell, 1986.

—. *Wittgenstein: A Life*. Berkeley: Univ. of California Press, 1988.

Mehta, Ved. *Fly and the Fly-Bottle: Encounters with British Intellectuals*. 1961. Baltimore: Pelican-Penguin, 1965.

Miesel, Victor H., ed. *Voices of German Expressionism*. Englewood Cliffs, NJ: Prentice-Hall, 1970.

Monk, Ray. *Ludwig Wittgenstein: The Duty of Genius*. New York: Free Press, 1990

O'Brien, Dennis. "The Unity of Wittgenstein's Thought." *International Philosophical Quarterly* 6 (1966): 45–70.

Pears, David. "Logical Atomism: Russell and Wittgenstein." *The Revolution in Philosophy*. Ed. A. J. Ayer. London: Macmillan, 1956. 41-55.

—, ed. *The Nature of Metaphysics*. London: MacMillan, 1957.

—. *Ludwig Wittgenstein*. New York: Viking, 1970.

—. *The False Prison*. 2 vols. Oxford: Clarendon, 1987.

Peterman, James F. *Philosophy as Therapy: An Interpretation and Defense of Wittgenstein's Later Philosophy Project*. Albany: SUNY, 1992.

Pitcher, George. *The Philosophy of Wittgenstein*. Englewood Cliffs, NJ: Prentice Hall, 1964.

—, ed. *Wittgenstein: The Philosophical Investigations*. Garden City, NY: Anchor-Doubleday, 1966.

Pitkin, Hanna Fenichel. *Wittgenstein and Justice*. Berkeley: Univ. of California Press, 1972.

Rajan, Sandara R. "Cassirer and Wittgenstein." *International Philosophical Quarterly* 7 (1967): 591-610.

Rhees, Rush. *Discussions of Wittgenstein*. New York: Schocken, 1970.

—, ed. *Ludwig Wittgenstein: Personal Recollections*. Totowa, NJ: Rowman and Littlefield, 1981.

Rorty, Richard, ed. *The Linguistic Turn: Recent Essays in Philosophical Method*. Chicago: Univ. of Chicago Press, 1967.

—. *Philosophy and the Mirror of Nature*.

Princeton, NJ: Princeton Univ. Press, 1979.

—. *Consequences of Pragmatism: Essays 1972–1980*. Minneapolis: Univ. of Minnesota Press, 1982.

Russell, Bertrand. *An Inquiry into Meaning and Truth*. 1940. Baltimore: Pelican-Penguin, 1962.

—. *Logic and Knowledge: Essays 1901–1950*. 1956. Ed. Robert C. Marsh. London: Allen & Unwin, 1966.

Scheffler, Israel. *Science and Subjectivity*. Indianapolis: Bobbs-Merrill, 1967.

Schulte, Joachim. *Wittgenstein: An Introduction*. Trans. William H. Brenner and John F. Holley. Albany: SUNY, 1992.

Schwyzer, H. R. G. "Wittgenstein's Picture-Theory of Language." *Essays on Wittgenstein's Tractatus*. Eds. I. M. Copi and R. W. Beard. New York: Macmillan, 1966.

Shanker, Stuart, ed. *Ludwig Wittgenstein: Critical Assessments*. Vol IV. London: Croom Helm, 1986.

Shields, Philip R. *Logic and Sin in the Writings of Ludwig Wittgenstein*. Chicago: Univ. of Chicago Press, 1993.

Specht, Ernst Konrad. *The Foundations of Wittgenstein's Late Philosophy*. 1963. Trans. D. E. Walford. New York: Manchester Univ. Press, 1969.

Spencer, Oswald. *The Decline of the West*. 1922. New York: Knopf, 1932.

Stenius, Erik. *Wittgenstein's Tractatus*. Ithaca, NY: Cornell Univ. Press, 1960.

Strawson, P. F. "Review of Wittgenstein's *Philosophical Investigations*." *Wittgenstein: The Philosophical Investigations*. Ed. George Pitcher. Garden City, NY: Anchor-Doubleday, 1966. 22–65.

Stroud, Barry. "Wittgenstein and Logical Necessity." *Wittgenstein: The Philosophical Investigations*. Ed. George Pitcher. Garden City, NY: Anchor-Doubleday, 1966. 477–96.

Suter, Ronald. *Interpreting Wittgenstein: A Cloud of Philosophy, a Drop of Grammar*. Philadelphia: Temple Univ. Press, 1989.

Takashi, Fujimoto. "The Notion of Erklärung." *Ludwig Wittgenstein: Philosophy and Language*. Eds., Alice Ambrose and Morris Lazerowitz. London: Allen & Unwin, 1972. 222–32.

Tilghman, B.R. *Wittgenstein, Ethics and Aesthetics: The View from Eternity*. Albany: SUNY, 1991.

Toulmin, Stephen. "Ludwig Wittgenstein." *Encounter* 32 (January 1969): 58–71.

Urban, Wilbur M. "Cassirer's Philosophy of Language." *The Philosophy of Ernst Cassirer*. Ed. Paul A. Schlipp. New York: Tudor, 1958. 403–41.

Urmson, J. O. *Philosophical Analysis*. 1956. London: Oxford Univ. Press, 1967.

Vesey, Godfrey, ed. *Understanding Wittgenstein*. 1974. Ithaca, NY: Cornell Univ. Press, 1976.

von Wright, G. H., ed. *Wittgenstein*. Oxford: Basil Blackwell, 1982.

—. *A Portrait of Wittgenstein as a Young Man: From the Diary of David Hume Pinsent 1912-1914*. Oxford: Basil Blackwell, 1990.

Waismann, F. "How I See Philosophy." *Logical Positivism*. Ed. A. J. Ayer. New York: Free Press, 1959. 345–80.

—. *The Principles of Linguistic Philosophy*. 1965. Ed. R. Harré. London: Macmillan, 1968.

Weiler, Gershon. *Mauthner's Critique of Language*. London: Cambridge Univ. Press, 1970.

—. "On Fritz Mauthner's Critique of Language." *Mind* LXVII (1958): 80–87.

Weiner, David Avraham. *Genius and Talent: Schopenhauer's Influence on Wittgenstein's Early Philosophy*. London: Associated Univ. Press, 1992.

Winch, Peter, ed. *Studies in the Philosophy of Wittgenstein*. London: Routledge & Kegan Paul, 1969.

Index